THE ANTARCTIC

An Anthology

Edited by Francis Spufford

GRANTA

Granta Publications, 12 Addison Avenue, London W11 4QR
First published in Great Britain by Granta Books, 2007 as
The Ends of the Earth Volume 2: The Antarctic
This edition published by Granta Books, 2008
Selection and introduction copyright © Francis Spufford, 2007

Various publishers and estates have generously given permission to use extracts from the following works: 'Antarctica: the Japanese South Polar Expedition of 1910–12', compiled and edited by Lt. Nobu Shirase and the Antarctic Expedition Supporters' Association, translated by Lara Dagnell and Hilary Shibata and published by Bluntisham Books. Originally published in Japanese as 'Nankyokuki' in 1913. Used by permission of Hilary Shibata. 'Scott Dies' by Francis Spufford from *I May Be Some Time*, copyright © 1997 by Francis Spufford. Used by permission of the author and Faber and Faber Ltd. 'The Blow' by Richard Byrd from *Alone*, copyright © 1938 by Richard E. Byrd, renewed 1966 by Marie A. Byrd. 'The Blasphemous City' by H.P. Lovecraft from *At the Mountains of Madness*, copyright © 1936 by Arkham House Publishers, Inc. First published in *Astounding Stories*. The definitive edition previously appeared in *At the Mountains of Madness*, published by Arkham House Publishers, Inc. in 1964. Copyright © 1964 by August Derleth. Copyright renewed 1992. 'White Lanterns' by Diane Ackerman from *The Moon by Whale Light*, copyright © 1991 by Diane Ackerman. Used by permission of Random House, Inc. 'Particles' by Bill Green from *Water, Ice and Stone*, copyright © 1995 by Bill Green. Used by permission of the author. 'Cabin 532' by Jenny Diski from *Skating to Antarctica*, copyright © 1997 by Jenny Diski. Used by permission of Granta Books. 'Hey, Woo' by Sara Wheeler from *Terra Incognita: Travels in Antarctica*, copyright © 1996 by Sara Wheeler. Used by permission of Random House, Inc. and by permission of the Random House Group Ltd. 'Blue Collar' by Nicholas Johnson from *Big Dead Place*, copyright © 2005 by Nicholas Johnson. Used by permission of Feral House and the author. 'In Amundsen's Footsteps, 2016' by Kim Stanley Robinson from *Antarctica*, copyright © 1998 by Kim Stanley Robinson. Used by permission of Bantam Books, a division of Random House, Inc. Bauche, Philippe (1700–1773) Map of Australasia and Antarctica, 1739. The map is accompanied by text describing, in French, the expedition, commanded by Bouvet, which led to the map's production. British Library, London, Great Britain. Photo Credit: HIP / Art Resource, NY.

Every effort has been made to contact copyright holders of the extracts used in this volume. However, the publisher would be happy to rectify any errors or omissions in future editions.

A CIP catalogue record for this book is available from the British Library.

1 3 5 7 9 10 8 6 4 2

ISBN 978-1-84708-028-8

Typeset by M Rules

Printed and bound in Great Britain by
J. H. Haynes & Co. Ltd., Sparkford

CONTENTS

INTRODUCTION

Francis Spufford

Polar explorers don't all come to an illustrious end. Nobu Shirase was famous once. A crowd of fifty thousand people turned out in the rain when his Japanese Antarctic Expedition sailed home in 1912. They sang patriotic songs and held up paper lanterns 'like wet peonies'. But at the age of 85, in the hungry year after the Second World War ended, he died of malnutrition in a rented room over a fish shop, almost completely forgotten. He left behind a farewell poem, in the traditional *waka* form of five lines and exactly thirty-one syllables. It said (in blunt English paraphrase): *Study the treasures of the Antarctic, even after I am dead.*

What treasures are these? From the financial point of view, no one got rich exploring the Antarctic in the 'heroic age' at the beginning of the twentieth century, despite the occasional fantasy of finding gold lying about in nuggets on some glacial moraine sealed away by ice and distance. Getting there cost so much that it took the equivalent of a space programme to land a few humans and their dogs or ponies on the shore of the southern continent. In effect, exploring the interior of Antarctica *was* a space programme, 1900-style; a venture into a white space on the map that was so inhospitable to life, you had to take along every scrap of food and fuel and equipment you needed, and every night retreat into a capsule of the warmer climate you came from. Only the air to breathe was provided, and that sometimes came choked with flying snow, or at temperatures that froze the moisture in your exhaled breaths till a crystalline mask, a beard of icicles, formed on your face. So there were no fortunes to be won at that time, no literal treasures to be had; just funding to find, through magic-lantern lecture tours, and rubber-chicken banquets with sceptical legislators, and weary presentations to patrons who might bring out the chequebook if you thrilled them enough.

Moreover, almost all Antarctic travellers seemed to insist, in what they wrote afterwards, on the physical misery of Antarctic living. 'Polar exploration,' runs the famous opening line of Apsley Cherry-Garrard's *Worst Journey in the World*, 'is at once the cleanest and the most isolated way of having a bad time which has been devised.' Or, as Shirase's own *Nankyokuki* put it, 'The whole enterprise was indescribably difficult and fraught with danger, and it was without doubt the worst of the trials and tribulations we had experienced since we left out mothers' wombs.' The human body, in the classic exploration narratives, was usually in a state of discomfort at best. It was chilled, it was soaked, it was contorted, it was blinded by glare, it craved for food to the point where its owner would dream happily of deep-fried sardines dipped in chocolate. Ernest Shackleton's sailing master, Frank Worsley, said the worst of their boat journey to South Georgia was the hanks of coarse reindeer hair they had to filter out of the soup with their teeth. And beyond discomfort, bodies were subject to a collection of utterly un-treasureable catastrophes. Sensations to look forward to included having the pus in your blisters turn to ice and expand, having wounds ten years old reopen, and having the soles of your feet fall off.

Yet these same books did indeed open Antarctica to their readers as a treasurehouse. They made it as self-evident that the snow has treasures as Shirase had found it; as almost everybody finds it who has been fortunate enough to go to the Antarctic themselves, and to feel the cold brilliance of the south light, and to see the enormity of the ice. Antarctica is rarely a continent that towers, rarely a place that overwhelms you with height. Its sublimity lies in width, in horizontals that go on and on. A tabular berg flecked with blue-green will lie across a whole quadrant of the horizon. The fractured white band of an ice shelf will stretch as far as the eye can see in both directions. The frieze of a far mountain range will be coloured by tender early light in a pattern that repeats; buttercup yellow where the snow's in the sun, a blue-yellow where it's not, chilled as the cream in some ultimately shaded dairy, over and over again horizon long. Antarctica reaches round you, on clear days. Its bigness takes you by the heart and squeezes. Once it has you, it tends to keep you. Whether you went there as an explorer or as a tourist, as a scientist or as a climber, as an administrator or as a cook, you start scheming, the moment you leave, to get back there again.

Oh yes, there are treasures. Antarctica is a wonder and a delight. But *how* it is treasured has changed with the changing perceptions of travellers. The human history of Antarctica is very short, barely more than a hundred years, for though James Clark Ross in Her Majesty's Ships *Erebus* and *Terror* made the first Antarctic landfall in the 1840s, serious exploration did not begin until the 1890s, and the layers of memory and story which make a place into a place were all laid down thereafter. Geologically speaking, Antarctica may be a piece of Gondwanaland; imaginatively, it is an artifact of the twentieth century, about as old as jazz or the Ford Motor Company. Yet the twentieth century was a densely packed one, for alterations in the understanding of nature, and science, and human society, and it is these that have played out, in displaced form, in the way we have seen Antarctica – in the way we've treasured it.

The first layer of Antarctic history was the heroic one. People usually put quote marks around 'heroic', and there is certainly a lot to be sceptical about in the nationalistic fervour that enfolded the great expeditions of the decade leading up to the First World War. But 'heroic' is the right word for the role those expeditions have played, ever after, in Antarctic memory. Together, the stories of them make up Antarctica's *Iliad* – a collective epic, in which figures not quite of human scale struggle and clash and sometimes die. Later times have endlessly reinterpreted its characters, but however much the interpretations change, the stories remain, because this barbarous beginning is the foundation of the human sense we've made of the continent, and is still the touchstone – the reference point – by which later generations of travellers understand what they themselves are doing there.

At the opening of the twentieth century, tiny gangs of human beings, all male, arrived on the margins of an unmapped space about the size of the continental United States, built themselves wooden cabins to live in, and set off inwards into the unknown. Ordinary-sized people when they were at home, they expanded, in their own conceptions of themselves, to match the giant scale of the landscape. Antarctica was an enormous stage which they were treading across virtually alone: how could they not feel as momentous, as *big* as the place, at the same time as they felt fragile, miniscule, infinitely vulnerable in relation to it? Antarctica made them big, first in the echo-chamber of their own breathing, as they sledged laboriously across the snow, then in the eager gaze of the world when they returned. Explorers had been famous figures for a long time, but mostly they had reported the strenuous discovery of populated places; they had been famous for encountering human otherness. Here, the explorers encountered only nature and themselves.

Or rather, nature and each other, because Antarctica like all deserts is an intensely gregarious place: the very few inhabitants necessarily live right on top of each other, getting to know each other's characteristics till they are either devoted friends, or maddened by homicidal irritation, or both. All sojourns in the ice accordingly generate emotions at high pressure. The difference of the Heroic Age was that, then, these were fused together with the business of dealing, for the very first time, from scratch, with the dangerous environment. The disagreements were disagreements about basic strategy for survival, about the elementary technology for moving around, about the proper way for authority to be exercised in an utterly isolated group.

Theoretically, the early explorers were engaged, in Antarctica, in a kind of romantic imperialism, and they did indeed try to claim what happened to them for various national stories, for the ongoing epics of British or Norwegian or German or Japanese or Australian identity – but, even in a world of empires, Antarctica was a domain where empire turned abstract, almost absurd; where you could clearly impose only a kind of vacuous diagram of possession on the snow if you claimed it for Queen Maud or King Edward VII or Emperor Meiji. Not surprisingly, what has survived of the Heroic Age in the modern imagination is more personal. It's a set of iconic figures, iconic events, iconic moments. Apsley Cherry-Garrard and his companions suffer through the horrors of the 'Winter Journey' in a state of unearthly calm and mutual kindness; Douglas Mawson loses both his sledging partners, over on the other side of the continent, and all their food, and walks home to base alone, holding his feet together with string. We look at what was endured, and ask if we could endure it. We look at the expeditions' famous leaders and ask ourselves who we resemble. Which are you? Are you a Captain Scott, tense, anxious, man-hauling your way through the snow by main force yet describing it brilliantly afterwards, relying for your authority on military rank and on charm? Are you a Shackleton, with exactly the same prejudice against dog-sledging as Scott, having learned it with him on the same disastrous journey in 1902, but allied to a wonderfully supple gift for managing people, maternally kind when you could be, unhesitatingly ruthless when you had to be? Are you Amundsen, driven, impeccably self-educated in polar technique, yet far more of a polar performance artist than a word man, and so best appreciated ever after by skiers, mountaineers, ice athletes who can dance through the same moves he made, on his way to the Pole in 1912? Are you, far more obscurely, a Shirase, scarcely noticed by the main contenders for the Pole when he turned up in the Ross Sea in 1912, yet determined to be there, to make a start?

So the main treasures of Antarctica's first age are pieces of human behaviour, far removed from the present sometimes in manners or sensibility, urgently sympathetic because they are the actions of our lone representatives amid a vast, cold, indifferent, wilderness. But there were treasures for the senses, too. The early explorers were romantic observers as well as romantic imperialists. They saw Antarctica with the eyes for wilderness that had been developed in Europe and North America by Romantic literature. Not too long before, wild landscapes had only looked to travellers like a barren mess; but now, thanks to Wordsworth and Keats and Goethe and Thoreau, people had learned to see beauty in the fractal, unplanned complexity of stone, of snow, of water, of ice. The journeys of the heroic age were often journeys into visual delight, reverently noted down by cold hands holding colder pencils. The Australian scientist Edgeworth David led a side trip on Shackleton's *Nimrod* expedition of 1907–9 to climb the great volcano Mount Erebus. From near the summit, he found, you could see a giant shadow of the mountain projected across the sea of cloud below. 'All within the shadow of Erebus was a soft bluish grey; all without was warm, bright and golden. Words fail to describe a scene of such transcendent majesty and beauty.' Antarctica, the explorers learned, was a place of sensory extremes. In the winter dark, or in the strange depthless glow of a white-out, it shut down your senses with tormenting thoroughness, but at other times it overloaded them with colour and dazzle. The Antarctic light refracted shades of cobalt or emerald or lilac off snow crystals that you would never see in any of the planet's other landscapes. Extra suns danced in the sky. The moon rose as a gilded smudge, as a burning slit, as a crimson block. The aurora shimmered against black, in slow gauzy pulses. But the explorers were also noting the porridge texture of new grey ice as it formed on a still sea, and the quiddity of individual boulders, perched like abandoned game pieces on low plinths of unmelted snow. All the detail of Antarctica, not just the spectacle, flooded into their willing eyes.

In this lay the seed of what the continent would become in the future. Many of the early expeditions did substantial scientific work: Scott's 1910–13 *Terra Nova* expedition produced its leader's heroic (or incompetent) defeat in the race for the pole, and a fist-ful of tragic death, but it also produced six closely printed blue and gold folio volumes of scientific results, in geology, marine biology, meteorology, measurement of the earth's magnetic field. Science, though, tended to be subordinated to the language of *conquest* which almost all the early explorers used, as if they were battling against a hostile nature in the Antarctic, and needed to assault it, attack it, overcome it. Knowledge came in as the prize, the suitably abstract prize, for victory: you struggled through the Antarctic's defences, and the unknown became known. The prize, of course, was never more abstract than in the competition to reach the South Pole itself, an unmarked spot corresponding to the geometry of human map-making, not to any physical feature a traveller could reach or see. It turned out to be located, this theoretical point where the earth's axis intersected its crust, on an ice plateau 10,000 feet high, beyond mountains you could only climb by mounting glaciers like ladders of smashed glass. And then the imaginary war cost real lives. But when the explorers of the Heroic Age were actually gazing, fascinated, at the intricacies of what was in front of them, the rhetoric of war sometimes went away. Scott has been much criticised for stopping, on the miserable homeward march from the Pole, to collect 35lb of rock specimens from exposed strata beside the Beardmore Glacier. But the fossil plant leaves in the samples, 170 million years old, were beautiful early evidence of the continent's Gondwanan past. Carrying them along was, perversely, among the most forward-looking things Scott ever did. It anticipated the coming time when scientists, not explorers, would be Antarctica's defining inhabitants; when under-standing, not surviving, would be the most pressing human business there.

But first came an interlude with aeroplanes. The Heroic Age ended with the coming of the First World War. The outbreak of the war itself was less decisive than the arrival of the news of its nature. Shackleton, having been baulked of the Pole by the Scott–Amundsen race of 1912, went back to the Antarctic for a quixotic attempt to cross it side to side in 1914. War was being declared as he left, but when he next caught up with the news, in 1917 – his ship having sunk, his men marooned on a speck of sub-antarctic rock, he himself having made a brilliant dash for help in an open boat across 800 miles of sea – the manager of the whaling station in South Georgia told him that 'Millions are dying. Europe is mad. The world is mad.' That was the age's end, in three sen-tences. The war spoiled public appetite for conquering nature; in

Europe, damaged the ability to pay the space-programme cost of it, too. And in the 1920s and 1930s, Antarctica was quiet again – except for the planes in its sky. The two expeditions of the American explorer Richard Byrd used dog sledges for land travel as a matter of course, since the motorized alternatives were still not reliable at low temperatures, but for covering distance, for his major forays into the unknown, he flew. The route to the Pole that had taken Amundsen a season to cover, there and back, took him two days, with views down onto the crumpled iceflows streaming over the Transantarctic Mountains which, for the first time, integrated the fragmented observations of the past into one dynamic map. This made a considerable psychological difference. A human being in Antarctica could now possess, imaginatively, a much wider spread of it than was visible through the eyeholes of any one knitted helmet. From ten thousand feet, you could begin to see how Antarctica worked; you could begin to see it as having a unity in which, paradoxically, humans played very little part. The other new technologies of communications changed Antarctica too. Even when Byrd wintered by himself in an isolated weather station on the Ross Ice Shelf, as described in his 1938 bestseller *Alone*, he was linked to the world beyond as his predecessors had never been, by radio. Leaking fumes from a heater almost killed him, and he went through a long dark night of hallucinatory self-examination, but he could get friendly voices to talk to every evening, and baseball scores, and news of his investments plummeting on Wall Street. Byrd's Antarctica was halfway between times. It was still a place of adventure and danger; and the ski-mounted biplanes could always be drafted in to serve in high-speed versions of the old fantasy of imperium. In 1939 a brief German expedition to the Weddell Sea claimed a swathe of the interior by the impatient method of over-flying it, and sprinkling the snow below with thousands of little metal swastikas.

War had stopped the expeditions; now war restarted them. A strategic worry about the Falkland Islands in 1944 put the British back into the long arm of Antarctica due south of the Americas, and as the Second World War segued into the Cold War, the continent became an arena for a confrontation between the two new superpowers, very much as if (to continue the space-programme analogy) the continent were a nearby planet, habitable if not very hospitable, which neither side could leave alone for fear the other one would have it. To add further complications, Latin American expeditions busily scribbled new land claims over the earlier European grabs for Antarctic territory, until the legal map of the continent resembled a logically impossible pie, where everyone's slice overlapped with everyone else's. The International Geophysical Year in 1957 brought activity to a new level. The US Navy started bulk construction of Antarctic facilities, with a giant base on Ross Island next door to Captain Scott's first hut, another logistically astonishing base at the South Pole itself, and a string of field camps and runways all over the million square miles of wilderness. Meanwhile, Soviet efforts went into building a chain of stations in the coldest, bleakest spots of the Weddell Sea sector, connected by mighty caterpillar convoys running on adapted artillery tractors. The scene seemed set for a mutually thwarting deadlock, in which humanity's primate instincts for power and territory took priority over all the actual qualities of the wilderness.

But instead, something remarkable happened. The deadlock metamorphosed into an international agreement to put Antarctica outside the reach of the global dispute. The Antarctic Treaty, signed in 1961 by the dozen nations active in Antarctica at the time, suspended all territorial claims and reserved the continent for science. Protocols added since have forbidden mining or oil drilling, protected Antarctica from human settlement except in very restricted ways, and put the continent under ecological quarantine. Cynics might say – did say – that the signatories' virtue did not cost them very much. As of 1961, Antarctica did not seem to contain much of economic value anyway. But the first indications appeared not long afterwards that there might, after all, be literal treasures under the snows, treasures of the mineral variety: and so far they have not been exploited. So far, despite it having no enforcement apparatus, the treaty has held. The United States' hasty collection of strategic assets in Antarctica became the main backbone of its transport infrastructure, with the US running the flights down from New Zealand to the great gateway at McMurdo Base, and onwards from there all over the continent. The Russians set records for enduring the lowest temperatures ever recorded on the planet: minus 80 centigrade, at Vostok station, which turned out, after the Soviet Union fell, to be sitting on top of one of the strangest of scientific surprises.

To begin with, the new, permanently inhabited Antarctica was still a noticeably military place. Into the 1970s and early 1980s, the navy ran the facilities at American bases, and still set the mood there, especially during the winters. McMurdo was officially designated as a ship, its residents ate in a galley and, like a submarine on Cold War missile patrol, it was powered by a small nuclear reactor, known affectionately to locals as 'Nukey-Poo'. But the patriarchal days of Antarctica were ending, both because something more routine and organized had taken over from the improvised tribal life of the Heroic Age, and also in the straightforward sense that the continent was no longer reserved exclusively for men. Women had first set foot in Antarctica in the 1950s, but only as naval wives. From the 1970s on, women were there in growing numbers in their own right, as scientists, as pilots, as support staff, as sailors or soldiers. The gender ratio on the continent remained bizarrely skewed, even in metropolitan McMurdo, but the perceptions and experiences of the other half of the human race did at last have the chance to inform Antarctic thinking and writing.

The sensibility that created the new consensual picture of Antarctica was the scientific one. After all, Antarctica was run *for* the scientists, who came to spend the polar summer searching for the trace gases of ancient climates in ice cores, or fossil-hunting in the Transantarctic Mountains, or teasing apart the molecular biology of the slow, slow bacteria of the Dry Valleys; often coming summer after summer, until they'd racked up totals of time on the ice that put the early explorers to shame. The scientists did not, of course, have a monopoly on access to Antarctica. Increasingly, as the twentieth century ended and the twenty-first century began, very expensive tourism was possible, often using the cast-off ice-breakers of the former Soviet Union as cruise ships; and for even more money, adventure travellers could fly into the private airstrip at Patriot Hills in West Antarctica, and ski to the Pole 'in the footsteps' of the Heroic Age explorers. But the scientists remained the dominant presence in Antarctic life. Travellers on the tour ships could gaze at the light and the wildlife, awestruck, heart-squeezed, and join what they saw to their own biographies, add it to their own treasuries of amazement. But the scientists were still the ones who got to set the meaning of the continent. It was theirs, to the point that support workers in Antarctica, flipping burgers or sorting garbage, sometimes became as pissed-off at the 'beakers' as long-ago geologists had once been at the Scotts and Shackletons who kept moulding a fabulous research opportunity into a narrative of adventure.

What the scientists learned to see was a kind of amplification, continent-wide and in immense detail, of the view from the early flights. Once again, there was a connection to technology. Because the scientists now had relative immunity from the dangers of the environment, because they could move around with relative ease, they could sink into the type of concentration which distributes itself through the material world it is thinking about. (This sort of disembodied attention is a lot easier if your body is, in fact, safe and warm.) From hundreds – thousands – of separate studies, a sense built up of Antarctica's unity as a physical system, with its separate components of ice and rock and air and sea all subtly dependent on one another; and the whole system, in turn, delicately interrelated with the functioning of the rest of the planet, from the world's weather to its ecosystems. This was another great change of perceptions, another great reframing of the whole idea of Antarctica. From the beginning, it had been crucial to its imaginative impact as a place that it was a place apart, locked away at the bottom of world, beyond terrible seas patrolled by a ring of storms. It was an icy South far less continuous with the rest of the world than the icy North was. You could, if you had a mind to, hail a taxi in New York or Berlin, and be driven to the Arctic: but the Antarctic was on a separate map. Now the separateness, though not the uniqueness, was going away. First came the awareness that the industrial processes of the populated planet off to the north did, indeed, reach down and touch the ice. Cans of oven spray hissing out chlorofluorocarbons in Tokyo could bore a hole in the atmosphere in the southern polar sky. Then, more troubling, came the realization that Antarctica could act back upon the rest of the planet. In the 1990s, it became plain that the Antarctic ice shelves, by locking away vast tonnages of fresh water, effectively governed world sea levels. If the CO_2 pumped out by humans raised global temperatures enough to loosen the ice sheets, the melt water from the Ross Sea and the Weddell Sea would come pouring down my street, your street, our street at home, if home happened to be any of the world's coastal cities. Now, Antarctica no longer looked like a fortress of ice to be conquered. It was a fragile panel in the fabric of the planet. It no longer threatened to overwhelm tiny humans doing epic deeds in a harsh landscape. The balance of threat had reversed. *We* could damage *it*, without ever leaving home – and might inadvertently summon down upon ourselves a disaster out of the ice which would dwarf the cold fate that Captain Scott had gone looking for in its indifferent spaces. The new treasure of Antarctica is knowledge. Knowledge for its own sake, for our delight; severely practical knowledge, about how we may hurt ourselves, in a world whose biological infrastructure does not grow stronger just because our economies do.

Change, change, change throughout the Antarctic century. What we think we see, in the far South, shifts with our own preoccupations, like the jumbled icefloes in Antarctic waters which have seemed to travellers to morph into very different architectures, depending on who was doing the looking, and when. Captain Scott's men saw the ruins of St Paul's Cathedral going by; Lieutenant Shirase's saw ruined temples. Look for modernist purity in the tabular bergs, and you find it. Look for tentacular, Gaudi-esque curlicues, and you find them too. Yet the ice's repertoire of shapes has been the same all century long.

When the Antarctic makes its astonishing impact on the senses, people try their damnedest to describe it. That's why there has been so much good writing about it, over the single century of its human history. People have constantly measured up the powers of language against it. But being in Antarctica is also a constant reminder of language's secondary status, of description's belated appearance on any scene. Nowhere else on Earth is it so clear that a place has an integrity apart from what we might say about it. Nowhere are words so obviously ineffectual a response to what just, massively, exists, whole and complete and in no real need of translation. Words, Antarctica teaches us, are not what the world is made of. Stop listening to me, then. Step aside, and sit down on that wind-carved boulder. Sit for a while: there are mountains in the distance to which the best response is hush. Take a long, silent look at the treasures of the snow.

But remember to get moving again while you can still feel your toes.

CHAPTER 1

'INTO THE NIGHT'

from *Through the First Antarctic Night* (1900)

Frederick A. Cook

Frederick Cook would win fame a decade after he wrote this, as one of the two claimants locked in dispute over the discovery of the North Pole. But here the young doctor from New York State, along with an equally young Roald Amundsen, is at the other end of the earth. The exploring vessel Belgica *has frozen fast into the Antarctic pack ice. As polar summer ends, the unprepared adventurers on board are about to become the first human beings to experience an Antarctic winter. Here, with the physical and psychological challenges of the long dark, the Heroic Age opens.*

March 4. – This morning a bunch of sharp rays of light pierced my port as the sun rose over the icy stillness of the north. It was like a bundle of frosted silver wire, and it served well the purpose of an eye-opener. Sleep here is an inexpressible dream. It does not matter how difficult the work, of how great the anxiety, we sink easily into prolonged restful slumbers. We awake rested, refreshed, and full of youthful vigour, always ready for the day's task. In the first days of our life in the pack we ate when we were hungry, slept when we were tired, and worked when the spirit moved us. (But later we were never hungry, always tired, and the spirit never moved us.)

We have wearied of pushing southward this season, and are discouraged in our ability to move in any direction, but we have tried hard to make a higher latitude. Nature frowns upon us and refuses to reward our dearly-bought venture. She guards the mysteries of the frozen south with much jealousy. She tempts us by permitting a small advance and a long look ahead, but when we have resolved to force on into the white blank, the icy gates close as if to say, 'You can look, but you must not enter.' A water sky, a land blink, or some other sign, indicative of land or open water, is constantly before us and these are, to the polar explorer, like the Star of Bethlehem to the children of Israel. They perpetually urge us on. We burn down the fires and wait impatiently for better success on the morrow, feeling always that we have won our success, thus far, by our own hard efforts, and by the same methods we hope to master the barriers now walled around us. Pressing ice, blasting head winds, blinding snow squalls, and all the worst elements of sea and weather combine to bewilder and defeat us.

The south polar lands are carefully shielded and fenced off by the circumpolar pack. The regions beyond the outer edge are not to be secured from the depths of mystery by a dash or an assault. The fortifications are more firmly laid than ever a human mind suggested. The prodigious depths of snow above, and the endless expanse of ensnaring sea around are mostly impregnable to man. He who contemplates an attack on this heatless undersurface of the globe will find many tempting allurements and many disheartening rebuffs. Such has been our experience. The battle, however, should be fought, though it promises to be the fiercest of all human engagements. Science demands it, modern progress calls for it, for in this age a blank upon our chart is a blur upon our prided enlightenment.

We are now again firmly stationed in a moving sea of ice, with no land and nothing stable on the horizon to warn us of our movements. Even the bergs, immense, mountainous masses, though apparently fixed and immovable, sail as we do, and with the same apparent ease. The astronomical positions which we obtain from the sun and from the stars indicate to us that we drift from five to ten miles per day. It is a strange sensation to know that, blown with the winds, you are moving rapidly over an unknown sea, and yet see nothing to indicate a movement. We pass no fixed point, and can see no pieces of ice stir; everything is quiet. The entire horizon drifts with us. We are part of an endless frozen sea. Our course is zigzag, but generally west – we do not know our destination, and are always conscious that we are the only human beings to be found in the entire circumpolar region at the bottom of the globe. It is a curious situation.

March 15. – The weather is remarkably clear. There is no wind, no noise, and no motion in the ice. During the night we saw the first aurora australis. I saw it first at eight o'clock, but it was so faint then that I could not be positively certain whether it was a cloud with an unusual ice-blink upon it or an aurora; but at ten o'clock we all saw it in a manner which was unmistakable. The first phenomenon was like a series of wavy fragments of cirrus clouds, blown by strong, high winds across the zenith. This entirely disappeared a few minutes after eight o'clock. What we saw later was a trembling lacework, draped like a curtain, on the southern sky. Various parts were now dark, and now light, as if a stream of electric sparks illuminated the fabric. The curtain seemed to move in response to these waves of light, as if driven by the wind which shook out old folds and created new ones, all of which made the scene one of new interest and rare glory.

That I might better see the new attraction and also experiment with my sleeping-bag, I resolved to try a sleep outside upon one of the floes. For several days I had promised myself the pleasure of this experience, but for one reason or another I had deferred it. At midnight I took my bag and, leaving the warmth and comfort of the cabin, I struggled out over the icy walls of the bark's embankment, and upon a floe three hundred yards east I spread out the bag. The temperature of the cabin was the ordinary temperature of a comfortable room; the temperature of the outside air was –20° C. (–4° F.) After undressing quickly, as one is apt to do in such temperatures, I slid into the fur bag and rolled over the ice until I found a depression suitable to my ideas of comfort. At first my teeth chattered and every muscle of my body quivered, but in a few minutes this passed off and there came a reaction similar to that after a cold bath. With this warm glow I turned from side to side and peeped past the fringe of accumulating frost, around my blow-hole through the bag, at the cold glitter of the stars. As I lay there alone, away from the noise of the ship, the silence and the solitude were curiously oppressive. There was not a breath of air stirring the glassy atmosphere, and not a sound from the ice-decked sea or its life to indicate movement or commotion. Only a day ago this same ice was a mass of small detached floes, moving and grinding off edges with a complaining squeak. How different it was now! Every fragment was cemented together into one heterogeneous mass and carpeted by a hard, ivory-like sheet of snow. Every move which I made in my bag was followed by a crackling complaint from the snow crust.

At about three o'clock in the morning a little wind came from the east. My blow-hole was turned in this direction, but the slow blast of air which struck my face kept my moustache and my whiskers, and every bit of fur near the opening, covered with ice. As I rolled over to face the leeward there seemed to be a misfit somewhere. The hood portion of the bag was as hard as if coated with sheet-iron, and my head was firmly encased. My hair, my face, and the under garments about my neck were frozen to the hood. With every turn I endured an agony of hair pulling. If I remained still my head became more and more fixed by the increasing condensation. In the morning my head was boxed like that of a deep sea-diver. But aside from this little discomfort I was perfectly at ease, and might have slept if the glory of the heavens and the charm of the scene about had not been too fascinating to permit restful repose.

The aurora, as the blue twilight announced the dawn, had settled into an arc of steady brilliancy which hung low on the southern sky, while directly under the zenith there quivered a few streamers; overhead was the southern cross, and all around the blue dome there were sparkling spots which stood out like huge gems. Along the horizon from south to east there was the glow of the sun, probably reflected from the unknown southern lands. This was a band of ochre tapering to gold and ending in orange red. At four o'clock the aurora was still visible but faint. The heavens were violet and the stars were now fading behind the increasing twilight. A zone of yellow extended from west around south to east, while the other half of the circle was a vivid purple. The ice was a dark blue. An hour later the highest icebergs began to glitter as if tipped with gold, and then the hummocks brightened. Finally, as the sun rose from her snowy bed, the whole frigid sea was coloured as if flooded with liquid gold. I turned over and had dropped into another slumber when I felt a peculiar tapping on the encasement of my face. I remained quiet, and presently I heard a loud chatter. It was uttered by a group of penguins who had come to interview their new companion. I hastened to respond to the call, and, after pounding my head and pulling out some bunches of hair, I jumped into my furs, bid the surprised penguins good morning, and went aboard. Here I learned that Lecointe, not knowing of my presence on the ice, had taken me for a seal, and was only waiting for better light to try his luck with the rifle.

April 16. – In this shiftless sea of ice everything depends upon the wind. If it is south, we have steady, clear, cold weather. If it is north we have a warm, humid air with snow and unsettled weather. If it is east or west it brings a tempest with great quantities of driving snow; but it never ceases blowing. It is blow, blow, from all points of the compass. It is because of this importance of the wind, because it is the key-note to the day which follows, that our first question in the morning is 'how is the wind?' To-day it is east, and has increased to a gale, in which it is absolutely impossible to take even a short walk on the pack. For recreation we have taken to mending. Racovitza is patching his pantaloons for the tenth time. This, he says, will be the last time, and I think he is right, for he has used leather to strengthen all the weak parts. Amundsen is patching boots; Lecointe is mending instruments; Danco and I are trying to repair watches. Nearly all of our good timepieces are out of commission. Our hands are better adapted for the trade of a blacksmith than that of a jeweller, but we are trying hard and have, to some extent, succeeded. Just at present it is the crystals which we wish to replace. We have no extra glasses, but we have found some small pocket compasses with crystals too small. How can we make them fit? Danco said, 'Try sealing wax,' which we did. We covered half of the watch and a good part of the crystal and thus made a very effective job, but in appearance it is a woeful object.

April 20. – The easterly storm which has raged unceasingly for a week, and almost continuously for a month, shows some signs this morning of ceasing. At 4 A.M. the barometer began to rise, and the temperature fell to –2° C. The wind shifted to the northeast, but its force was soon spent. During the day the wind came only in intermittent puffs. The mouse-coloured clouds separated, permitting an occasional sunburst to light up the awful gloom which has so long hung over us. To-night, at ten o'clock, it is actually calm, and snow is falling lightly in huge, feathery flakes. This sudden calmness and dark unbroken silence, after the many days of boisterous gales, instill within us a curious sensation. The ship no longer quivers and groans. The ropes about the rigging have ceased their discordant music, and the floes do not utter the usual nerve-despairing screams. This sudden stillness, seemingly increased by the falling snow, brings to us a notion of impending danger.

May 16. – The long night began at 12 o'clock last night. We did not know this until this afternoon. At 4 o'clock Lecointe got an observation by two stars which placed us in latitude 71° 34′ 30″, longitude 89° 10′. According to a careful calculation from these figures the captain announces the melancholy news that there will be no more day – no more sun for seventy days, if our position remains about the same. If we drift north the night will be shorter, if south it will be longer. Shortly before noon the long prayed-for southerly wind came, sweeping from the pack the warm, black atmosphere, and replacing it with a sharp air and a clearing sky. Exactly at noon we saw a brightening in the north. We expected to see the sun by refraction, though we knew it was actually below the horizon, but we were disappointed. The cold whiteness of our earlier surroundings has now been succeeded by a colder blackness. Even the long, bright twilight, which gladdened our hearts on first entering the pack, has been reduced to but a fraction of its earlier glory; this now takes the place of our departed day.

May 17. – At about seven o'clock the captain went out to find two stars from which to obtain an observation for position. The sky was too hazy to give him an observation, but his eye rested upon an inexplicable speck of light in the west. He stood and looked at it for some moments. It did not change in position, but sparkled now and then like a star. The thing came suddenly, disappeared and again reappeared in exactly the same spot. It was so curious and assumed so much the nature of a surprise, that Lecointe came into the cabin and announced the news. We accused him of having had too early an eye-opener, but we went out quickly to see the mystery. It was about eight o'clock; the sky was a streaky mouse colour. The ice was gray, with a slight suggestion of lilac in the high lights, but the entire outline of the pack was vague under a very dark twilight. We looked for some time in the direction in which Lecointe pointed, but we saw only a gloomy waste of ice, lined in places by breaks in the pack from which oozed a black cloud of vapour. We were not sure that the captain's eyesight was not defective, and began to black-guard him afresh.

After we had stood on the snow-decked bridge for ten minutes, shivering and kicking about to keep our blood from freezing, we saw on a floe some distance westward a light like that of a torch. It flick-ered, rose and fell, as if carried by some moving object. We went forward to find if anybody was missing – for we could only explain the thing by imagining a man carrying a lantern. Everybody was found to be on board, and then the excitement ran high. Soon all hands were on deck and all seemed to think that the light was being moved towards us. Is it a human being? Is it perhaps some one from an unknown south polar race of people? For some minutes no one ventured out on the pack to meet the strange messenger. We were, indeed, not sufficiently dressed for this mission. Few had had break-fast; all were without mittens and hats, some without coats, and others without trousers. If it were a diplomatic visitor we were certainly in an uncomfortable and undignified uniform with which to receive him. Amundsen, who was the biggest, the strongest, the bravest, and generally the best dressed man for sudden emergencies, slipped into his *annorak*, jumped on his *ski* and skated rapidly over the gloomy blackness of the pack to the light. He lingered about the spot a bit, and then returned without company and without the light, looking somewhat sheepish. It proved to be a mass of phosphorescent snow which had been newly charged by sea algae, and was occasionally raised and brushed by the pressure of the ice.

May 18. – During the few hours of midday dawn we made an excursion to a favourite iceberg to view the last signs of the departing day. It was a weird jaunt. I shall always remember the peculiar impression it produced upon me. When we started almost all the party were outside, standing about in groups of three or four, discussing the prospects of the long winter night and the short glory of the scene about. A thing sadder by far than the fleeing sun was the illness of our companion, Lieutenant Danco, which was emphasised to us now by his absence from all the groups, his malady confining him to the ship. We knew at this time that he would never again see a sunrise, and we felt that perhaps others might follow him. 'Who will be here to greet the returning sun?' was often asked.

My companions on the excursion were Gerlache and Amundsen. Slowly and lazily we skated over the rough surface of the snow to the northward. The pack, with the strange play of deflected light upon it, the subdued high lights, the softened shadows, the little speck of human and wild life, and our good ship buried under its snows, should have been interesting to us; but we were interested only in the sky and in the northern portion of it. A few moments before twelve the cream-coloured zone in the north brightened to an orange hue, and precisely at noon half of the form of the sun ascended above the ice. It was a misshapen, dull semicircle of gold heatless, rayless, and sad. It sank again in a few moments, leaving almost no colour and nothing cheerful to remember through the seventy long days of darkness which followed. We returned to the ship and during the afternoon laid out the plans for our midwinter occupation.

May 20. – It is the fifth day of the long night and it certainly seems long, very long, since we have felt the heat of the sun. Since entering the pack our spirits have not improved. The quantity of food which we have consumed, individually and collectively, has steadily decreased and our relish for food has also slowly but steadily failed. There was a time when each man enjoyed some special dish and by distributing these favoured dishes at different times it was possible to have some one gastronomically happy every day. But now we are tired of everything. We despise all articles which come out of tin, and a general dislike is the normal air of the *Belgica*. The cook is entitled, through his efforts to please us, to kind consideration, but the arrangement of the menu is condemned, and the entire food store is used as a subject for bitter sarcasm. Everybody having any connection with the selection or preparation of the food, past or present, is heaped with some criticism. Some of this is merited, but most of it is the natural outcome of our despairing isolation from accustomed comforts.

I do not mean to say that we are more discontented than other men in similar conditions. This part of the life of polar explorers is usually suppressed in the narratives. An almost monotonous discontent occurs in every expedition through the polar night. It is natural that this should be so, for when men are compelled to see one another's faces, encounter the few good and the many bad traits of character for weeks, months, and years, without any outer influence to direct the mind, they are apt to remember only the rough edges which rub up against their own bumps of misconduct. If we could only get away from each other for a few hours at a time, we might learn to see a new side and take a fresh interest in our comrades; but this is not possible. The truth is, that we are at this moment as tired of each other's company as we are of the cold monotony of the black night and of the unpalatable sameness of our food. Now and then we experience affectionate moody spells and then we try to inspire each other with a sort of superficial effervescence of good cheer, but such moods are short-lived.

Physically, mentally, and perhaps morally, then, we are depressed. and from my past experience in the Arctic I know that this depression will increase with the advance of the night, and far into the increasing dawn of next summer.

The mental conditions have been indicated above. Physically we are steadily losing strength, though our weight remains nearly the same, with a slight increase in some. All seem puffy about the eyes and ankles, and the muscles, which were hard earlier, are now soft, though not reduced in size. We are pale, and the skin is unusually oily. The hair grows rapidly, and the skin about the nails has a tendency to creep over them, seemingly to protect them from the cold. The heart action is failing in force and is decidedly irregular. Indeed, this organ responds to the slightest stimulation in an alarming manner. If we walk hurriedly around the ship the pulse rises to 110 beats, and if we continue for fifteen minutes it intermits, and there is also some difficulty of respiration. The observers, going only one hundred yards to the observatories, come in almost breathless after their short run. The usual pulse, too, is extremely changeable from day to day. Now it is full, regular, and vigorous; again it is soft, intermittent and feeble. In one case it was, yesterday, 43, to-day it is 98, but the man complains of nothing and does his regular work. The sun seems to supply an indescribable something which controls and steadies the heart. In its absence it goes like an engine without a governor.

There is at present no one disabled, but there are many little complaints. About half of the men complain of headaches and insomnia; many are dizzy and uncomfortable about the head, and others are sleepy at all times, though they sleep nine hours. All of the secretions are reduced, from which it follows that digestion is difficult. Acid dyspepsia and frequent gastric discomforts are often mentioned. There are also rheumatic and neuralgic pains, muscular twitchings, and an indefinite number of small complaints, but there is but one serious case on hand. This is Danco. He has an old heart lesion, a leak of one of the valves, which has been followed by an enlargement of the heart and a thickening of its walls. In ordinary conditions, when there was no need for an unusual physical or mental strain, and when liberal fresh food and bright sunshine were at hand, he felt no defect. But these conditions are now changed. The hypertrophied muscular tissue is beginning to weaken, and atrophy of the heart is the result, dilating and weakening with a sort of measured step, which, if it continues at the present rate, will prove fatal within a month.

May 27. – The little dusk at midday is fading more and more. A feeble deflected light falls upon the elevations, the icebergs, and the hummocks, offering a faint cheerfulness, but this soon withdraws and leaves a film of blackness. The pack presents daily the same despondent surface of gray which, by contrast to the white sparkle of some time ago, makes our outlook even more melancholy. The weather is now quite clear and in general more settled. The temperature ranges from 5° to 10° C. below zero. We have frequent falls of snow, but the quantity is small and the period is short. Generally we are able to see the stars from two in the afternoon until ten in the morning. During the four hours of midday the sky is generally screened by a thick icy vapour. There are a few white petrels about daily, and in the sounding hole we have noticed a seal occasionally, but there is now no other life. All have an abundance of work, but our ambition for regular occupation, particularly anything which requires prolonged mental concentration, is wanting; even the task of keeping up the log is too much. There is nothing new to write about, nothing to excite fresh interest. There are now no auroras, and no halos; everything on the frozen sea and over it is sleeping the long sleep of the frigid night.

May 31. – The regular routine of our work is tiresome in the extreme, not because it is difficult of execution or requires great physical exertion, but because of its monotony. Day after day, week after week, and month after month we rise at the same hour, eat the same things, talk on the same subjects, make a pretense of doing the same work, and look out upon the same icy wilderness. We try hard to introduce new topics for thought and new concoctions for the weary stomach. We strain the truth to introduce stories of home and of flowery future prospects, hoping to infuse a new cheer; but it all fails miserably. We are under the spell of the black Antarctic night, and, like the world which it darkens, we are cold, cheerless, and inactive. We have aged ten years in thirty days.

June 1. – It is now difficult to get out of our warm beds in the morning. There is no dawn, – nothing to mark the usual division of night and morning until nearly noon. During the early part of the night it is next to impossible to go to sleep, and if we drink coffee we do not sleep at all. When we do sink into a slumber, it is so deep that we are not easily awakened. Our appetites are growing smaller and smaller, and the little food which is consumed gives much trouble. Oh, for that heavenly ball of fire! Not for the heat – the human economy can regulate that – but for the light – the hope of life.

June 3. – The weather is unendurable, the temperature is –30° C. and an easterly gale is burying us in a huge drift of snow. With a high wind, an air thick with flying snow, and a temperature such as we have had for the past three days, ranging from –28° to –30°, it is utterly impossible to exist outside in the open blast. In calm weather such a temperature causes delight, but in a storm it gives rise to despair. I think it is Conan Doyle who says, 'What companion is there like the great restless, throbbing polar sea? What human mood is there which it does not match and sympathise with?' I should like Mr. Doyle to spend one month with us on this great, restless, throbbing sea, under this dense, restless, throbbing blackness of the antarctic night. I am sure he would find conditions to drive his pen, but where is the companionship of a sea which with every heave brings a block of ice against your berth making your only hope of life, the bark, tremble from end to end? Where is the human being who will find sympathy in the howling winds under the polar night?

June 4. – The ice is again breaking and the pressure of the floes, as they ride over each other, makes a noise converting the otherwise dark quietude into a howling scene of groans. It is again snowing and the wind keeps veering from the north-west to north-east.

Whenever we have advanced on our mysterious drift with the restless pack, either far east or far south, or both, we are arrested in our progress and the temperature falls. In the east there is also great pressure, and it is only in the far east or south that we get easterly or southerly winds. These winds have the character of land breezes – extremely dry, with a low temperature – followed by delightful, clear weather. From these facts we must conclude that the east and south are lined with land of large proportions or islands united by ice. An easy wind south or west drives us quickly; indeed, at times we drift northward without wind. The bergs now seem to press north and east.

June 5. – To-day we have to record the darkest page in our log – the death of our beloved comrade, Danco. It has not been unexpected, for we have known that he could not recover, but the awful blank left by his demise is keenly felt, and the sudden gloom of despair, thus thrown over the entire party, is impossible of description. Poor fellow! in the past forty-eight hours he had been steadily improving, and, although we were not encouraged by this, he felt so much better that he was cheerful and altogether more like his

former self, but it was the calm before the storm. Without any pre-
monition of his coming death Danco passed away easily tonight;
his last words to me were, 'I can breathe lighter and will soon get
strength.' A companion with noble traits has left us. The event is
too sad to note in detail. His life has steadily and persistingly sunk
with the northerly setting of the sun. In ordinary health, his circulation was so nicely balanced that it needed but the unbalancing
element of the prolonged darkness to disturb the equilibrium, and
send him to a premature grave.

June 7. – We have made a bag of sail-cloth, and into it the
remains of Danco have been sewn. This morning we searched the
crevasses for an opening which might serve as a grave. We found no
place sufficiently open, but with axes and chisels we cut an aperture
through the young ice in a recent lead, about one hundred yards
from the bark. Owing to the depressing effect upon the party, we
found it necessary to place the body outside on the ice upon a sledge
the day after the death. At a few minutes before noon to-day the
commandant, followed by the officers and scientific staff came to
this sledge. The crew, dressed in an outer suit of duck, then marched
out and, taking the drag rope, they proceeded over the rough drifts
southerly to the lead. The day was bitterly cold, with a wind coming
out of the south-west. Much snow in fine crystals was driven
through the air, and it pierced the skin like needles. The surface of
the ice was gray, but the sky had here and there a touch of brightness. In the north there was a feeble metallic glow, and directly
overhead there were a few stratus of rose-coloured clouds. The
moon, fiery, with a ragged edge, hung low on the southern sky.
There was light enough to read ordinary print, but it was a weird
light. Danco was a favourite among the sailors, and his departure
was as keenly felt in the forecastle as among us. The men expressed
this in the funeral procession. Slowly but steadily they marched over
the rough surface of the ice with an air of inexpressible sadness. The

sledge was brought to the freezing water. Here the commandant made a few fitting remarks, and then two heavy weights were attached to the feet, and the body was entrusted to the frosted bosom of the Antarctic ocean.

June 8. – The melancholy death, and the incidents of the melancholy burial of Danco, have brought over us a spell of despondency which we seem unable to conquer. I fear that this feeling will remain with us for some time, and we can ill afford it. Though there are none among us sick at this time, we may at any moment have small complaints which will become serious under this death-dealing spell of despair. We are constantly picturing to ourselves the form of our late companion floating about in a standing position, with the weights to his feet, under the frozen surface and perhaps under the *Belgica*.

June 22. – It is midnight and midwinter. Thirty-five long, day-less nights have passed. An equal number of dreary, cheerless days must elapse before we again see the glowing orb, the star of day. The sun has reached its greatest northern declination. We have thus passed the antarctic midnight. The winter solstice is to us the merid-ian day, the zenith of the night as much so as twelve o'clock is the meridian hour to those who dwell in the more favoured lands, in the temperate and tropical zones, where there is a regular day and night three hundred and sixty-five times in the yearly cycle. Yesterday was the darkest day of the night; a more dismal sky and a more depress-ing scene could not be imagined, but to-day the outlook is a little brighter. The sky is lined with a few touches of orange. The frozen sea of black snow is made more cheerful by the high lights, with a sort of dull phosphorescent glimmer of the projecting peaks of ice.

July 12. – The light is daily increasing at midday, which should be a potent encouragement, but we are failing in fortitude and in

physical force. From day to day we all complain of a general enfee-
blement of strength, of insufficient heart action, of a mental
lethargy, and of a universal feeling of discomfort. There has, however, been one exception; one among us who has not fallen into the
habit of being a chronic complainer. This is Captain Lecointe. The
captain has had to do the most trying work, that of making the nau-
tical observations, which often keeps him handling delicate
instruments outside and in trying positions in the open blast for an
hour at a time. He has come in with frosted fingers, frozen ears, and
stiffened feet, but with characteristic good humour he has passed
these discomforts off. His heart action has steadily remained full
and regular. The only other man in the party of equal strength is
the cook, Michotte. But to-day I have to record the saddening news
that Lecointe is suddenly failing. Not that he has complained of any
ill-feeling, for he still maintains that he feels well; but in the usual
daily examination, I notice that his pulse is intermitting, the first
sign of coming debility. He is assuming a deathly pallor, does not
eat, and finds it difficult to either sleep or breathe. There is a puffiness under the eyes, his ankles are swollen, and the entire skin has
a dry, glossy appearance. The symptoms are all similar to those of
Danco in his last stages; but Lecointe has a steady heart and sound
organs, which augur in his favour.

July 14. – Lecointe has given up all hope of ever recovering,
and has made out his last instructions. His case seems almost hopeless to me. The unfavourable prognosis has sent another wave of
despair over the entire party. Almost everybody is alarmed and
coming to me for medical treatment, for real or imaginary troubles. The complaints differ considerably, but the underlying cause
is the same in all. We are developing a form of anaemia peculiar
to the polar regions. An anaemia which I had noticed before
among the members of the first Peary Arctic edition, but our conditions are much more serious. To overcome this trouble I have

devised a plan of action, which the sailors call the 'baking treatment'. As soon as the pulse becomes irregular and rises to one hundred beats per minute, with a puffiness of the eyes and swollen ankles, the man is stripped and placed close to a fire for one hour each day. I prohibit all food except milk, cranberry sauce, and fresh meat, either penguin or seal steaks fried in oleomargarine. The patient is not allowed to do anything which will seriously tax the heart. His bedding is dried daily, and his clothing is carefully adjusted to the needs of his occupation. Laxatives are generally necessary: and vegetable bitters, with mineral acids, are a decided help. Strychnine is the only remedy which has given me any service in regulating the heart, and this I have used as a routine. But surely one of the most important things was to raise the patient's hopes and instil a spirit of good humour. When at all seriously afflicted, the men felt that they would surely die, and to combat this spirit of abject hopelessness was my most difficult task. My comrades, however, were excellent aids, for as soon as one of our number was down, everybody made it his business to create an air of good cheer about him.

The first upon whom I tried this system of treatment systematically was Lecointe. I had urged part of it upon Danco, but he could not eat the penguin, and when I told him he must, he said he would rather die. When Lecointe came under treatment I told him that if he would follow the treatment carefully I thought he would be out of bed in a week. I did not have this faith in the treatment at that time, but I had confidence in the soundness of Lecointe's organs and I wished to boom up the man. Lecointe replied by saying, 'I will sit on the stove for a month and eat penguins for the rest of my polar life if that will do me good.' (He did sit beside the stove two hours daily for a month, and he ate, by his own choosing, penguin steaks for the balance of his stay in the polar circle. In a week he was about, and in a fortnight he again made his observations, and for the rest of his polar existence he was again one of the strongest men on the *Belgica*.)

July 15. – The weather continues cold, but clear and calm, the only three qualities which make the antarctic climate endurable during the night. There is now much light. One can read ordinary print at 9 A.M., and at noon the north is flushed with a glory of green and orange and yellow. We are still very feeble. An exercise of one hour sends the pulse up to 130, but we have all learned to like and crave penguin meat. To sleep is our most difficult task, and to avoid work is the mission of everybody. Arctowski says, 'We are in a mad-house,' and our humour points that way.

July 21. – The night is clear and sharp, with a brightness in the sky and a blueness on the ice which we have not seen since the first few days after sunset. An aurora of unusual brightness is arched across the southern sky. The transformation in its figure is rapid, and the wavy movement is strikingly noticeable. We are all out looking at the aurora, some by way of curiosity, but others are seriously studying the phenomenon. Arctowski, bundled in a wealth of Siberian furs, is walking up and down the deck, ascending to the bridge and passing in and out of the laboratory, as if some great event were about to transpire. Racovitza, with a pencil in his bare hand, in torn trousers, and without a coat or a hat, comes out every few minutes and, with a shiver, returns to make serious sketches of the aurora and humorous drafts of the unfortunate workers in the 'cold, ladyless south.' These daily touches of humour by 'Raco' are bitterly sarcastic but extremely amusing. Lecointe, lost in a Nansen suit of furs, has been out on the pack in his observatory, which he calls the 'Hotel,' and is particularly elated because he has succeeded in getting an observation. 'Now,' says he, 'we will know when this bloody sun will rise.' Our position is latitude 70° 36′ 19″, longitude 86° 34′ 19″. If we continue to drift northerly a little, if the temperature remains low enough to give a great refraction, and if the weather remains clear, the captain promises us a peep of the sun for a few moments to-morrow. This is the happiest bit of news which has come to us, and it sends a thrill of joy from the cabin to the fore-castle.

July 22. – Every man on board has long since chosen a favourite elevation from which to watch the coming sight. Some are in the crow's nest, others on the ropes and spars of the rigging; but these are the men who do little travelling. The adventurous fellows are scattered over the pack upon icebergs and high hummocks. These positions were taken at about eleven o'clock. The northern sky at this time was nearly clear and clothed with the usual haze. A bright lemon glow was just changing into an even glimmer of rose. At about half-past eleven a few stratus clouds spread over the rose, and under these there was a play in colours, too complex for my powers of description. The clouds were at first violet, but they quickly caught the train of colours which was spread over the sky beyond. There were spaces of gold, orange, blue, green, and a hundred harmonious blends, with an occasional strip like a band of polished silver to set the colours in bold relief. Precisely at twelve o'clock a fiery cloud separated, disclosing a bit of the upper rim of the sun.

All this time I had been absorbed by the pyrotechnic-like display, but now I turned about to see my companions and the glory of the new sea of ice, under the first light of the new day. Looking towards the sun the fields of snow had a velvety aspect in pink. In the opposite direction the pack was noticeably flushed with a soft lavender light. The whole scene changed in colour with every direction taken by the eye, and everywhere the ice seemed veiled by a gauzy atmosphere in which the colour appeared to rest. For several minutes my companions did not speak. Indeed, we could not at that time have found words with which to express the buoyant feeling of relief, and the emotion of the new life which was sent coursing through our arteries by the hammer-like beats of our enfeebled hearts.

Lecointe and Amundsen were standing on an iceberg close to me. They faced the light, and watched the fragment of the sun slide under bergs, over hummocks, and along the even expanse of the frozen sea, with a worshipful air. Their eyes beamed with delight, but under this delight there was noticeable the accumulated suffering of seventy dayless nights. Their faces were drawn and thin, though the weight of their bodies was not reduced. The skin had a sickly, jaundiced colour, green, and yellow, and muddy. Altogether, we accused each other of appearing as if we had not been washed for months.

CHAPTER 2

'LANDFALL'

from *To the South Polar Regions* (1901)

Louis Bernacchi

Bernacchi, an Australian geologist on the Southern Cross expedition led by the quarrelsome Norwegian-Australian Carsten Borchgrevink, was not describing an unknown landscape in this account of the party's landfall at Cape Adare. James Clark Ross's ships back in the 1840s had discovered and named the rocky angle of Antarctica that greets you first, when you sail south from Tasmania. But Bernacchi and his companions were seeing it with a difference. Now humanity had come to stay; now they had arrived to find out where the astonishing vistas led, to learn what lay beyond the mountains. Bernacchi gazes south, and the curtain rises on a continent.

We were now in the open sea to the south, for not a particle of ice was visible in any direction. Large flocks of brown-backed petrels were seen, and numbers of whales of the finner type. A sharp look-out was kept for land, and at 7 P.M. on the 15th of February it was sighted; but it was only a glimpse we caught of it through the dense canopy of clouds. Since noon the wind had increased steadily in force, until towards evening it was blowing a furious gale from the southeast and was accompanied by clouds of drifting snow. All that night and the following day the storm raged with full fury and the ship laboured heavily in the heavy seas. She lay to under half topsails, plunging fiercely into the seas and sometimes burying her whole bows beneath the waves, whilst ever and anon mighty green billows would pour over our decks and rush down into the cabins below. Our horizon was narrowly limited by the sheets of spray borne by the wind and the drifting snow, so we could see no land although we were not far from it.

The storm gradually abated towards the afternoon of the 17th, and we were able to stand in once more for the coast. The weather continued to improve and the dense mist cleared a little. At two o'clock in the afternoon land was again sighted distant some twenty-five miles, and we headed for a dark and high mass of rock which was evidently Cape Adare. It was a Cape of a very dark basaltic appearance, with scarcely any snow laying upon it, thus forming a strong contrast to the rest of the snow-covered coast. This lack of snow is principally due to the very exposed position of the Cape to the south-east winds, and, perhaps, also to the steep and smooth nature of its sides, which afford no hold for any snowfall. As we approached the coast it changed continually in aspect. Sometimes dense clouds of mist would envelop it; at other times the clouds would roll up like a great curtain, disclosing to our eyes a long chain of snow-clad mountains, the peaks of which tapered up one above the other like the tiers of an amphitheatre or those of the Great Pyramid of Cheops; but it was only a momentary vision, quickly disappearing, then all was again sombre, nothing but the heaving mass of waters, the whistle of the wind in the cordage, and the blinding snow across our decks.

Although we were certainly twenty miles distant from the land, the intervening space seemed infinitely less; in those high latitudes the eye is constantly liable to be deceived in the estimate it forms of distances. Apart from the contrast of light and shade, the great height of the mountain ranges and their bareness (they being destitute of any trees, etc., whereby to afford a point of comparison) augment this singular deception.

The wind decreased in fury as we got under the lee of the shore, but the whole heavens were still overcast with a dark mantle of tempestuous clouds, which now and then enshrouded the land in its folds, hiding it entirely from our view. The Bay (Robertson Bay) was clear of ice excepting for a huge stranded and weather beaten iceberg in its centre, into the cavities of which the seas ever and anon rushed with a great roar. As we drew closer, the coast assumed a most formidable aspect. The most striking features were the stillness and deadness and impassibility of the new world. Nothing around but ice and rock and water. No token of vitality anywhere; nothing to be seen on the steep sides of the excoriated hills. Igneous rocks and eternal ice constituted the landscape. Here and there enormous glaciers fell into the sea, the extremities of some many miles in width. Afterwards, when the mist had cleared away, we counted about a dozen of them around the Bay, rising out of the waters like great crystal walls. Approaching this sinister coast for the first time, on such a boisterous, cold and gloomy day, our decks covered with drift snow and frozen sea water, the rigging encased in ice, the heavens as black as death, was like approaching some unknown land of punishment, and struck into our hearts a feeling preciously akin to fear when calling to mind that there, on that terrible shore, we were to live isolated from all the world for many long months to come. It was a scene, terrible in its austerity, that can only be witnessed at that extremity of the globe; truly, a land of unsurpassed desolation.

The bay, into which we had entered, was about forty miles in width, and appeared to be well sheltered from the south-west, south-south-east, and east winds, but was exposed to those from the north-west. At its southern extremity, one recognised the great peak of Mount Sabine, rising up in weird majesty to some 12,000 feet. We were now close in under the shore and in smooth water. How delightful it was to be in calm water under the lee of the cold high peaks, after being so long involved in the din of the roaring elements.

The Commander now decided to effect a landing and requested Mr. Fougner and me to accompany him ashore in a small canvas boat. We got into the frail craft and rowed her ashore, but it took nearly a quarter of an hour to reach the land, for, although the distance from the ship appeared small, it was actually great. The place of landing was a shelving beach, formed of gravel and pebbles; slight surf was breaking upon it and the boat had to be handled carefully so as to avoid capsizing.

Thus, after many months, we had attained our destination, notwithstanding the numerous obstacles with which our path had been beset.

After having hoisted up our boat out of reach of the sea, we commenced an examination of the place. We had not walked many yards before we met the secluded and melancholy inhabitants of that South Polar land; these were the penguins scattered about it in groups of a hundred and more. They extended us but cold courtesy and gravely regarded us from a distance; but on our approaching closer they evinced more interest and commenced talking loquaciously together in their own particular vernacular. They had evidently discovered that there was something unusual about our appearance, and some were commissioned to investigate matters. These, with perfect *sang-froid*, slowly marched right up to our feet and ogled up at us in a most ludicrous fashion. Having finished this scrutiny, they returned to their fellows as sedately as they had come, and thenceforth took no more notice of us. What impressed us greatly was the general appearance of sadness prevailing amongst them; they seemed to be under the shadow of some great trouble. It is no small matter that will arouse them from their stolidity. There were many young birds among them; no doubt most of the older ones had already migrated northwards, it being late in the year for them. The effluvium from the guano was very powerful. The strong ammoniacal odour at first gave us a sensation of nausea, but we soon got used to it and never afterwards suffered any unpleasantness. There was, however, no large accumulation of guano of any commercial value, for in no place was it deeper than from three to four inches, and this only in very small patches of only a few feet in extent. The powerful winds prevent any extensive formation by sweeping all accumulations into the sea.

Bleached remains of thousands of penguins were scattered all over the platform, mostly young birds that had succumbed to the severity of the climate. Thousands of years hence, if the species should become extinct, those remains, frozen and buried among the debris, will be available as a proof of what once existed in these gelid regions now just habitable, then, perhaps, not at all. Stretched out on their backs along the beach were many seals enjoying their quiet, hitherto undisturbed, siesta. They were of the species *Leptonychotes Weddelli*, of which we had not met one in the ice-pack; these were of a dark colour with light spots. As we approached them they opened their beautiful and large intelligent eyes, gazed at us nonchalantly, snorted, blinked, and went to sleep again. Fear with these animals, as also with the penguins, is evidently an acquired, and not an hereditary habit. Numerous mummified carcases of these seals were observed lying about.

We also saw a few Giant Petrels *(Ossifraga gigantea)* and a great number of skua-gulls *(Megalestris Maccormicki)*. These latter seemed to resent our visit, for they repeatedly darted at our heads and made a noisy outcry.

Satisfied with our preliminary survey of the place, we returned on board. The ship was brought in close to the shore and anchor let go in about eleven fathoms of water. Then, after some champagne-drinking and speech-making, we went on shore again, for all wanted to feel the rocks beneath their feet and to climb up the cliffs and get a look round.

It was nearly midnight when Mr. Hugh Evans and I commenced the ascent of Cape Adare. The light was still fairly strong at that time, nor was the temperature at all low. By following a ridge of craggy rocks we found the climbing tolerably easy and reached the top in less than an hour. We were thus the first human beings to set foot on the summit of South Victoria Land, and we felt full compensation for our climb. On the way up, we saw a few penguins, and even at the top (950 feet by aneroid) there were traces of them.

The scene before us looked inexpressibly desolate. A more barren desert cannot be conceived, but one of immense interest from a geological point of view.

From the end of the Cape to the foot of the mountain-range beyond, a great waste of hollows and ridges lay before our eyes; ridges rising beyond ridges like ocean waves, whose tumult had been suddenly frozen into stone. Beds of snow and ice filled up some of these extensive hollows, which had been scooped out by glacier action.

Never before had I seen the evidences of volcanic and of glacier action laying side by side – the hobnobbing of extreme heat and extreme cold. Great fire-scathed masses of rock rose out of the *debris* formed by the glaciers that had passed over the land. Vast convulsions must at one time have shaken the foundations of this land. But now silence and deep peace brooded over the scene that once had been so fearfully convulsed.

When we had set out the weather was fine, but later on the sky became overcast, as dark ominous clouds rolled up from the north-east.

The prospect from where we were was extensive, but scarcely beautiful. Down at our feet lay the sea, almost free of ice-pack. Huge stranded icebergs, defying the power of the solar beams, were visible in various directions along the coast. Behind us lay the great Antarctic Land; snow peaks rising beyond one another until by distance they dwindled away to insignificancy. The silence and immobility of the scene was impressive; not the slightest animation or vitality anywhere. It was like a mental image of our globe in its primitive state – a spectacle of Chaos.

Around us ice and snow and the remnants of internal fires; above, a sinister sky; below, the sombre sea; and over all, the silence of the sepulchre!

CHAPTER 3

'SLEDGE DOGS AND ENGLISHMEN'

from *Diary of the Discovery Expedition, 1901–4* (1967)

Edward Wilson

The Discovery's *voyage to the Ross Sea in 1900 to 1904 was an expedition on a different scale from any of the nimble scouting-parties that had gone before. It was imperial Britain's grand, official effort, masterminded at home by a fantasizing octogenarian savant, and equipped with no expense spared. But out in the great whiteness, as a pioneer party went south across the Ross Ice Shelf, the* Discovery's *big plans still came down to three men and a dog team, facing the cold. In this journal kept by the biologist-surgeon Edward Wilson, you won't find more than faint traces of one of the two crises that struck the travellers. Wilson's eye was too kind, perhaps too unearthly, for him to record the rivalry that unfolded between Robert Scott, the leader, and the third man, the Anglo-Irish merchant marine lieutenant Ernest Shackleton. But his journal is full of the other problem that made this trip such a disastrous influence on later British expedition, such a crucible for trouble yet to come. Here we watch all three of them struggle, and fail, to master dog-driving — the only technology that could have made their passage through the snow something better than an ordeal.*

Sunday, 16 Nov. — Twenty-fifth Sunday after Trinity. A perfectly beautiful day, and we turned out at 6 A.M. We first tried the dogs with the total weights and six sledges. They were altogether too much for them on this surface, so we decided to start relay work. We did 2½ miles three times over before lunch, bringing up 3 sledges at a time, then taking the dogs back and bringing up the other three. We did the same after lunch, covering 15 geographical miles in the day and making 5 miles good to the south. Tedious work. We had most brilliant sunshine all day. After camping, there was a fine dog fight in which every one of the team succeeded in joining, as both the dog pickets were dragged out. A white low mist rises over the Barrier surface during the small hours of the night after these sunny cloudless days, and in the mist is nearly always to be seen a white fog-bow facing the sun.

Wed 19 Nov. – Weather as before. Dead calm all day and very misty. Ice crystals falling all day, very thickly tonight. Altogether beautiful weather as the sun breaks through now and again and patches of blue sky overhead. Hard day's work. 15 miles covered to make 5 miles southing. Dogs getting very tired and very slow. We were at it from 11.30 A.M. till 9.30 P.M. and now at 11.15 P.M. we are at last in our sleeping bags. Surface worse than ever, with a thick coating of loose ice crystals like fine sand. We pray for a wind to sweep it all off and give us a hard surface again. This is wearing us out and the dogs, and yet we cover no ground. And the exertion of driving the poor beasts is something awful. Fine halo with brilliant prismatic parhelia round the sun today. There was a double halo for a while at 4 P.M., the outer one having the more marked prismatic colours and a radius about twice that of the inner. Thick fall of ice crystals again tonight. Have seen no land today, flat Barrier surface all round, very few sastrugi visible. Seriously thinking of giving the dogs a day off to rest.

Sat 22 Nov. – Northerly breeze, sufficient to just help us with both sails set. Beautiful day, but threatening to become overcast and

windy from the northwest. Turned out at 9 A.M. Made 2½ miles
southing before lunch, covering 7½ to do it, pulling hard with the
dogs all the way. After lunch we made 2¼ miles, 4¾ to the S.S.W.
during the day, and fourteen miles covered to make that. More new
land appearing to the southwest, and during the afternoon land
appeared right ahead to the S.S.W., which is very satisfactory, as we
can now make straight for it and leave a depot, and so reduce our
weights considerably. Altogether much more promising than this
slow and tedious plod to the south on an ice plain simply to beat a
southern record. Now we have new land to survey, and I have the
prospect of sketching, and we may find out something too which
will explain this extraordinary Great Barrier, as we are so to speak
getting to the back of it.

The surface today is very soft and heavy. We tried the dogs with
the whole weights today, but they could hardly move them. Very
tedious this relay work.

Tues 2 Dec. – 5 A.M. really begins the day, when we are writing up
our diaries in our sleeping bags after a long night's work, preparatory to turning in for the day. Slept nine hours solid. Turned out at
3 P.M. Covered 13 miles in making 4¼ to the southwest. My full day
on. The Captain had the luncheon camping and in preparing our
hot stuff set the tent alight, luckily just as we came up with the
second loads, or the blessed thing would have been burnt.
Providentially I was able to grab the thing the moment the flame
came through to the outside and put it out, so that the only damage
was a hole you could put your head through.

We had a heavy day and turned in late about 6 A.M. The weather
from 5 P.M. till midnight was overcast and we could see nothing.
Then it cleared quickly and the new land all came in sight ahead

of us, more and more new land appearing to the south. One can now see a lot of detail in it, and it seems to consist of a series of fine bold mountain ranges with splendid peaks, all snow-clad to the base of course, but here and there rocky precipices, too steep to hold the snow, stood out bold and dark. It was a wonderful sight, the pale blue shadows in the white ranges standing against a greenish sky.

The dogs pulled well until the last lap when the sun was very hot and they 'threw their 'ands in', and refused to do anything. The only thing then is to beat them and get them on yard by yard, sickening work. Many of them are badly chafed by the harness.

Fri 5 Dec. – Just turned in, 4 A.M. Turned out again at 4 P.M. Nearly every night now we dream of eating and food. Very hungry always, our allowance being a very bare one. Dreams as a rule of splendid food, ball suppers, sirloins of beef, caldrons full of steaming vegetables. But one spends all one's time shouting at waiters who won't bring one a plate of anything, or else one finds the beef is only ashes when one gets it, or a pot full of honey has been poured out on a sawdusty floor. One very rarely gets a feed in one's sleep, though occasionally one does. For one night I dreamed that I ate the whole of a large cake in the hall at Westal without thinking and was horribly ashamed when I realized it had been put there to go in for drawing room tea, and everyone was asking where the cake was gone. These dreams were very vivid, I remember them now, though it is two month since I dreamed them. One night I dreamed that Sir David Gill at the Cape was examining me in Divinity and I told him I had only just come back from the farthest south journey and was frightfully hungry, so he got in a *huge* roast sirloin of beef and insisted on filling me up to the brim before he examined me.

Glorious day again, without a cloud. New plan today. We did 4 miles straight off with the first half load, then had our cold lunch as we went back for the second half with the dogs. Twelve miles we covered to make this four towards our depot. At a mile and a half from camp I went on ahead on ski and prepared the tent and got the supper under way. My eyes are a bit touched by the sun glare today. On these night marches we have the sun straight in our faces to the south and so strong is the glare that it catches one, notwithstanding all one's care. I have worn snow goggles every day since our start.

Tues 9 Dec. – 2 A.M. Just turned in. Warm sunny morning. Beautiful range of rugged snowcovered mountains before us, with a long rounded snow hill at the foot. Did some darning. Woke up at 10 A.M. and as it was very hot in the tent, I sat outside in the hot sun and made a sketch of the panorama of new land before us. The heat was intense and there was no breeze. So one could easily sketch in bare hands and they got sun scorched. Turned in again when I had finished and slept till 4 P.M. when we had breakfast. Broiling hot sun all day. The dogs managed 2½ miles with half loads, but Snatcher died in the night and on opening him I found he had died of an acute peritonitis.

The snow today was soft, ankle deep, and the work very hot and heavy. No breeze except an occasional puff from the north. No clouds, the sun scorching down on us the whole march. We turned in at 4 A.M., no one having had a rest in camp today, as all three are needed to haul and help the dogs.

Thurs 11 Dec. – 5 A.M. Just turned in. The skua is still with us. Turned out at 4 P.M. after another very hot night in the tent. We started seal meat with our breakfast, as well as having it for lunch today. Very heavy day's work. Covered nine miles and made 3 good towards the land. Soft and heavy snow, the dogs constantly stopping all together and refusing to pull on. The Captain had the camp shift. The dogs seem a trifle better in health for the pieces of their companion, whom I cut up and distributed among them. Not one refused to eat it, indeed most of them neglected their fish for it. There was no hesitation. 'Dog don't eat dog' certainly doesn't hold down here, any more than does Ruskin's aphorism in *Modern Painters* that 'A fool always wants to shorten space and time; a wise man wants to lengthen both'. We must be awful fools at that rate, for our one desire is to shorten the space between us and the land. Perhaps Ruskin would agree that we are awful fools to be here at all, though I think if he saw these new mountain ranges he might think perhaps it was worth it.

The snow is soft and one sinks in at every step, making the walking very fatiguing. Supper, sleeping bag and breakfast are joys worth living for under these conditions. Only our appetites have clean outgrown our daily rations and we are always ravenously hungry, before meals painfully so for an hour or two.

Wed 17 Dec. – 4 A.M. and a well marked fog-bow of white light. Just turned into our bags after camping and supper. I act as butcher every night now, killing a dog when necessary and cutting him up to feed the others. Slept well and woke at 11.20 when all the fog was gone and it was a brilliantly clear hot sunny day. No breeze. So I left my bag and the tent and sat sketching on the sledges for nearly three hours, when the others turned out and we had breakfast. We spent

an hour upon odd jobs and started away south or a trifle east of south towards the land farthest visible.

I was leading, but after 3 hours got such a violent attack of sunglare in my eyes that I could see nothing. Yet I had worn grey glasses all the time sketching, and grey glasses as well as leather snow goggles on the march. I put in some drops and for the remaining five hours pulled behind with both eyes blindfold. They were very painful and streaming with water. By the time we camped they were better. We had lovely weather and the dogs pulled fairly well, making in all some 8 miles during the day. We passed some very splendid cliffs of rock and ice and glaciated land. The sun's heat was intense today, scorching our faces and hands. Noses constantly skinning, lips very painful, swollen and raw.

Sun 21 Dec. – Fourth Sunday in Advent. I now save half a biscuit from supper to eat when I wake at night, otherwise I simply can't sleep again. I have never experienced such craving for more food before. We turned out about 7 A.M. and after breakfast made 2¼ miles when the dogs became so utterly rotten that we camped. It was very hot and close and we decided to start again at night time. Soft snowflakes falling, no sun, but low stratus. We eat our cold lunch and then slumbered and did odd jobs from 1 till 7 P.M. when we had some hot Bovril chocolate with somatose, and made another start.

The dogs were worse than ever and after a mile and a half we had to give it up. They simply wouldn't attempt to pull and seem as weak as kittens. We then tried some experiments – uncoupled all the dogs and took off all the food we were carrying for them, leaving only our own kit and food for the month. The surface was so heavy that we three could hardly budge it at all. We camped and had supper and turned in for a short night, intending to get back to the day routine again tomorrow.

The night was as raw and cold as the day had been oppressively hot, up to plus 28° F. by the sling thermometer. Did my butcher's job and turned in.

Wed 24 Dec. – Christmas Eve. 2 A.M. In our bags writing up diaries or talking of food, letters and the relief ship. Turned out at 9.30 A.M. to a bright sunny morning, nice and warm. We had several jobs to do. We discarded and left the large sledge which carried all the dogs' fish and cut in two our own provision tank to take also the remains of the fish and carry the dog flesh. This meant a good bit of sewing as they are canvas tanks. Shackle and I did this, while the Captain took a round of angles and a sight, which put 81° 33½′ S.lat. We started away about 1 P.M. and made 5 miles by 6 P.M. Camped for lunch and then did 3 more by 9 P.M. when we camped for the night. As a result of today's medical examination I told the Captain that both he and Shackleton had suspicious looking gums, though hardly enough to swear to scurvy in them. No sketching today, very hazy light and excessive mirage. Surface rather better and dogs pulling better. My eyes touched by sun glare very painful during the night.

Fri 26 Dec. – Woke up at 5 A.M. and as the left eye is still uncomfortable, made a sketch, using the right eye only. About 10 A.M. we started off and made nearly 5 miles, when my left eye got so intensely painful and watered so profusely that I could see nothing and could hardly stand the pain. I cocainized it repeatedly on the march, but the effect didn't last for more than a few minutes. For two days too I have had this eye blind-fold for a trifling grittiness and now it came to this, while the right eye, which I had been using freely, was perfectly well. The Captain decided we should camp for lunch and the pain got worse and worse. I never had such pain in the eye before, and all the afternoon it was all I could do to lie still in my sleeping bag, dropping in cocaine from time to time. We tried ice, and zinc solution as well. After supper I tried hard to sleep, but after two hours of misery I gave myself a dose of morphia and then slept soundly the whole night and woke up practically well.

Sat 27 Dec. – Turned out at 7 A.M. Again a bright sunny day and no wind. I lay in my bag with my eyes bandaged while all the cooking was done, for fear of starting off again. The Captain and Shackle did everything for me. Nothing could have been nicer than the way I was treated. We started off at 10 A.M. and without camping for lunch, made a good march of 10 miles by 7 P.M., through a long day with a scorching sun. We then camped for the night.

From start to finish today I went blindfold both eyes, pulling on ski. Luckily the surface was smooth and I only fell twice. I had the strangest thoughts or day dreams as I went along, all suggested by the intense heat of the sun I think. Sometimes I was in beech woods, sometimes in fir woods, sometimes in the Birdlip woods, all sorts of places connected in my mind with a hot sun. And the swish-swish of the ski was as though one's feet were brushing through dead leaves, or cranberry undergrowth or heather or juicy blue-bells. One could almost see them and smell them. It was delightful. I had no pain in the eyes all day, a trifling headache. Towards evening we came in sight of a splendid new range of mountains still farther to the south.

❋

Wed 31 Dec. – Turned out at 6 A.M. NAO ration breakfast. Sun coming out and clouds rapidly clearing. We started off and made 4 or 5 miles by 2 P.M., watching the strait all the while to see if the head of it would clear. The mountains were perfectly beautiful today in the sunshine. As far as we could see, and apparently it was a blue horizon line, there was no land blocking the strait, so we must suppose this southernmost high land of 13,000 ft. to be insular perhaps. The strait was about 20 miles or more across and ran in due west, I should say. But all these details will appear when the Captain's map has been made out. He took a sort of running survey of the whole coast line.

All the morning we were crossing very immense pressure ridges radiating from the cape which formed the northern boundary of the strait. They were cut up in all directions by immense crevasses which were all filled in and bridged over with compacted snow. Sometimes from edge to edge the crevasse would measure 50 to 60 ft. and the whole train of sledges, dogs and all would be on the bridge at once. Only at the edges was there a risk of going through and some of the narrow crevasses too let one down suddenly.

At 2 P.M. we camped and after lunch, with some food in our pockets, we started off on ski to try and reach bare rock and bring back some specimens for the geologist. We also wanted to know whether there was anything in the way of a tide crack on shore or not, as this would practically decide whether the Barrier was afloat or aground. We ran in some 4 miles over smooth rounded pressure ridges, hills and vales and then were brought up by a perfect chaos of pressure and crevasses. We roped ourselves together, took off and left our ski at the edge and commenced to try and cross what appeared to be a gigantic tide crack, extending about a mile and a half across to the snow slopes that came off the land. Once across this, we could get our rock specimens which appeared quite close, but we had more than we could manage before us.

We started by going down steps cut in an ice slope, then by continual winding from side to side we made our way gradually across what at first looked like impassable crevasses, but in places they were filled in, though 50 to 80 ft. deep and blue ice, and in places they were bridged over. But after a while we were faced by more and more precarious bridges, and they got narrower and fewer, and were constantly giving way as we crossed them one by one on the rope. We never unroped the whole time, as there were crevasses everywhere and not a sign of some of them, till one of us went in and saw blue depths below to any extent you like. Shackleton was tied up in the middle, and the Captain and I at each end. Sometimes he led, sometimes I, if he came to an impasse and we had to go back.

As we got deeper and deeper in among this chaos of ice, the travelling became more and more difficult, and the ice all more recently broken up, so that no snow bridges had formed and we were faced by crevasses, ten, twenty, and thirty feet across, with sheer cliff ice sides to a depth of 50 or 80 ft. Unknown depths sometimes, because the bottom seemed a jumble of ice and snow and frozen pools of water and great screens of immense icicles. A very beautiful sight indeed, but an element of uncertainty about it, as one was always expecting to see someone drop in a hole, and while keeping your rope taut in case that happened, you would suddenly drop in a hole yourself. We tried hard to cross all this and reach the rock, but after covering a mile or more of it we came to impassable crevasses, and then saw that the land snow slope ended in a sheer ice cliff, a true ice foot, of some 40 ft. which decided us to retrace our steps, as even if we reached it, this ice foot would prevent our reaching rock.

The sun's heat was intense and not a breath of wind stirring. The heat has a very great power on these ice masses, as is evidenced by the immense icicles and frozen pools of what has been water. The colours, all shades of blue and pale green and shimmering lights were to be seen among these crevasses. The prismatic colours of the ice crystals were wonderful too today, forming what looked literally like a carpet of snow, glittering with gems of every conceivable colour, crimson, blue, violet, yellow, green and orange, and of a brilliance that would put any jewel in the shade. Our supper got upset in the tent sad to say, and we are so short of food that we scraped it all up off the floor cloth and cooked it up again. It was a soup so didn't suffer much. Another dog died today from sheer weakness.

Thurs 1 Jan. – New Year's Day. Best wishes to all at home, and the best of good luck to all of us. We turned out at 8 A.M. to breakfast. Fine hot sunny day again, slightly overcast by cirro-stratus. Got away by 11 A.M. and made 4½ miles by 2.30. Camped for an hour for lunch and then made 4 miles more by 7.30, when we camped for supper. 8½ miles in the day, homewards now. We had sail set all the afternoon with a fair breeze. The dogs are terribly weak and of very little use. Another dog dropped on the march today, too weak even to walk. We put him on the sledge till evening, and when we had fed them and gone into the tent, he was killed by his neighbour in the trace, for his food. Our tent floor cloth, a large square of Willesden canvas, we use as a sail and it makes an excellent one.

What we have to consider is that we shall soon have no dogs at all and shall have to pull all our food and gear ourselves. And we don't know anything about the snow surface of the Barrier during summer. It may be quite different to what it was on the way south. One *must* leave a margin for heavy surfaces, bad travelling, and weather, difficulty in picking up depots, and of course the possibility of one of us breaking down. We have been making outwards from the coast today and find the surface improving as we do so. Close in shore it is apparently windless, and there is evidently a tremendous precipitate every night during the summer of fog-crystals, which lie inches deep, feet deep in places, forming a smooth, soft, crustless surface of flocculent snow.

Mon 5 Jan. – Turned out 6.30 A.M. Fine sunny morning with northerly breeze and a little cirrus about. Made 4¼ miles in the morning, lunching at one. I sketched outside on my bag as the sun was warm and the breeze had dropped. Our lunch is a meagre meal – a biscuit and a half, eight lumps of sugar and a piece of sealmeat. One can hold it all in one hand, but it serves to carry us on for three hours' hauling in the afternoon. During this we covered 3¾ miles today in very deep soft ice crystals. We can now pull the sledges ourselves, so we have given up driving the dogs. They are doing no work at all.

We had yesterday the most beautiful cloud colouring round the sun, and again today much the same. There were cirrus clouds on a blue sky round the sun and these were beautifully edged with a vivid scarlet – a real vermilion, which ran into orange, yellow and pure violet on white cirrus clouds. The breeze today continued northerly, but the sun on the snow crystals made the sledges run very easily on the whole. One sweats very freely all day long. We have got into a routine now which balances our work and our food supply to a nicety, keeping us always hungry.

Wed 7 Jan. – Turned out at 6 A.M. Bright warm and sunny morning. Started off with a light head wind from the northwest. Cast all

the remaining dogs adrift and pulled the sledges ourselves on foot. Good surface. Made 5½ miles by 12.30. Camped for lunch. All the land partly obscured by low stratus. After lunch made up the 10 miles and camped at 5 P.M. Very hot sun, but more or less overcast sky. Very free perspiration, wet through all day. Washed our feet and hands in the snow on camping. Another dog dropped today.

The cloud effects over the land have been very fine all day, rolling cumulus clouds among the snow mountains and deep shadows, alternating with bright sunlight. It was a great relief to us today to plod along with no worry from the dogs. They all followed at their own pace. We had spells of conversation and long spells of silence, during which my thoughts wandered on ahead of me to the days that are yet to come.

CHAPTER 4

'FARTHEST SOUTH'

from *The Heart of the Antarctic* (1909)

Ernest Shackleton

*Shackleton came back to Antarctica in 1907 as the leader of his own
expedition, outraging Scott, who believed Shackleton had promised to
leave alone the whole Ross Sea route to the Pole. What really petrified
Scott, of course, was the astonishing hair's-breadth failure to reach the
Pole excerpted here. With a man-hauling technique for travel as dogged
and painful as his rival's, Shackleton had nonetheless traversed the Ice
Shelf, discovered a glacier leading up through the blockading mountains, and burst out into the globe's very last terrain, the high ice plateau
where the South Pole lay. Frantically calculating and recalculating his
supplies, Shackleton discovered that even starvation rations would not
let him take the last steps – and turned for home ninety-seven miles from
glory, a decision with a humane magnificence about it that still endures,
even if luck then played a part in bringing him back alive from the risks
he had already taken to reach his Farthest South.*

December 21. Midsummer Day, with 28° of frost! We have frost-
bitten fingers and ears, and a strong blizzard wind has been blowing
from the south all day, all due to the fact that we have climbed to an
altitude of over 8000 ft. above sea-level. From early morning we
have been striving to the south, but six miles is the total distance

gained, for from noon, or rather from lunch at 1 P.M., we have been hauling the sledges up, one after the other, by standing pulls across crevasses and over great pressure ridges. When we had advanced one sledge some distance, we put up a flag on a bamboo to mark its position, and then roped up and returned for the other. The wind, no doubt, has a great deal to do with the low temperature, and we feel the cold, as we are going on short commons. The altitude adds to the difficulties, but we are getting south all the time. We started away from camp at 6.45 A.M. to-day, and except for an hour's halt at lunch, worked on until 6 P.M. Now we are camped in a filled-up crevasse, the only place where snow to put round the tents can be obtained, for all the rest of the ground we are on is either névé or hard ice. We little thought that this particular pressure ridge was going to be such an obstacle; it looked quite ordinary, even a short way off, but we have now decided to trust nothing to eyesight, for the distances are so deceptive up here. It is a wonderful sight to look down over the glacier from the great altitude we are at, and to see the mountains stretching away east and west, some of them over 15,000 ft. in height. We are very hungry now, and it seems as cold almost as the spring sledging. Our beards are masses of ice all day long. Thank God we are fit and well and have had no accident, which is a mercy, seeing that we have covered over 130 miles of crevassed ice.

December 22. All day long, from 7 A.M., except for the hour when we stopped for lunch, we have been relaying the sledges over the pressure mounds and across crevasses. Our total distance to the good for the whole day was only four miles southward, but this evening our prospects look brighter, for we must now have come to the end of the great glacier. It is flattening out, and except for crevasses there will not be much trouble in hauling the sledges to-morrow. One sledge to-day, when coming down with a run over a pressure ridge, turned a complete somersault, but nothing was damaged, in spite of the total weight being over 400 lb. We are now dragging 400 lb. at a time up the steep slopes and across the ridges, working with the alpine rope all day, and roping ourselves together when we go back for the second sledge, for the ground is so treacherous that many times during the day we are saved only by the rope from falling into fathomless pits. Wild describes the sensation of walking over this surface, half ice and half snow, as like walking over the glass roof of a station. The usual query when one of us falls into a crevasse is: 'Have you found it?' One gets somewhat callous as regards the immediate danger, though we are always glad to meet crevasses with their coats off, that is, not hidden by the snow covering. To-night we are camped in a filled-in crevasse. Away to the north down the glacier a thick cumulus cloud is lying, but some of the largest mountains are standing out clearly. Immediately behind us lies a broken sea of pressure ice. Please God, ahead of us there is a clear road to the Pole.

December 23. Eight thousand eight hundred and twenty feet up, and still steering upwards amid great waves of pressure and ice-falls, for our plateau, after a good morning's march, began to rise in higher ridges, so that it really was not the plateau after all. To-day's crevasses have been far more dangerous than any others we have crossed, as the soft snow hides all trace of them until we fall through. Constantly to-day one or another of the party has had to be hauled out from a chasm by means of his harness, which had alone saved him from death in the icy vault below. We started at 6.40 A.M. and worked on steadily until 6 P.M., with the usual lunch hour in the middle of the day. The pony maize does not swell in the water now, as the temperature is very low and the water freezes. The result is that it swells inside after we have eaten it. We are very hungry indeed, and talk a great deal of what we would like to eat. In spite of the crevasses, we have done thirteen miles to-day to the south, and we are now in latitude 85° 41′ South. The temperature at noon was plus 6° Fahr. and at 6 P.M. it was minus 1° Fahr., but it is much lower at night. There was a strong south-east to south-south-east wind blowing all day, and it was cutting to our noses and burst lips. Wild was frost-bitten. I do trust that to-morrow will see the end of this bad travelling, so that we can stretch out our legs for the Pole.

December 24. A much better day for us; indeed, the brightest we have had since entering our Southern Gateway. We started off at 7 A.M. across waves and undulations of ice, with some one or other of our little party falling through the thin crust of snow every now and then. At 10.30 A.M. I decided to steer more to the west, and we soon got on to a better surface, and covered 5 miles 250 yards in the forenoon. After lunch, as the surface was distinctly improving, we discarded the second sledge, and started our afternoon's march with one sledge. It has been blowing freshly from the south and drifting all day, and this, with over 40° of frost, has coated our faces with ice. We get superficial frost-bites every now and then. During the afternoon the surface improved greatly, and the cracks and crevasses disappeared, but we are still going uphill, and from the summit of one ridge saw some new land, which runs south-south-east down to latitude 86° South. We camped at 6 P.M., very tired and with cold feet. We have only the clothes we stand up in now, as we depoted everything else, and this continued rise means lower temperatures than I had anticipated. To-night we are 9095 ft. above sea-level, and the way before us is still rising. I trust that it will soon level out, for it is hard work pulling at this altitude. So far there is no sign of the very hard surface that Captain Scott speaks of in connection with his journey on the Northern Plateau. There seem to be just here regular layers of snow, not much wind-swept, but we will see better the surface conditions in a few days. To-morrow will be Christmas Day, and our thoughts turn to home and all the attendant joys of the time. One longs to hear 'the hansoms slurring through the London mud.' Instead of that, we are lying in a little tent, isolated high on the roof of the end of the world, far, indeed, from the ways trodden of men. Still, our thoughts can fly across the wastes of ice and snow and across the oceans to those whom we are striving for and who are thinking of us now. And, thank God, we are nearing our goal. The distance covered to-day was 11 miles 250 yards.

December 25. Christmas Day. There has been from 45° to 48° of frost, drifting snow and a strong biting south wind, and such has been the order of the day's march from 7 A.M. to 6 P.M. up one of the steepest rises we have yet done, crevassed in places. Now, as I write, we are 9500 ft. above sea-level, and our latitude at 6 P.M. was 85° 55' South. We started away after a good breakfast, and soon came to soft snow, through which our worn and torn sledge-runners dragged heavily. All morning we hauled along, and at noon had done 5 miles 250 yards. Sights gave us latitude 85° 51' South. We had lunch then, and I took a photograph of the camp with the Queen's flag flying and also our tent flags, my companions being in the picture. It was very cold, the temperature being minus 16° Fahr., and the wind went through us. All the afternoon we worked steadily uphill, and we could see at 6 P.M. the new land plainly trending to the south-east. This land is very much glaciated. It is comparatively bare of snow, and there are well-defined glaciers on the side of the range, which seems to end up in the south-east with a large mountain like a keep. We have called it 'The Castle.' Behind these the mountains have more gentle slopes and are more rounded. They seem to fall away to the south-east, so that, as we are going south, the angle opens and we will soon miss them. When we camped at 6 P.M. the wind was decreasing. It is hard to understand this soft snow with such a persistent wind, and I can only suppose that we have not yet reached the actual plateau level, and that the snow we are travelling over just now is on the slopes, blown down by the south and south-east wind. We had a splendid dinner. First came hoosh, consisting of pony ration boiled up with pemmican and some of our emergency Oxo and biscuit. Then in the cocoa water I boiled our little plum pudding, which a friend of Wild's had given him. This, with a drop of medical brandy, was a luxury which Lucullus himself might have envied; then came cocoa, and lastly cigars and a spoonful of *creme de menthe* sent us by a friend in Scotland. We are full to-night, and this is the last time we will be for many a long day. After dinner we discussed the situation, and we have decided to still further reduce our food. We have now nearly 500 miles, geographical, to do if we are to get to the Pole and back to the spot where we are at the present moment. We have one months' food, but only three weeks' biscuit, so we are going to make each week's food last ten days. We will have one biscuit in the morning, three at mid-day, and two at night. It is the only thing to do. To-morrow we will throw away everything except the most absolute necessities. Already we are, as regards clothes, down to the limit, but we must trust to the old sledge-runners and dump the spare ones. One must risk this. We are very far away from all the world, and home thoughts have been much with us to-day, thoughts interrupted by pitching forward into a hidden crevasse more than once. Ah, well, we shall see all our own people when the work here is done. Marshall took our temperatures to-night. We are all two degrees sub normal, but as fit as can be. It is a fine open-air life and we are getting south.

December 26. Got away at 7 A.M. sharp, after dumping a lot of gear. We marched steadily all day except for lunch, and we have done 14 miles 480 yards on an uphill march, with soft snow at times and a bad wind. Ridge after ridge we met, and though the surface is better and harder in places, we feel very tired at the end of ten hours' pulling. Our height to-night is 9590 ft. above sea-level according to the hypsometer. The ridges we meet with are almost similar in appearance. We see the sun shining on them in the distance, and then the rise begins very gradually. The snow gets soft, and the weight of the sledge becomes more marked. As we near the top the soft snow gives place to a hard surface, and on the summit of the ridge we find small crevasses. Every time we reach the top of a ridge we say to ourselves: 'Perhaps this is the last,' but it never is the last; always there appears away ahead of us another ridge. I do not think that the land lies very far below the ice-sheet, for the crevasses on the summits of the ridges suggest that the sheet is moving over land at no great depth. It would seem that the descent towards the glacier proper from the plateau is by a series of terraces. We lost sight of the land to-day, having left it all behind us, and now we have the waste of snow all around. Two more days and our maize will be finished. Then our hooshes will be more woefully thin than ever. This shortness of food is unpleasant, but if we allow ourselves what, under ordinary circumstances, would be a reasonable amount, we would have to abandon all idea of getting far south.

December 27. If a great snow plain, rising every seven miles in a steep ridge, can be called a plateau, then we are on it at last, with an altitude above the sea of 9820 ft. We started at 7 A.M. and marched till noon, encountering at 11 A.M. a steep snow ridge which pretty well cooked us, but we got the sledge up by noon and camped. We are pulling 150 lb. per man. In the afternoon we had good going till 5 P.M. and then another ridge as difficult as the previous one, so that our backs and legs were in a bad way when we reached the top at 6 P.M., having done 14 miles 930 yards for the day. Thank heaven it has been a fine day, with little wind. The temperature is minus 9° Fahr. This surface is most peculiar, showing layers of snow with little sastrugi all pointing south-south-east. Short food make us think of plum puddings, and hard half-cooked maize gives us indigestion, but we are getting south. The latitude is 86° 19' South to-night. Our thoughts are with the people at home a great deal.

December 28. If the Barrier is a changing sea, the plateau is a changing sky. During the morning march we continued to go up hill steadily, but the surface was constantly changing. First there was soft snow in layers, then soft snow so deep that we were well over our ankles, and the temperature being well below zero, our feet were cold through sinking in. No one can say what we are going to find next, but we can go steadily ahead. We started at 6.55 A.M., and had done 7 miles 200 yards by noon, the pulling being very hard. Some of the snow is blown into hard sastrugi, some that look perfectly smooth and hard have only a thin crust through which we break when pulling; all of it is a trouble. Yesterday we passed our last crevasse, though there are a few cracks or ridges fringed with crystals shining like diamonds, warning us that the cracks are open. We are now 10,199 ft. above sea-level, and the plateau is gradually flattening out, but it was heavy work pulling this afternoon. The high altitude and a temperature of 48° of frost made breathing and work difficult. We are getting south – latitude 86° 31′ South to-night. The last sixty miles we hope to rush, leaving everything possible, taking one tent only and using the poles of the other as marks every ten miles, for we will leave all our food sixty miles off the Pole except enough to carry us there and back. I hope with good weather to reach the Pole on January 12, and then we will try and rush it to get to Hut Point by February 28. We are so tired after each hour's pulling that we throw ourselves on our backs for a three minutes' spell. It took us over ten hours to do 14 miles 450 yards to-day, but we did it all right. It is a wonderful thing to be over 10,000 ft. up, almost at the end of the world. The short food is trying, but when we have done the work we will be happy. Adams had a bad headache all yesterday, and to-day I had the same trouble, but it is better now. Otherwise we are all fit and well. I think the country is flattening out more and more, and hope to-morrow to make fifteen miles, at least.

December 29. Yesterday I wrote that we hoped to do fifteen miles to-day, but such is the variable character of this surface that one cannot prophesy with any certainty an hour ahead. A strong southerly wind, with from 44° to 49° of frost, combined with the effect of short rations, made our distance 12 miles 600 yards instead. We have reached an altitude of 10,310 ft., and an uphill gradient gave us one of the most severe pulls for ten hours that would be possible. It looks serious, for we must increase the food if we are to get on at all, and we must risk a depot at seventy miles off the Pole and dash for it then. Our sledge is badly strained, and on the abominably bad surface of soft snow is dreadfully hard to move. I have been suffering from a bad headache all day, and Adams also was worried by the cold. I think that these headaches are a form of mountain sickness, due to our high altitude. The others have bled from the nose, and that must relieve them. Physical effort is always trying at a high altitude, and we are straining at the harness all day, sometimes slipping in the soft snow that overlies the hard sastrugi. My head is very bad. The sensation is as though the nerves were being twisted up with a corkscrew and then pulled out. Marshall took our temperatures to-night, and we are all at about 94°, but in spite of this we are getting south. We are only 198 miles off our goal now. If the rise would stop the cold would not matter, but it is hard to know what is man's limit. We have only 150 lb. per man to pull, but it is more severe work than the 250 lb. per man up the glacier was. The Pole is hard to get.

December 30. We only did 4 miles 100 yards to-day. We started at 7 A.M., but had to camp at 11 A.M., a blizzard springing up from the south. It is more than annoying. I cannot express my feelings. We were pulling at last on a level surface, but very soft snow, when at about 10 A.M. the south wind and drift commenced to increase, and at 11 A.M. it was so bad that we had to camp. And here all day we have been lying in our sleeping-bags trying to keep warm and listening to the threshing drift on the tent-side. I am in the cooking-tent, and the wind comes through, it is so thin. Our precious food is going and the time also, and it is so important to us to get on. We lie here and think of how to make things better, but we cannot reduce food now, and the only thing will be to rush all possible at the end. We will do and are doing all humanly possible. It is with Providence to help us.

December 31. The last day of the old year, and the hardest day we have had almost, pushing through soft snow uphill with a strong head wind and drift all day. The temperature is minus 7° Fahr., and our altitude is 10,477 ft. above sea-level. The altitude is trying. My head has been very bad all day, and we are all feeling the short food, but still we are getting south. We are in latitude 86° 54' South to-night, but we have only three weeks' food and two weeks' biscuit to do nearly 500 geographical miles. We can only do our best. Too tired to write more to-night. We all get iced-up about our faces, and are on the verge of frost-bite all the time. Please God the weather will be fine during the next fourteen days. Then all will be well. The distance to-day was eleven miles.

January 1, 1909. Head too bad to write much. We did 11 miles 900 yards (statute) to-day, and the latitude at 6 P.M. was 87° 6½' South, so we have beaten North and South records. Struggling uphill all day in very soft snow. Every one done up and weak from want of food. When we camped at 6 P.M. fine warm weather, thank God. Only 172½ miles from the Pole. The height above sea-level, now 10,755 ft., makes all work difficult. Surface seems to be better ahead. I do trust it will be so to-morrow.

January 2. Terribly hard work to-day. We started at 6.45 A.M. with a fairly good surface, which soon became very soft. We were sinking in over our ankles, and our broken sledge, by running side-ways, added to the drag. We have been going uphill all day, and to-night are 11,034 ft. above sea-level. It has taken us all day to do

10 miles 450 yards, though the weights are fairly light. A cold wind, with a temperature of minus 14° Fahr., goes right through us now, as we are weakening from want of food, and the high altitude makes every movement an effort, especially if we stumble on the march. My head is giving me trouble all the time. Wild seems the most fit of us. God knows we are doing all we can, but the outlook is serious if this surface continues and the plateau gets higher, for we are not travelling fast enough to make our food spin out and get back to our depot in time. I cannot think of failure yet. I must look at the matter sensibly and consider the lives of those who are with me. I feel that if we go on too far it will be impossible to get back over this surface, and then all the results will be lost to the world. We can now definitely locate the South Pole on the highest plateau in the world, and our geological work and meteorology will be of the greatest use to science; but all this is not the Pole. Man can only do his best, and we have arrayed against us the strongest forces of nature. This cutting south wind with drift plays the mischief with us, and after ten hours of struggling against it one pannikin of food with two biscuits and a cup of cocoa does not warm one up much. I must think over the situation carefully to-morrow, for time is going on and food is going also.

January 3. Started at 6.55 A.M., cloudy but fairly warm. The temperature was minus 8° Fahr. at noon. We had a terrible surface all the morning, and did only 5 miles 100 yards. A meridian altitude gave us latitude 87° 22′ South at noon. The surface was better in the afternoon, and we did six geographical miles. The temperature at 6 P.M. was minus 11° Fahr. It was an uphill pull towards the evening, and we camped at 6.20 P.M., the altitude being 11,220 ft. above the sea. To-morrow we must risk making a depot on the plateau, and make a dash for it, but even then, if this surface continues, we will be two weeks in carrying it through.

January 4. The end is in sight. We can only go for three more

days at the most, for we are weakening rapidly. Short food and a
blizzard wind from the south, with driving drift, at a temperature
of 47° of frost, have plainly told us to-day that we are reaching our
limit, for we were so done up at noon with cold that the clinical
thermometer failed to register the temperature of three of us at 94°.
We started at 7.40 A.M., leaving a depot on this great wide plateau,
a risk that only this case justified, and one that my comrades agreed
to, as they have to every one so far, with the same cheerfulness and
regardlessness of self that have been the means of our getting as far
as we have done so far. Pathetically small looked the bamboo, one
of the tent poles, with a bit of bag sewn on as a flag, to mark our
stock of provisions, which has to take us back to our depot, one
hundred and fifty miles north. We lost sight of it in half an hour,
and are now trusting to our footprints in the snow to guide us back
to each bamboo until we pick up the depot again. I trust that the
weather will keep clear. To-day we have done 13⅓ geographical
miles, and with only 70 lb. per man to pull it is as hard, even harder,
work than the 100 odd lb. was yesterday, and far harder than the 250
lb. were three weeks ago, when we were climbing the glacier. This,
I consider, is a clear indication of our failing strength. The main
thing against us is the altitude of 11,200 ft. and the biting wind. Our
faces are cut, and our feet and hands are always on the verge of
frost-bite. Our fingers, indeed, often go, but we get them round
more or less. I have great trouble with two fingers on my left hand.
They had been badly jammed when we were getting the motor up
over the ice face at winter quarters, and the circulation is not good.
Our boots now are pretty well worn out, and we have to halt at
times to pick the snow out of the soles. Our stock of sennegrass is
nearly exhausted, so we have to use the same frozen stuff day after
day. Another trouble is that the lamp-wick with which we tie the
finnesko is chafed through, and we have to tie knots in it. These
knots catch the snow under our feet, making a lump that has to be

cleared every now and then. I am of the opinion that to sledge even in the height of summer on this plateau, we should have at least forty ounces of food a day per man, and we are on short rations of the ordinary allowance of thirty-two ounces. We depoted our extra underclothing to save weight about three weeks ago, and are now in the same clothes night and day. One suit of underclothing, shirt and guernsey, and our thin Burberries, now all patched. When we get up in the morning, out of the wet bag, our Burberries become like a coat of mail at once, and our heads and beards get iced-up with the moisture when breathing on the march. There is half a gale blowing dead in our teeth all the time. We hope to reach within 100 geographical miles of the Pole; under the circumstances we can expect to do very little more. I am confident that the Pole lies on the great plateau we have discovered, miles and miles from any out-standing land. The temperature to-night is minus 24° Fahr.

January 5. To-day head wind and drift again, with 50° of frost, and a terrible surface. We have been marching through 8 in. of snow, covering sharp sastrugi, which plays havoc with our feet, but we have done 13½ geographical miles, for we increased our food, seeing that it was absolutely necessary to do this to enable us to accomplish anything. I realise that the food we have been having has not been sufficient to keep up our strength, let alone supply the wastage caused by exertion, and now we must try to keep warmth in us, though our strength is being used up. Our temperatures at 5 A.M. were 94° Fahr. We got away at 7 A.M. sharp and marched till noon, then from 1 P.M. sharp till 6 P.M. All being in one tent makes our camp-work slower, for we are so cramped for room, and we get up at 4.40 A.M. so as to get away by 7 A.M. Two of us have to stand outside the tent at night until things are squared up inside, and we find it cold work. Hunger grips us hard, and the food-supply is very small. My head still gives me great trouble. I began by wishing that my worst enemy had it instead of myself, but now I don't wish even my worst enemy to have such a headache; still, it is no use talking about it. Self is a subject that most of us are fluent on. We find the utmost difficulty in carrying through the day, and we can only go for two or three more days. Never once has the temperature been above zero since we got on to the plateau, though this is the height of summer. We have done our best, and we thank God for having allowed us to get so far.

January 6. This must be our last outward march with the sledge and camp equipment. To-morrow we must leave camp with some food, and push as far south as possible, and then plant the flag. To-day's story is 57° of frost, with a strong blizzard and high drift; yet we marched 13¼ geographical miles through soft snow, being helped by extra food. This does not mean full rations, but a bigger ration than we have been having lately. The pony maize is all finished. The most trying day we have yet spent, our fingers and faces being frost-bitten continually. To-morrow we will rush south with the flag. We are at 88° 7' South to-night. It is our last outward march. Blowing hard to-night. I would fail to explain my feelings if I tried to write them down, now that the end has come. There is only one thing that lightens the disappointment, and that is the feeling that we have done all we could. It is the forces of nature that have prevented us from going right through. I cannot write more.

January 7. A blinding, shrieking blizzard all day, with the temperature ranging from 60° to 70° of frost. It has been impossible to leave the tent, which is snowed up on the lee side. We have been lying in our bags all day, only warm at food time, with fine snow making through the walls of the worn tent and covering our bags. We are greatly cramped. Adams is suffering from cramp every now and then. We are eating our valuable food without marching. The wind has been blowing eighty to ninety miles an hour. We can hardly sleep. To-morrow I trust this will be over. Directly the wind drops we march as far south as possible, then plant the flag, and turn homeward. Our chief anxiety is lest our tracks may drift up, for to them we must trust mainly to find our depot; we have no land bearings in this great plain of snow. It is a serious risk that we have taken, but we had to play the game to the utmost, and Providence will look after us.

January 8. Again all day in our bags, suffering considerably physically from cold hands and feet, and from hunger, but more mentally, for we cannot get on south, and we simply lie here shivering. Every now and then one of our party's feet go, and the unfortunate beggar has to take his leg out of the sleeping-bag and have his frozen foot nursed into life again by placing it inside the shirt, against the skin of his almost equally unfortunate neighbour. We must do something more to the south, even though the food is going, and we weaken lying in the cold, for with 72° of frost the wind cuts through our thin tent, and even the drift is finding its way in and on to our bags, which are wet enough as it is. Cramp is not uncommon every now and then, and the drift all round the tent has made it so small that there is hardly room for us at all. The wind has been blowing hard all day; some of the gusts must be over seventy or eighty miles an hour. This evening it seems as though it were going to ease down, and directly it does we shall be up and away south for a rush. I feel that this march must be our limit. We are so short of food, and at this high altitude, 11,600 ft., it is hard to keep any warmth in our bodies between the scanty meals. We have nothing to read now, having depoted our little books to save weight, and it is dreary work lying in the tent with nothing to read, and too cold to write much in the diary.

January 9. Our last day outwards. We have shot our bolt, and the tale is latitude 88° 23' South, longitude 162° East. The wind eased down at 1 A.M., and at 2 A.M. we were up and had breakfast. At 4 A.M. started south, with the Queen's Union Jack, a brass cylinder containing stamps and documents to place at the furthest south point, camera, glasses, and compass. At 9 A.M. we were in 88° 23′ South, half running and half walking over a surface much hardened by the recent blizzard. It was strange for us to go along without the nightmare of a sledge dragging behind us. We hoisted Her Majesty's flag and the other Union Jack afterwards, and took possession of the plateau in the name of His Majesty. While the Union Jack blew out stiffly in the icy gale that cut us to the bone, we looked south with our powerful glasses, but could see nothing but the dead white snow plain. There was no break in the plateau as it extended towards the Pole, and we feel sure that the goal we have failed to reach lies on this plain. We stayed only a few minutes, and then, taking the Queen's flag and eating our scanty meal as we went, we hurried back and reached our camp about 3 P.M. We were so dead tired that we only did two hours' march in the afternoon and camped at 5.30 P.M. The temperature was minus 19° Fahr. Fortunately for us, our tracks were not obliterated by the blizzard; indeed, they stood up, making a trail easily followed. Homeward bound at last. Whatever regrets may be, we have done our best.

CHAPTER 5

'LT. SHIRASE'S CALLING CARD'

from *Nankyokuki* (1913)

Nobu Shirase

In January 1912, the race to the Pole between Scott's unwieldy British expedition and Amundsen's sleek Norwegian team was already working itself out, deep in the interior of the continent. But these two competing heavyweights were not the only ones in Antarctica. Almost unnoticed, Nobu Shirase's Japanese 'Dash Patrol' had moored near to Amundsen's ship in the Bay of Whales, and were unloading supplies onto the ice shelf for their own polar adventure. Very enthusiastic, very patriotic, and very much novices in the polar environment, Shirase's group depended on the dog-sledding skills of two Ainu he had brought along, from the indigenous community of the northern island of Hokkaido. With the guidance — not always acknowledged — of these experts, the Dash Patrol in fact managed to set a sledging speed record during their brief foray south. But the interest of Shirase's story lies not so much in what was achieved, as in how it filters the common themes of the Heroic Age through a strikingly different sensibility, and claims Antarctica as the imaginative possession of a world wider than Europe.

At 2 A.M. we made out a faint pale grey line on the horizon to port, which we thought must be either a mountain or a cloud. Not until 4:20 A.M. did we see that it was actually the undulating wall of the

Great Ice Barrier itself. As we drew nearer we could see it more and more clearly. At first sight the Barrier appeared as a sweeping crescent of ice about 150 *shaku* high; it was like a series of pure white folding screens, or perhaps a gigantic white snake at rest. The sea was fortunately clear of ice, and as we looked about us we were surrounded by the rippling greasy blue-green waters so characteristic of the Ross Sea. The ship was by now surging forward, with all sails set and engine full ahead.

We were now at a point some thirty miles east of the Bay of Whales, so this led to a suggestion that we change our plans and make a landing in King Edward VII Land. This was decided upon, and bringing the ship to within a mile of the Barrier, we sailed eastward along it in search of a place to land.

Looking to starboard there were numerous caves and fissures in the Barrier, the nearer ones reflecting a deep blue onto the sea, and the further ones black as a scattering of brush strokes on the surface. From projections along the walls of these fissures hung icicles, like glass rods suspended in festoons, and these caught the lapis lazuli reflection of the ever-moving waters below.

Suddenly, a gunshot echoed round the deck. It was Takeda testing the strength of the ice by firing a shot at an overhanging section which looked about to fall. The results only led us to conclude that for all its delicate appearance we were looking at an extremely tough form of ice. Takeda leant on his rifle and sighed. 'If only we had a 120 mm cannon! Just one shot with that would knock such a hole in this ice that we could land wherever we wanted.'

At 7:30 A.M. we rounded a promontory and came upon a small bay approximately two miles wide and running inland for about a mile. At the far end of the bay the ice rose steeply in a series of ridges, on one side the Barrier formed a cliff, and on the other the shore was low and flat rather like a harbour quay. It seemed a suitable place to land, and we brought *Kainan-maru* into the bay.

As soon as the ship hove to the stern the boat was lowered and Takeda, Tsuchiya, Onitaro Watanabe and Hanamori all clambered aboard. Lt. Shirase instructed them to reconnoitre the area around the bay, and they rowed off. With perfect timing, the sun came out from behind the clouds and the silver of the Barrier on both sides of us shone brilliantly on the blue-green waves. The boat slowly neared the shore, the red of its ensign plain to see as it fluttered on high. *Kainan-maru* followed it into the bay.

On the right-hand side of the bay was a big ice cave which cast a deep blue reflection on the water, and just at that moment we spotted a large seal lying on the ice at the entrance to this cave. We called out to the men on the boat, and they made fast to a corner of the ice and went for the seal, full of courage and shouting with excitement now that they had at last found a worthy opponent. Their four poles came down on the seal again and again, but the enemy bared its fangs and fought back. Its mouth opened wide and it stuck out its blood-red tongue like some huge serpent. The four men finally subdued their foe by a concerted attack from all sides during which it was surrounded and beaten down in a veritable frenzy of blows. This battle lasted a full thirty minutes, and all the combatants were showered with blood and drenched with sweat.

No sooner was the battle over than the four warriors shouted a loud *Banzai!* and started climbing the steep slope. They disappeared behind one of the ridges and then reappeared further up, moving towards the left. Advancing in single file, frequently stumbling and getting to their feet again, but all the while going onwards and upwards, they soon reached the top of the Barrier, from where they continued to march inland.

Back on the ship we waited impatiently for a sign of the four men. Forty minutes later, we saw their distant silhouettes moving on the Barrier. We could see the red of their raised ensign as they drew up in a line beneath it. We could hear them in the distance as they shouted *Banzai!* three times, and we saw four pairs of arms raised and lowered in salute as they shouted. They had just completed this little ceremony and started back when the seal with which they had done battle earlier suddenly revived. Slowly lifting its head it took a quiet look around and seeing that its enemies had gone started crawling towards the water's edge. 'Look out! The seal's come back to life! Oh no! It's going to get away!' We all shouted and gesticulated wildly from the deck, but our warriors had only just set off on their way back and couldn't possibly have got there in time to stop it.

We could only stamp our feet in frustration, and shout 'Oh! What a shame!' but it was all to no avail. The seal was already nearing the water's edge and was just about to dive in when Muramatsu could stand it no longer, and raising his gun took a pot-shot at it. Unfortunately he missed. Startled by the report, the seal quickened its pace and finally disappeared into the depths of the ocean. It seems that seals recover completely the moment they are back in the sea, however badly injured they may have seemed when out of the water. The creatures would appear to enjoy some kind of divine protection.

The boat returned with the four men at around 9:20 A.M. and Takeda gave Lt. Shirase a detailed description of what they had found.

From the landing place, which had been excellent, they had seen what looked like a whole range of icy peaks in the distance. When they had gone a little further these turned out to be not distant mountains but the end of a vast glacier which attended for tens of *ri* [200 km] inland. Such terrain would make the Dash Patrol wellnigh impossible. One side of the glacier was as precipitous as the other and there were crevasses running in all directions. Many of these were covered with a thin crust of ice which made the surface look safe where in fact it was extremely dangerous. Hanamori, who was in the lead, put his foot right through this icy crust and fell into a crevasse about three *skaku* [1 m] across and stretching north-south for many *ri*. Luckily Tsuchiya was right beside him and managed to haul him out, otherwise he would certainly have perished, but it was an extremely dangerous place, and after that incident they thought it best to give up all idea of landing there. They had lowered Lt. Shirase's visiting card into a deep crack in the ice, and come straight back.

We were all very disappointed, not least Lt. Shirase. However, Takeda urged us not to lose heart. He was convinced that our efforts in exploring the bay had not been wasted, and spoke with great feeling about the solemn grandeur of the Barrier. They had seen icicles the size of elephant's tusks, and just the opportunity of studying these at close quarters had made it all worth while.

Lt. Shirase named the huge glacier they had surveyed Yonin Hyōga and decided to call this bay Kainan Bay. The position is 78° 17′ S and 162° 50′ W. When the naming ceremony was over *Kainan-maru* put back out to sea.

After a general discussion about where to land, it was agreed that only the Main Landing Party would go ashore at the Bay of Whales, and that *Kainan-maru* would then take a Coastal Party back to explore King Edward VII Land. We altered course at 10 A.M., and started to steam westwards.

During the afternoon the sky gradually clouded over. The wind blew mournfully, the temperature dropped, and snow squalls drove sporadically across the deck. Then suddenly we realised that the dark shape we could just make out about twenty miles ahead was a ship. 'Look! Pirates!' said one of the sailors to Yoshino, who happened to be on deck.

Total panic ensued! Yoshino was so astonished he went round telling the whole ship, and everyone crowded on deck in disbelief. As we drew nearer, we could see that it was a lone sailing ship, but we were still uncertain where she was from. Just as the Japanese flag flew from the mast of *Kainan-maru*, this vessel was also flying a flag, but because of the distance and poor visibility we were unable to see it properly.

Eventually when only about five miles remained between the two ships, we managed to identify their flag. It was a blue cross on a red ground, and we were now in no doubt that she was *Fram*, the ship of the Norwegian Polar Expedition.

Soon after this we sailed into the Bay of Whales as planned. Unlike Kainan Bay which we had just left, the sea here was quite frozen over and we were unable to take *Kainan-maru* very far in. There was no helping it, so at 10 P.M. we rammed *Kainan-maru*'s bow into the ice edge to the east of *Fram* and approximately one and a half miles west of the eastern limit of the bay, and there we moored her to the ice.

On examining our surroundings we saw that the sea ice extended all the way to where the Barrier rose at the end of the bay, which was about fifteen miles from the ice edge. The bay was indeed enormous, and we had a truly panoramic view. The sea ice was thick and smooth and stretched rigid across from east to west, linking the ice cliffs of the Barrier which rose on either hand. Seals and penguins were dotted around on this vast white plain, and skuas and snow petrels swooped to left and right. Pods of whales swam about rippling the surface swell of the silent deep-blue sea, coming up close to the ship and emitting loud and eerie sounds as they blew fountains of water into the air.

The day had started snowy, but later as the dark clouds cleared it had turned into one of bright sunshine. Although it was almost midnight, the south polar sun shone tirelessly on and on, and we were blessed with light and warmth around the clock. This enabled us to carry out our work aboard according to plan.

No sooner had we made fast than Lt. Shirase gave orders for all expedition members to get ready to go ashore and explore. At this everyone's spirits rose, and we made an immediate start on all the rigorous preparations required. It was 11 P.M. when we left the ship and set off. As the crow flies it was about two miles from *Kainan-maru* to the Barrier, and our way lay over a sheet of ice which was three or four *shaku* [1 m] thick, but with only about five or six *sun* [18 cm] showing above water. Its level surface promised well for our advance.

However, it seemed that the season was approaching when this sheet of ice would float out to sea, and there were several cracks running in various directions, along the edges of which small embankments had formed which reminded one of the dykes separating paddy fields back home. It looked as if a sudden gust of wind from the south would blow it all straight out into the ocean. Moreover, some of the cracks were about seven or eight *sun* [22 cm] wide and we could see the deep blue of the sea and in it a large number of minnow-like fish swimming around. We had to exercise the greatest caution as we advanced and all felt that we really were walking on thin ice.

Our group advanced in a straight line towards the Barrier ahead, our feet making strange and ghostly squeaks as we trod on the half-frozen snow. We spied two or three seals along the way. Their coats, spotted but dark and glossy as lacquer, together with their general corpulence, were sufficient for us to surmise that there were plenty of fish in the surrounding seas. These seals seemed to be of a somewhat different species to those found in northern waters, and also to those we had caught so far.

We were all dressed alike with three shirts and two pairs of long underpants, over which we wore our uniforms complete with hoods, snow goggles, ear-muffs and gloves. On our feet we wore soft felt boots with metal crampons, and we each carried a long bamboo pole to steady us as we walked. As we advanced further and further onto the ice, the heat of the sun beat down on us from above and reflected up at us from the snow, and we began to feel uncomfortably hot. Soon the sweat was streaming off us and we were completely soaked. Those with overcoats took them off and walked on panting, with the coats slung over their shoulders. To make matters worse, the steam rising from our bodies condensed so as to form an extremely disagreeable mist on the dark lenses of the goggles we wore as protection against snowblindness. However, as we couldn't take them off, we just had to carry on walking in increasing discomfort, occasionally mopping the lenses as we went.

Eventually, after marching across the sea ice for about an hour, we reached the foot of the Barrier. A great wall of ice towered steeply more than two hundred *shaku* [60 m] above us with blue and purple lights rising like flames overhead, and as we gazed up in horror our skin turned to goose flesh at the sight that met our eyes. We could see that anything much stronger than a breeze would bring some of the steepest parts crashing straight down. Protruding blocks of ice, avalanches past and yet to come, precariously jutting chunks and lumps, all these contrasted with strangely carved shapes of a polished chalky whiteness. The blocks of ice continually falling from this cliff had smashed the sea ice below to such an extent that in places you could even see the water beneath it. Some of the floes were ratted on top of one another and as the great swells of the ocean surged to and fro beneath them they moved slowly up and down, sending strange rending noises like ripping silk echoing across the silent land and the sky. From holes in the ice seals occasionally showed their heads, baring their cruel fangs as they came up for air. Such awesome sights and stirrings are unique to the polar regions.

As you will have gathered from this description, the climb up the Barrier looked like being an extremely difficult one. However, our position as we attempted to walk along beneath the cliffs was no less dangerous.

We therefore decided to press on. Muramatsu, Yoshino and Hanamori took the lead and started to advance. They struck out

with caution, their poles in their hands, picking their way across the
rotten sea ice, scrambling on their bellies to climb atop a huge block
of fallen ice, then leaping a yawning chasm. Picking their way carefully to left and right they slowly advanced until at last they reached
the foot of the cliff itself. Ahead of them a recent mighty avalanche
had left a terrifying scar, and this was where their labours really
started. The ice ahead was steep, smooth and slippery, but before
they could even start their assault on the cliff they had to cross a
deep crevasse which barred their way. Glancing up they saw above
them an overhanging section of the Barrier which showed every
sign of imminent collapse, and they knew they were in mortal
danger. To put it bluntly, the slightest lapse of attention and their
fates would be sealed, either crushed beneath a block of ice or sent
plummeting into the depths of a crevasse. However, only by sur-
mounting the obstacle of the ice cliff would there be any further
advance, and as they had already pledged their very lives to this
venture they gathered their courage and determination in both
hands and fought with all their might, brandishing their snow-
shovels as weapons. The method was for one man to forge ahead
and dig a pathway through the snow and ice, while the others
waited behind him holding the rope attached to his waist as a safety
precaution in case he fell. They did not dare to raise their voices.
They took their turns to lead the way with apprehensive awe, as if
looking into the depths of a bottomless pool, or walking on tip-toe
across very thin ice.

However, their patient labours brought them step by step
towards the top. On reaching a smooth plateau of ice they looked
down, and saw the narrow path which they had cut snaking endlessly through the snow like a sheep's intestines. Then, turning
around, they suddenly realised that they had at last arrived on the
Barrier itself! Without a moment's pause to catch their breath or
mop away the sweat which now drenched their bodies, they shouted

loud *Banzais!*, raising both hands high in triumphal salute. The second and third units echoed their *Banzais!* from below, and soon to a succession of *Banzai! Banzai!* their fellow explorers emerged to join them at the top. Glancing at their watches they saw it was precisely midnight.

A minute later it was the morning of the following day, the 17th. As we all looked back at the way we had come, we saw the blue sea lying in an almost flat calm, the white ice floes scattered on its surface, and the two ships, *Kainan-maru* and *Fram*, floating in lonely isolation alongside the expanse of sea ice which covered the entire bay. This was a *sumie* world painted in Indian ink on white paper. On the ice around *Kainan-maru* we could just make out the black shapes of people dotted about and moving hither and thither to the sound of occasional gun shots, and surmised that the ship's crew were out and about on the ice, hunting penguins, seals and suchlike to dissipate the weariness of the long voyage, like little birds let out of their cage.

Turning to look in the other direction, we saw a boundless plain of white ice stretching undisturbed into infinity, meeting the blue sky and continuing beyond. Though we could sense the many secrets hidden in its depths, there was not a shadow to be seen. The sun was reflected off the white snow with dazzling brightness, and we were all struck to the very heart by a feeling of awe.

CHAPTER 6

'THE WINTER JOURNEY'

from *The Worst Journey in the World* (1922)

Apsley Cherry-Garrard

Probably the greatest piece of writing in all exploration literature, Cherry-Garrard's Worst Journey *is an account of the whole of Scott's catastrophic return to Antarctica, the* Terra Nova *expedition of 1910–13, as witnessed by a shy, impressionable, intensely short-sighted 'gentleman volunteer', whose experiences left him grief-struck almost to the point of madness. But the core of the book is the 'worst journey' itself, this unforgettable description of a side trip made in the subzero stillness of the winter before Scott started for the Pole. Cherry-Garrard and his companions, Edward Wilson ('Bill') and Herbert Bowers ('Birdie'), set off to collect the eggs of the Emperor Penguin, which only nests at the darkest point of the polar year. The near-impossibility of the route, given their primitive polar equipment, made the sixty-mile walk into a miniature epic of endurance. Wilson and Bowers would both die with Scott on the polar journey; but here, Cherry-Garrard remembers his friends at a time of paradoxical triumph, rising to the occasion with a devoted, graceful stoicism. No one in this very British trio ever curses, snaps or grumbles. Understatement does all their screaming for them.*

The horror of the nineteen days it took us to travel from Cape Evans to Cape Crozier would have to be re-experienced to be appreciated; and any one would be a fool who went again: it is not possible to describe it. The weeks which followed them were comparative bliss, not because later our conditions were better – they were far worse – but because we were callous. I for one had come to that point of suffering at which I did not really care if only I could die without much pain. They talk of the heroism of the dying – they little know – it would be so easy to die, a dose of morphia, a friendly crevasse, and blissful sleep. The trouble is to go on.

It was the darkness that did it. I don't believe minus seventy temperatures would be bad in daylight, not comparatively bad, when you could see where you were going, where you were stepping, where the sledge straps were, the cooker, the primus, the food; could see your footsteps lately trodden deep into the soft snow that you might find your way back to the rest of your load; could see the lashings of the food bags; could read a compass without striking three or four different boxes to find one dry match; could read your watch to see if the blissful moment of getting out of your bag was come without groping in the snow all about; when it would not take you five minutes to lash up the door of the tent, and five hours to get started in the morning . . .

But in these days we were never less than four hours from the moment when Bill cried 'Time to get up' to the time when we got into our harness. It took two men to get one man into his harness, and was all they could do, for the canvas was frozen and our clothes were frozen until sometimes not even two men could bend them into the required shape.

The trouble is sweat and breath. I never knew before how much of the body's waste comes out through the pores of the skin. On the most bitter days, when we had to camp before we had done a four-hour march in order to nurse back our frozen feet, it seemed that we must be sweating. And all this sweat, instead of passing away through the porous wool of our clothing and gradually drying off us, froze and accumulated. It passed just away from our flesh and then became ice: we shook plenty of snow and ice down from inside our trousers every time we changed our foot-gear, and we could have shaken it from our vests and from between our vests and shirts, but of course we could not strip to this extent. But when we got into our sleeping-bags, if we were fortunate, we became warm enough during the night to thaw this ice: part remained in our clothes, part passed into the skins of our sleeping-bags, and soon both were sheets of armour-plate.

As for our breath – in the daytime it did nothing worse than cover the lower parts of our faces with ice and solder our bala-clavas tightly to our heads. It was no good trying to get your balaclava off until you had had the primus going quite a long time, and then you could throw your breath about if you wished. The trouble really began in your sleeping-bag, for it was far too cold to keep a hole open through which to breathe. So all night long our breath froze into the skins, and our respiration became quicker and quicker as the air in our bags got fouler and fouler: it was never possible to make a match strike or burn inside our bags!

Of course we were not iced up all at once: it took several days of this kind of thing before we really got into big difficulties on this score. It was not until I got out of the tent one morning fully ready to pack the sledge that I realized the possibilities ahead. We had had our breakfast, struggled into our foot-gear, and squared up inside the tent, which was comparatively warm. Once outside, I raised my head to look round and found I could not move it back. My clothing had frozen hard as I stood – perhaps fifteen seconds. For four hours I had to pull with my head stuck up, and from that time we all took care to bend down into a pulling position before being frozen in.

By now we had realized that we must reverse the usual sledging routine and do everything slowly, wearing when possible the fur mitts which fitted over our woollen mitts, and always stopping whatever we were doing, directly we felt that any part of us was getting frozen, until the circulation was restored. Henceforward it was common for one or other of us to leave the other two to continue the camp work while he stamped about in the snow, beat his arms, or nursed some exposed part. But we could not restore the circulation of our feet like this – the only way then was to camp and get some hot water into ourselves before we took our footgear off. The difficulty was to know whether our feet were frozen or not, for the only thing we knew for certain was that we had lost all feeling in them. Wilson's knowledge as a doctor came in here: many a time he had to decide from our descriptions of our feet whether to camp or to go on for another hour. A wrong decision meant disaster, for if one of us had been crippled the whole party would have been placed in great difficulties. Probably we should all have died.

We were now getting into that cold bay which lies between the Hut Point Peninsula and Terror Point. In consequence of the lack of high winds the surface of the snow is never swept and hardened and polished as elsewhere: it was now a mass of the hardest and smallest snow crystals, to pull through which in cold temperatures was just like pulling through sand. I have spoken elsewhere of Barrier surfaces, and how, when the cold is very great, sledge runners cannot melt the crystal points but only advance by rolling them over and over upon one another. That was the surface we met on this journey, and in soft snow the effect is accentuated. Our feet were sinking deep at every step.

And so when we tried to start on June 30 we found we could not move both sledges together. There was nothing for it but to take one on at a time and come back for the other. This has often been done in daylight when the only risks run are those of blizzards which may spring up suddenly and obliterate tracks. Now in darkness it was more complicated. From 11 A.M. to 3 P.M. there was enough light to see the big holes made by our feet, and we took on one sledge, trudged back in our tracks, and brought on the second. Bowers used to toggle and untoggle our harnesses when we changed sledges. Of course in this relay work we covered three miles in distance for every one mile forward, and even the single sledges were very hard pulling. When we lunched the temperature was −61°. After lunch the little light had gone, and we carried a naked lighted candle back with us when we went to find our second sledge. It was the weirdest kind of procession, three frozen men and a little pool of light. Generally we steered by Jupiter, and I never see him now without recalling his friendship in those days.

We were very silent, it was not very easy to talk: but sledging is always a silent business. I remember a long discussion which began just now about cold snaps – was this the normal condition of the Barrier, or was it a cold snap? – what constituted a cold snap? The discussion lasted about a week. Do things slowly, always slowly, that was the burden of Wilson's leadership: and every now and then the question, Shall we go on? and the answer Yes. 'I think we are all right as long as our appetites are good,' said Bill. Always patient, self-possessed, unruffled, he was the only man on earth, as I believe, who could have led this journey.

That day we made three miles, and travelled ten miles to do it. The temperature was −66° when we camped, and we were already pretty badly iced up. That was the last night I lay (I had written slept) in my big reindeer bag without the lining of eider-down which we each carried. For me it was a very bad night: a succession of shivering fits which I was quite unable to stop, and which took possession of my body for many minutes at a time until I thought my back would break, such was the strain placed upon it.

They talk of chattering teeth: but when your body chatters you may call yourself cold. I can only compare the strain to that which I have been unfortunate enough to see in a case of lock-jaw.

We did the same relay work on July 1, but found the pulling still harder; and it was all that we could do to move the one sledge forward. From now onwards Wilson and I, but not to the same extent Bowers, experienced a curious optical delusion when returning in our tracks for the second sledge. I have said that we found our way back by the light of a candle, and we found it necessary to go back in our same footprints. These holes became to our tired brains not depressions but elevations: hummocks over which we stepped, raising our feet painfully and draggingly. And then we remembered, and said what fools we were, and for a while we compelled ourselves to walk through these phantom hills. But it was no lasting good, and as the days passed we realized that we must suffer this absurdity, for we could not do anything else. But of course it took it out of us.

During these days the blisters on my fingers were very painful. Long before my hands were frost-bitten, or indeed anything but cold, which was of course a normal thing, the matter inside these big blisters, which rose all down my fingers with only a skin between them, was frozen into ice. To handle the cooking gear or the food bags was agony, to start the primus was worse and when, one day, I was able to prick six or seven of the blisters after supper and let the liquid matter out, the relief was very great. Every night after that I treated such others as were ready in the same way until they gradually disappeared. Sometimes it was difficult not to howl.

I *did* want to howl many times every hour of these days and nights, but I invented a formula instead, which I repeated to myself continually. Especially, I remember, it came in useful when at the end of the march with my feet frost-bitten, my heart beating slowly, my vitality at its lowest ebb, my body solid with cold, I used to seize the shovel and go on digging snow on to the tent skirting while the cook inside was trying to light the primus. 'You've got it in the neck – stick it – stick it – you've got it in the neck,' was the refrain, and I wanted every little bit of encouragement it would give me: then I would find myself repeating 'Stick it – stick it – stick it – stick, it,' and then 'You've got it in the neck.' One of the joys of summer sledging is that you can let your mind wander thousands of miles away for weeks and weeks. Oates used to provision his little yacht (there was a pickled herring he was going to have): I invented the compactest little revolving bookcase which was going to hold not books, but pemmican and chocolate and biscuit and cocoa and sugar, and have a cooker on the top, and was going to stand always ready to quench my hunger when I got home: and we visited restaurants and theatres and grouse moors, and we thought of a pretty girl, or girls, and . . . But now that was all impossible. Our conditions forced themselves upon us without pause: it was not possible to think of anything else. We got no respite. I found it best to refuse to let myself think of the past or the future – to live only for the job of the moment, and to compel myself to think only how to do it most efficiently. Once you let yourself imagine . . .

I have met with amusement people who say, 'Oh, we had minus fifty temperatures in Canada; they didn't worry *me*,' or 'I've been down to minus sixty something in Siberia.' And then you find that they had nice dry clothing, a nice night's sleep in a nice aired bed, and had just walked out after lunch for a few minutes from a nice warm hut or an overheated train. And they look back upon it as an experience to be remembered. Well! of course as an experience of cold this can only be compared to eating a vanilla ice with hot chocolate cream after an excellent dinner at Claridge's. But in our present state we began to look upon minus fifties as a luxury which we did not often get.

That evening, for the first time, we discarded our naked candle in favour of the rising moon. We had started before the moon on purpose, but as we shall see she gave us little light. However, we owed our escape from a very sticky death to her on one occasion.

It was a little later on when we were among crevasses, with Terror above us, but invisible, somewhere on our left, and the Barrier pressure on our right. We were quite lost in the darkness, and only knew that we were running downhill, the sledge almost catching our heels. There had been no light all day, clouds obscured the moon, we had not seen her since yesterday. And quite suddenly a little patch of clear sky drifted, as it were, over her face, and she showed us three paces ahead a great crevasse with just a shining icy lid not much thicker than glass. We should all have walked into it, and the sledge would certainly have followed us down. After that I felt we had a chance of pulling through: God could not be so cruel as to have saved us just to prolong our agony.

But at present we need not worry about crevasses; for we had not reached the long stretch where the moving Barrier, with the weight of many hundred miles of ice behind it, comes butting up against the slopes of Mount Terror, itself some eleven thousand feet high. Now we were still plunging ankle-deep in the mass of soft sandy snow which lies in the windless area. It seemed to have no bottom at all, and since the snow was much the same temperature as the air, our feet, as well as our bodies, got colder and colder the longer we marched: in ordinary sledging you begin to warm up after a quarter of an hour's pulling, here it was just the reverse. Even now I find myself unconsciously kicking the toes of my right foot against the heel of my left: a habit I picked up on this journey by doing it every time we halted. Well no. Not always. For there was one halt when we just lay on our backs and gazed up into the sky, where, so the others said, there was blazing the most wonderful aurora they had ever seen. I did not see it, being so near-sighted and unable to wear spectacles owing to the cold. The aurora was always before us as we travelled east, more beautiful than any seen by previous expeditions wintering in McMurdo Sound, where Erebus must have hidden the most brilliant displays. Now most of the sky was covered with swinging, swaying curtains which met in a great whirl overhead: lemon yellow, green and orange.

We got forward only 2 miles, and by this time I had silently made up my mind that we had not the ghost of a chance of reaching the penguins. I am sure that Bill was having a very bad time these nights, though it was an impression rather than anything else, for he never said so. We knew we did sleep, for we heard one another snore, and also we used to have dreams and nightmares; but we had little consciousness of it, and we were now beginning to drop off when we halted on the march.

Our sleeping-bags were getting really bad by now, and already it took a long time to thaw a way down into them at night. Bill spread his in the middle, Bowers was on his right, and I was on his left. Always he insisted that I should start getting my legs into mine before *he* started: we were rapidly cooling down after our hot supper, and this was very unselfish of him. Then came seven shivering hours and first thing on getting out of our sleeping-bags in the morning we stuffed our personal gear into the mouth of the bag before it could freeze: this made a plug which when removed formed a frozen hole for us to push into as a start in the evening.

We got into some strange knots when trying to persuade our limbs into our bags, and suffered terribly from cramp in consequence. We would wait and rub, but directly we tried to move again down it would come and grip our legs in a vice. We also, especially Bowers, suffered agony from cramp in the stomach. We let the primus burn on after supper now for a time – it was the only thing which kept us going – and when one who was holding the primus was seized with cramp we hastily took the lamp from him until the spasm was over. It was horrible to see Birdie's stomach cramp sometimes: he certainly got it much worse than Bill or I. I suffered a lot from heartburn, especially in my bag at nights: we were eating a great proportion of fat and this was probably the cause. Stupidly I said nothing about it for a long time. Later when Bill found out, he soon made it better with the medical case.

Birdie always lit the candle in the morning – so called, and this was an heroic business. Moisture collected on our matches if you looked at them. Partly I suppose it was bringing them from outside into a comparatively warm tent; partly from putting boxes into pockets in our clothing. Sometimes it was necessary to try four or five boxes before a match struck. The temperature of the boxes and matches was about a hundred degrees of frost, and the smallest touch of the metal on naked flesh caused a frost-bite. If you wore mitts you could scarcely feel anything – especially since the tips of our fingers were already very callous. To get the first light going in the morning was a beastly cold business, made worse by having to make sure that it was at last time to get up. Bill insisted that we must lie in our bags seven hours every night.

In civilization men are taken at their own valuation because there are so many ways of concealment, and there is so little time, perhaps even so little understanding. Not so down South. These two men went through the Winter Journey and lived: later they went through the Polar Journey and died. They were gold, pure, shining, unalloyed. Words cannot express how good their companionship was.

Through all these days, and those which were to follow, the worst I suppose in their dark severity that men have ever come through alive, no single hasty or angry word passed their lips. When, later, we were sure, so far as we can be sure of anything, that we must die, they were cheerful, and so far as I can judge their songs and cheery words were quite unforced. Nor were they ever flurried, though always as quick as the conditions would allow in moments of emergency. It is hard that often such men must go first when others far less worthy remain.

There are those who write of Polar Expeditions as though the whole thing was as easy as possible. They are trusting, I suspect, in a public who will say, 'What a fine fellow this is! we know what horrors he has endured, yet see, how little he makes of all his difficulties and hard-ships.' Others have gone to the opposite extreme. I do not know that there is any use in trying to make a −18° temperature appear formidable to an uninitiated reader by calling it fifty degrees of frost. I want to do neither of these things. I am not going to pretend that this was anything but a ghastly journey, made bearable and even pleasant to look back upon by the qualities of my two companions who have gone. At the same time I have no wish to make it appear more horrible than it actually was: the reader need not fear that I am trying to exaggerate.

Luckily we were spared wind. Our naked candle burnt steadily as we trudged back in our tracks to fetch our other sledge, but if we touched metal for a fraction of a second with naked fingers we were frost-bitten. To fasten the strap buckles over the loaded sledge was difficult: to handle the cooker, or mugs, or spoons, the primus or oil can was worse. How Bowers managed with the meteorological instruments I do not know, but the meteorological log is perfectly kept. Yet as soon as you breathed near the paper it was covered with a film of ice through which the pencil would not bite. To handle rope was always cold and in these very low temperatures dreadfully cold work. The toggling up of our harnesses to the sledge we were about to pull, the untoggling at the end of the stage, the lashing up of our sleeping-bags in the morning, the fastening of the cooker to the top of the instrument box, were bad, but not nearly so bad as the smaller lashings which were now strings of ice. One of the worst was round the weekly food bag, and those round the pemmican, tea and butter bags inside were thinner still. But the real devil was the lashing of the tent door: it was like wire, and yet had to be tied tight. If you had to get out of the tent during the seven hours spent in our sleeping-bags you must tie a string as stiff as a poker, and re-thaw your way into a bag already as hard as a board. Our paraffin was supplied at a flash point suitable to low temperatures and was only a little milky: it was very difficult to splinter bits off the butter.

The temperature that night was −75.8°, and I will not pretend that it did not convince me that Dante was right when he placed the circles of ice below the circles of fire. Still we slept sometimes, and always we lay for seven hours. Again and again Bill asked us how about going back, and always we said no. Yet there was nothing I should have liked better: I was quite sure that to dream of Cape Crozier was the wildest lunacy. That day we had advanced 1½ miles by the utmost labour, and the usual relay work. This was quite a good march – and Cape Crozier is 67 miles from Cape Evans!

More than once in my short life I have been struck by the value of the man who is blind to what appears to be a common-sense certainty: he achieves the impossible. We never spoke our thoughts: we discussed the Age of Stone which was to come, when we built our cosy warm rock hut on the slopes of Mount Terror, and ran our stove with penguin blubber, and pickled little Emperors in warmth and dryness. We were quite intelligent people, and we must all have known that we were not going to see the penguins and that it was folly to go forward. And yet with quiet perseverance, in perfect friendship, almost with gentleness those two men led on. I just did what I was told.

Bill was anxious. It seems that Scott had twice gone for a walk with him during the Winter, and tried to persuade him not to go, and only finally consented on condition that Bill brought us all back unharmed: we were Southern Journey men. Bill had a tremendous respect for Scott, and later when we were about to make an effort to get back home over the Barrier, and our case was very desperate, he was most anxious to leave no gear behind at Cape Crozier, even the scientific gear which could be of no use to us and of which we had plenty more at the hut. 'Scott will never forgive me if I leave gear behind,' he said. It is a good sledging principle, and the party which does not follow it, or which leaves some of its load to be fetched in later is seldom a good one: but it is a principle which can be carried to excess.

And now Bill was feeling terribly responsible for both of us. He kept on saying that he was sorry, but he had never dreamed it was going to be as bad as this. He felt that having asked us to come he was in some way chargeable with our troubles. When leaders have this kind of feeling about their men they get much better results, if the men are good: if men are bad or even moderate they will try and take advantage of what they consider to be softness.

In the early morning of the next day snow began to fall and the fog was dense: when we got up we could see nothing at all anywhere. After the usual four hours to get going in the morning we settled that it was impossible to relay, for we should never be able to track ourselves back to the second sledge. It was with very great relief that we found we could move both sledges together, and I think this was mainly due to the temperature which had risen to −36°.

This was our fourth day of fog in addition to the normal darkness, and we knew we must be approaching the land. It would be Terror Point, and the fog is probably caused by the moist warm air coming up from the sea through the pressure cracks and crevasses; for it is supposed that the Barrier here is afloat.

I wish I could take you on to the great Ice Barrier some calm evening when the sun is just dipping in the middle of the night and show you the autumn tints on Ross Island. A last look round before turning in, a good day's march behind, enough fine fat pemmican inside you to make you happy, the homely smell of tobacco from the tent, a pleasant sense of soft fur and the deep sleep to come. And all the softest colours God has made are in the snow; on Erebus to the west, where the wind can scarcely move his cloud of smoke; and on Terror to the east, not so high, and more regular in form. How peaceful and dignified it all is.

That was what you might have seen four months ago had you been out on the Barrier plain. Low down on the extreme right or east of the land there was a black smudge of rock peeping out from great snow-drifts: that was the Knoll, and close under it were the cliffs of Cape Crozier, the Knoll looking quite low and the cliffs invisible, although they are eight hundred feet high, a sheer precipice falling to the sea.

It is at Cape Crozier that the Barrier edge, which runs for four hundred miles as an ice-cliff up to 200 feet high, meets the land. The Barrier is moving against this land at a rate which is sometimes not much less than a mile in a year. Perhaps you can imagine the chaos which it piles up: there are pressure ridges compared to which the waves of the sea are like a ploughed field. We had therefore to find our way along the pressure to the Knoll, and thence penetrate *through* the pressure to the Emperors' Bay. And we had to do it in the dark.

Terror Point, which we were approaching in the fog, is a short twenty miles from the Knoll, and ends in a long snow-tongue running out into the Barrier. The way had been travelled a good many times in daylight, and Wilson knew there was a narrow path, free from crevasses, which skirted along between the mountain and the pressure ridges running parallel to it. But it is one thing to walk along a corridor by day, and quite another to try to do so at night, especially when there are no walls by which you can correct your

course – only crevasses. Anyway, Terror Point must be somewhere close to us now, and vaguely in front of us was that strip of
snow, neither Barrier nor mountain, which was our only way forward.

We began to realize, now that our eyes were more or less out of
action, how much we could do with our feet and ears. The effect
of walking in finnesko is much the same as walking in gloves, and
you get a sense of touch which nothing else except bare feet could
give you. Thus we could feel every small variation in surface,
every crust through which our feet broke, every hardened patch
below the soft snow. And soon we began to rely more and more
upon the sound of our footsteps to tell us whether we were on crevasses or solid ground. From now onwards we were working
among crevasses fairly constantly. I loathe them in full daylight
when much can be done to avoid them, and when if you fall into
them you can at any rate see where the sides are, which way they
run and how best to scramble out; when your companions can see
how to stop the sledge to which you are all attached by your harness; how most safely to hold the sledge when stopped; how, if you
are dangling fifteen feet down in a chasm, to work above you to
get you up to the surface again. And then our clothes were generally something like clothes. Even under the ideal conditions of
good light, warmth and no wind, crevasses are beastly, whether
you are pulling over a level and uniform snow surface, never
knowing what moment will find you dropping into some bottomless pit, or whether you are rushing for the Alpine rope and the
sledge, to help some companion who has disappeared. I dream
sometimes now of bad days we had on the Beardmore and elsewhere, when men were dropping through to be caught up and
hang at the full length of the harnesses and toggles many times in
an hour. On the same sledge as myself on the Beardmore one man
went down once head first, and another eight times to the length

of his harness in 25 minutes. And always you wondered whether your harness was going to hold when the jerk came. But those days were a Sunday School treat compared to our days of blind-man's buff with the Emperor penguins among the crevasses of Cape Crozier.

Our troubles were greatly increased by the state of our clothes. If we had been dressed in lead we should have been able to move our arms and necks and heads more easily than we could now. If the same amount of icing had extended to our legs I believe we should still be there, standing unable to move: but happily the forks of our trousers still remained movable. To get into our canvas harnesses was the most absurd business. Quite in the early days of our journey we met with this difficulty, and somewhat foolishly decided not to take off our harness for lunch. The harnesses thawed in the tent, and froze back as hard as boards. Likewise our clothing was hard as boards and stuck out from our bodies in every imaginable fold and angle. To fit one board over the other required the united efforts of the would-be wearer and his two companions, and the process had to be repeated for each one of us twice a day. Goodness knows how long it took; but it cannot have been less than five minutes' thumping at each man.

As we approached Terror Point in the fog we sensed that we had risen and fallen over several rises. Every now and then we felt hard slippery snow under our feet. Every now and then our feet went through crusts in the surface. And then quite suddenly, vague, indefinable, monstrous, there loomed a something ahead. I remember having a feeling as of ghosts about as we untoggled our harnesses from the sledge, tied them together, and thus roped walked upwards on that ice. The moon was showing a ghastly ragged mountainous edge above us in the fog, and as we rose we found that we were on a pressure ridge. We stopped, looked at one another, and then *bang* – right under our feet. More bangs, and creaks and groans; for that ice was moving and splitting like glass. The cracks went off all round us, and some of them ran along for hundreds of yards. Afterwards we got used to it, but at first the effect was very jumpy. From first to last during this journey we had plenty of variety and none of that monotony which is inevitable in sledging over long distances of Barrier in summer. Only the long shivering fits following close one after the other all the time we lay in our dreadful sleeping-bags, hour after hour and night after night in those temperatures – they were as monotonous as could be. Later we got frost-bitten even as we lay in our sleeping-bags. Things are getting pretty bad when you get frost-bitten in your bag.

There was only a glow where the moon was; we stood in a moonlit fog, and this was sufficient to show the edge of another ridge ahead, and yet another on our left. We were utterly bewildered. The deep booming of the ice continued, and it may be that the tide has something to do with this, though we were many miles from the ordinary coastal ice. We went back, toggled up to our sledges again and pulled in what we thought was the right direction, always with that feeling that the earth may open underneath your feet which you have in crevassed areas. But all we found were more mounds and banks of snow and ice, into which we almost ran before we saw them. We were clearly lost. It was near midnight, and I wrote, 'it may be the pressure ridges or it may be Terror, it is impossible to say, – and I should think it is impossible to move till it clears. We were steering N.E. when we got here and returned S. W. till we seemed to be in a hollow and camped.'

The temperature had been rising from −36° at 11 A.M. and it was now −27°; snow was falling and nothing whatever could be seen. From under the tent came noises as though some giant was banging a big empty tank. All the signs were for a blizzard, and indeed we had not long finished our supper and were thawing our way little by little into our bags when the wind came away from the south. Before it started we got a glimpse of black rock, and knew we must be in the pressure ridges where they nearly join Mount Terror.

I will not say that I was entirely easy in my mind as we lay out that blizzard somewhere off Terror Point; I don't know how the others were feeling. The unearthly banging going on underneath us may have had something to do with it. But we were quite lost in the pressure and it might be the deuce and all to get out in the dark. The wind eddied and swirled quite out of its usual straightforward way, and the tent got badly snowed up: our sledge had disappeared long ago. The position was not altogether a comfortable one.

Tuesday night and Wednesday it blew up to force 10, temperature from –7° to + 2°. And then it began to modify and get squally. By 3 A.M. on Thursday (July 13) the wind had nearly ceased, the temperature was falling and the stars were shining through detached clouds. We were soon getting our breakfast, which always consisted of tea, followed by pemmican. We soaked our biscuits in both. Then we set to work to dig out the sledges and tent, a big job taking several hours. At last we got started. In that jerky way in which I was still managing to jot a few sentences down each night as a record, I wrote:

'Did 7½ miles during day – seems a marvellous run – rose and fell over several ridges of Terror – in afternoon suddenly came on huge crevasse on one of these – we were quite high on Terror – moon saved us walking in – it might have taken sledge and all.'

To do seven miles in a day, a distance which had taken us nearly a week in the past, was very heartening. The temperature was between –20° and –30° all day, and that was good too. When crossing the undulations which ran down out of the mountain into the true pressure ridges on our right we found that the wind which

came down off the mountain struck along the top of the undula-
tion, and flowing each way, caused a N.E. breeze on one side and
a N.W. breeze on the other. There seemed to be wind in the sky,
and the blizzard had not cleared as far away as we should have
wished.

During the time through which we had come it was by burning
more oil than is usually allowed for cooking that we kept going at
all. After each meal was cooked we allowed the primus to burn on
for a while and thus warmed up the tent. Then we could nurse
back our frozen feet and do any necessary little odd jobs. More
often we just sat and nodded for a few minutes, keeping one
another from going too deeply to sleep. But it was running away
with the oil. We started with 6 one-gallon tins (those tins Scott had
criticized), and we had now used four of them. At first we said we
must have at least two one-gallon tins with which to go back; but
by now our estimate had come down to one full gallon tin, and two
full primus lamps. Our sleeping-bags were awful. It took me, even
as early in the journey as this, an hour of pushing and thumping
and cramp every night to thaw out enough of mine to get into it
at all. Even that was not so bad as lying in them when we got there.

Only −35° but 'a very bad night' according to my diary. We got
away in good time, but it was a ghastly day and my nerves were
quivering at the end, for we could not find that straight and
narrow way which led between the crevasses on either hand. Time
after time we found we were out of our course by the sudden fall
of the ground beneath our feet – in we went and then – 'are we too
far right?' – nobody knows – 'well let's try nearer in to the mountain,' and so forth! 'By hard slogging 2¾ miles this morning – then
on in thick gloom which suddenly lifted and we found ourselves
under a huge great mountain of pressure ridge looking black in
shadow. We went on, bending to the left, when Bill fell and put his
arm into a crevasse. We went over this and another, and some time

after got somewhere up to the left, and both Bill and I put a foot into a crevasse. We sounded all about and everywhere was hollow, and so we ran the sledge down over it and all was well.' Once we got right into the pressure and took a longish time to get out again. Bill lengthened his trace out with the Alpine rope now and often afterwards, so he found the crevasses well ahead of us and the sledge: nice for us but not so nice for Bill. Crevasses in the dark *do* put your nerves on edge.

When we started next morning (July 15) we could see on our left front and more or less on top of us the Knoll, which is a big hill whose precipitous cliffs to seaward form Cape Crozier. The sides of it sloped down towards us, and pressing against its ice-cliffs on ahead were miles and miles of great pressure ridges, along which we had travelled, and which hemmed us in. Mount Terror rose ten thousand feet high on our left, and was connected with the Knoll by a great cup-like drift of wind-polished snow. The slope of this in one place runs gently out on to the corridor along which we had sledged, and here we turned and started to pull our sledges up. There were no crevasses, only the great drift of snow, so hard that we used our crampons just as though we had been on ice, and as polished as the china sides of a giant cup which it resembled. For three miles we slogged up, until we were only 150 yards from the moraine shelf where we were going to build our hut of rocks and snow. This moraine was above us on our left, the twin peaks of the Knoll were across the cup on our right; and here, 800 feet up the mountain side, we pitched our last camp.

We had arrived.

The view was magnificent and I got my spectacles out and cleared the ice away time after time to look. To the east a great field of pressure ridges below, looking in the moonlight as if giants had been ploughing with ploughs which made furrows fifty or sixty feet deep: these ran right up to the Barrier edge, and beyond was the frozen Ross Sea, lying flat, white and peaceful as though such things as blizzards were unknown. To the north and northeast the Knoll. Behind us Mount Terror on which we stood, and over all the grey limitless Barrier seemed to cast a spell of cold immensity, vague, ponderous, a breeding-place of wind and drift and darkness. God! What a place!

CHAPTER 7

'TOPSY-TURVY'

from *The South Pole* (1912)

Roald Amundsen

It was the Norwegian explorer Roald Amundsen's misfortune as a writer that he tended to make his adventures sound, perversely, a little too easy. They were not, of course. His victorious advance to the Pole in December 1911 was a wonder of tenacity, judgement, physical courage and intelligent risk-taking. Here, with the dangerous ice-falls of the Axel Heiberg glacier successfully navigated, we see him at full stretch, accelerating across the last bleak miles of the polar plateau to reach a place which (he engagingly admits) was not the goal of all his dreams. But as an explorer he always valued skilful actions above skilful descriptions of those actions; and so he does not quite know now how to realize on the page – for us, reading – his own state of quizzical, physical exhilaration.

The weather did not continue fine for long. Next day (December 5) there was a gale from the north, and once more the whole plain was a mass of drifting snow. In addition to this there was thick falling snow, which blinded us and made things worse, but a feeling of security had come over us and helped us to advance rapidly and without hesitation, although we could see nothing. That day we encountered new surface conditions – big, hard snow-waves (sastrugi). These were anything but pleasant to work among, especially when one could not see them. It was of no use for us 'forerunners' to think of going in advance under these circumstances, as it was impossible to keep on one's feet. Three or four paces was often the most we managed to do before falling down. The sastrugi were very high, and often abrupt; if one came on them unexpectedly, one required to be more than an acrobat to keep on one's feet. The plan we found to work best in these conditions was to let Hanssen's dogs go first; this was an unpleasant job for Hanssen, and for his dogs too, but it succeeded, and succeeded well. An upset here and there was, of course, unavoidable, but with a little patience the sledge was always righted again. The drivers had as much as they could do to support their sledges among these sastrugi, but while supporting the sledges, they had at the same time a support for themselves. It was worse for us who had no sledges, but by keeping in the wake of them we could see where the irregularities lay, and thus get over them. Hanssen deserves a special word of praise for his driving on this surface in such weather. It is a difficult matter to drive Eskimo dogs forward when they cannot see; but Hanssen managed it well, both getting the dogs on and steering his course by compass. One would not think it possible to keep an approximately right course when the uneven ground gives such violent shocks that the needle flies several times round the compass, and is no sooner still again than it recommences the same dance; but when at last we got an observation, it turned out that Hanssen had steered to a hair, for the observations and dead reckoning agreed to a mile. In spite of all hindrances, and of being able to see nothing, the sledge-meters showed nearly twenty-five miles.

December 6 brought the same weather: thick snow, sky and plain all one, nothing to be seen. Nevertheless we made splendid progress. The sastrugi gradually became levelled out, until the surface was perfectly smooth; it was a relief to have even ground to go upon once more. These irregularities that one was constantly falling over were a nuisance; if we had met with them in our usual surroundings it would not have mattered so much; but up here on the high ground, where we had to stand and gasp for breath every time we rolled over, it was certainly not pleasant.

That day we passed 88° S. 23' S, and camped in 88° 9' S. A great surprise awaited us in the tent that evening. I expected to find, as on the previous evening, that the boiling-point had fallen somewhat; in other words, that it would show a continued rise of the ground, but to our astonishment this was not so. The water boiled at exactly the same temperature as on the preceding day. I tried it several times, to convince myself that there was nothing wrong, each time with the same result. There was great rejoicing among us all when I was able to announce that we had arrived on the top of the plateau.

December 7 began like the 6th, with absolutely thick weather, but, as they say, you never know what the day is like before sunset. Possibly I might have chosen a better expression than this last – one more in agreement with the natural conditions – but I will let it stand. Though for several weeks now the sun had not set, my readers will not be so critical as to reproach me with inaccuracy. With a light wind from the north-east, we now went southward at a good speed over the perfectly level plain, with excellent going. The uphill work had taken it out of our dogs, though not to any serious extent. They had turned greedy – there is no denying that – and the half kilo of pemmican they got each day was not enough to fill their stomachs. Early and late they were looking for something – no matter what – to devour. To begin with they contented themselves with such loose objects as ski-bindings, whips, boots, and the like; but as we came to know their proclivities, we took such care of everything that they found no extra meals lying about. But that was not the end of the matter. They then went for the fixed lashings of the sledges, and – if we had allowed it – would very quickly have resolved the various sledges into their component parts. But we found a way of stopping that: every evening, on halting, the sledges were buried in the snow, so as to hide all the lashings. That was successful; curiously enough, they never tried to force the 'snow rampart.' I may mention as a curious thing that these ravenous animals, that devoured everything they came across, even to the ebonite points of our ski-sticks, never made any attempt to break into the provision cases. They lay there and went about among the sledges with their noses just on a level with the split cases, seeing and scenting the pemmican, without once making a sign of taking any. But if one raised a lid, they were not long in showing themselves. Then they all came in a great hurry and flocked about the sledges in the hope of getting a little extra bit. I am at a loss to explain this behaviour; that bashfulness was not at the root of it, I am tolerably certain.

During the forenoon the thick, grey curtain of cloud began to grow thinner on the horizon, and for the first time for three days we could see a few miles about us. The feeling was something like that one has on waking from a good nap, rubbing one's eyes and looking around. We had become so accustomed to the grey twilight that this positively dazzled us. Meanwhile, the upper layer of air seemed obstinately to remain the same and to be doing its best to prevent the sun from showing itself. We badly wanted to get a meridian altitude, so that we could determine our latitude. Since 86° 47' S. we had had no observation, and it was not easy to say when we should get one. Hitherto, the weather conditions on the high ground had not been particularly favourable. Although the prospects were not very promising, we halted at 11 a.m. and made ready to catch the sun if it should be kind enough to look out. Hassel and Wisting used one sextant and artificial horizon, Hanssen and I the other set.

I don't know that I have ever stood and absolutely pulled at the sun to get it out as I did that time. If we got an observation here which agreed with our reckoning, then it would be possible, if the worst came to the worst, to go to the Pole on dead reckoning; but if we got none now, it was a question whether our claim to the Pole would be admitted on the dead reckoning we should be able to produce. Whether my pulling helped or not, it is certain that the sun appeared. It was not very brilliant to begin with, but, practised as we now were in availing ourselves of even the poorest chances, it was good enough. Down it came, was checked by all, and the altitude written down. The curtain of cloud was rent more and more, and before we had finished our work – that is to say, caught the sun at its highest, and convinced ourselves that it was descending again – it was shining in all its glory. We had put away our instruments and were sitting on the sledges, engaged in the calculations. I can safely say that we were excited. What would the result be, after marching blindly for so long and over such impossible ground, as we had been doing? We added and subtracted, and at last there was the result. We looked at each other in sheer incredulity: the result was as astonishing as the most consummate conjuring trick – 88° 16' S., precisely to a minute the same as our reckoning, 88° 16' S. If we were forced to go to the Pole on dead reckoning, then surely the most exacting would admit our right to do so. We put away our observation books, ate one or two biscuits, and went at it again.

We had a great piece of work before us that day, nothing less than carrying our flag farther south than the foot of man had trod. We had our silk flag ready; it was made fast to two ski-sticks and laid on Hanssen's sledge. I had given him orders that as soon as we had covered the distance to 88° S., which was Shackleton's farthest south, the flag was to be hoisted on his sledge. It was my turn as forerunner, and I pushed on. There was no longer any difficulty in holding one's course; I had the grandest cloud-formations to steer by, and everything now went like a machine. First came the fore-runner for the time being, then Hanssen, then Wisting, and finally Bjaaland. The forerunner who was not on duty went where he liked; as a rule he accompanied one or other of the sledges. I had long ago fallen into a reverie – far removed from the scene in which I was moving; what I thought about I do not remember now, but I was so preoccupied that I had entirely forgotten my surroundings. Then suddenly I was roused from my dreaming by a jubilant shout, followed by ringing cheers. I turned round quickly to discover the reason of this unwonted occurrence, and stood speechless and over-come.

I find it impossible to express the feelings that possessed me at this moment. All the sledges had stopped, and from the foremost of them the Norwegian flag was flying. It shook itself out, waved and flapped so that the silk rustled; it looked wonderfully well in the pure, clear air and the shining white surroundings. 88° 23' was past; we were farther south than any human being had been. No other moment of the whole trip affected me like this. The tears forced their way to my eyes; by no effort of will could I keep them back. It was the flag yonder that conquered me and my will. Luckily I was some way in advance of the others, so that I had time to pull myself together and master my feelings before reaching my comrades. We all shook hands, with mutual congratulations; we had won our way far by holding together, and we would go farther yet – to the end.

We did not pass that spot without according our highest tribute of admiration to the man, who – together with his gallant com-panions – had planted his country's flag so infinitely nearer to the goal than any of his precursors. Sir Ernest Shackleton's name will always be written in the annals of Antarctic exploration in letters of fire. Pluck and grit can work wonders, and I know of no better example of this than what that man has accomplished.

The cameras of course had to come out, and we got an excellent photograph of the scene which none of us will ever forget. We went on a couple of miles more, to 88° 25', and then camped. The weather had improved, and kept on improving all the time. It was now almost perfectly calm, radiantly clear, and, under the circumstances, quite summer-like: – 0.4° F. Inside the tent it was quite sultry. This was more than we had expected.

After much consideration and discussion we had come to the conclusion that we ought to lay down a depot – the last one – at this spot. The advantages of lightening our sledges were so great that we should have to risk it. Nor would there be any great risk attached to it, after all, since we should adopt a system of marks that would lead even a blind man back to the place. We had determined to mark it not only at right angles to our course – that is, from east to west – but by snow beacons at every two geographical miles to the south.

We stayed here on the following day to arrange this depot. Hanssen's dogs were real marvels, all of them; nothing seemed to have any effect on them. They had grown rather thinner, of course, but they were still as strong as ever. It was therefore decided not to lighten Hanssen's sledge, but only the two others; both Wisting's and Bjaaland's teams had suffered, especially the latter's. The reduction in weight that was effected was considerable – nearly 110 pounds on each of the two sledges; there was thus about 220 pounds in the depot. The snow here was ill-adapted for building, but we put up quite a respectable monument all the same. It was dogs' pemmican and biscuits that were left behind; we carried with us on the sledges provisions for about a month. If, therefore, contrary to expectation, we should be so unlucky as to miss this depot, we should nevertheless be fairly sure of reaching our depot in 86° 21' before supplies ran short. The cross-marking of the depot was done with sixty splinters of black packing-case on each side, with 100 paces between each. Every other one had a shred of black cloth on the top. The splinters on the east side were all marked, so that on seeing them we should know instantly that we were to the east of the depot. Those on the west had no marks.

The warmth of the past few days seemed to have matured our frost-sores, and we presented an awful appearance. It was Wisting, Hanssen, and I who had suffered the worst damage in the last south-east blizzard; the left side of our faces was one mass of sore, bathed in matter and serum. We looked like the worst type of tramps and ruffians, and would probably not have been recognized by our nearest relations. These sores were a great trouble to us during the latter part of the journey. The slightest gust of wind produced a sensation as if one's face were being cut backwards and forwards with a blunt knife. They lasted a long time, too; I can remember Hanssen removing the last scab when we were coming into Hobart – three months later. We were very lucky in the weather during this depot work; the sun came out all at once, and we had an excellent opportunity of taking some good azimuth observations, the last of any use that we got on the journey.

December 9 arrived with the same fine weather and sunshine. True, we felt our frost-sores rather sharply that day, with –18.4° F. and a little breeze dead against us, but that could not be helped. We at once began to put up beacons – a work which was continued with great regularity right up to the Pole. These beacons were not so big as those we had built down on the Barrier; we could see that they would be quite large enough with a height of about 3 feet, as it was very easy to see the slightest irregularity on this perfectly flat sur-face. While thus engaged we had an opportunity of becoming thoroughly acquainted with the nature of the snow. Often – very often indeed – on this part of the plateau, to the south of 88° 25′, we had difficulty in getting snow good enough – that is, solid enough for cutting blocks. The snow up here seemed to have fallen very quietly, in light breezes or calms. We could thrust the tent-pole, which was 6 feet long, right down without meeting resistance, which showed that there was no hard layer of snow. The surface was also perfectly level; there was not a sign of sastrugi in any direction.

Every step we now took in advance brought us rapidly nearer the goal; we could feel fairly certain of reaching it on the afternoon of the 14th. It was very natural that our conversation should be chiefly concerned with the time of arrival. None of us would admit that he was nervous, but I am inclined to think that we all had a little touch of that malady. What should we see when we got there? A vast, endless plain, that no eye had yet seen and no foot yet trodden; or – No, it was an impossibility; with the speed at which we had travelled, we must reach the goal first, there could be no doubt about that. And yet – and yet – Wherever there is the smallest loophole, doubt creeps in and gnaws and gnaws and never leaves a poor wretch in peace. 'What on earth is Uroa scenting?' It was Bjaaland who made this remark, on one of these last days, when I was going by the side of his sledge and talking to him. 'And the strange thing is that he's scenting to the south. It can never be –' Mylius, Ring, and Suggen showed the same interest in the southerly direction; it was quite extraordinary to see how they raised their heads, with every sign of curiosity, put their noses in the air, and sniffed due south. One would really have thought there was something remarkable to be found there.

From 88° 25′ S. the barometer and hypsometer indicated slowly but surely that the plateau was beginning to descend towards the other side. This was a pleasant surprise to us; we had thus not only found the very summit of the plateau, but also the slope down on the far side. This would have a very important bearing for obtaining an idea of the construction of the whole plateau. On December 9 observations and dead reckoning agreed within a mile. The same result again on the 10th: observation 2 kilometres behind reckoning. The weather and going remained about the same as on the preceding days: light south-easterly breeze, temperature −18.4° F. The snow surface was loose, but ski and sledges glided over it well. On the 11th, the same weather conditions. Temperature −13° F. Observation and reckoning again agreed exactly. Our latitude was 89° 15′ S. On the 12th we reached 89° 30′, reckoning 1 kilometre behind observation. Going and surface as good as ever. Weather splendid – calm with sunshine. The noon observation on the 13th gave 89° 37′ S. Reckoning 89° 38.5′ S. We halted in the afternoon, after going eight geographical miles, and camped in 89° 45′, according to reckoning.

The weather during the forenoon had been just as fine as before; in the afternoon we had some snow-showers from the south-east. It was like the eve of some great festival that night in the tent. One could feel that a great event was at hand. Our flag was taken out again and lashed to the same two ski-sticks as before. Then it was rolled up and laid aside, to be ready when the time came. I was awake several times during the night, and had the same feeling that I can remember as a little boy on the night before Christmas Eve – an intense expectation of what was going to happen. Otherwise I think we slept just as well that night as any other.

On the morning of December 14 the weather was of the finest, just as if it had been made for arriving at the Pole. I am not quite sure, but I believe we despatched our breakfast rather more quickly than usual and were out of the tent sooner, though I must admit that we always accomplished this with all reasonable haste. We went in the usual order – the forerunner, Hanssen, Wisting, Bjaaland, and the reserve forerunner. By noon we had reached 89° 53′ by dead reckoning, and made ready to take the rest in one stage. At 10 a.m. a light breeze had sprung up from the south-east, and it had clouded over, so that we got no noon altitude; but the clouds were not thick, and from time to time we had a glimpse of the sun through them.

The going on that day was rather different from what it had been; sometimes the ski went over it well, but at others it was pretty bad. We advanced that day in the same mechanical way as before; not much was said, but eyes were used all the more. Hanssen's neck grew twice as long as before in his endeavour to see a few inches farther. I had asked him before we started to spy out ahead for all he was worth, and he did so with a vengeance. But, however keenly he stared, he could not descry anything but the endless flat plain ahead of us. The dogs had dropped their scenting, and appeared to have lost their interest in the regions about the earth's axis.

At three in the afternoon a simultaneous 'Halt!' rang out from the drivers. They had carefully examined their sledge-meters, and they all showed the full distance – our Pole by reckoning. The goal was reached, the journey ended. I cannot say – though I know it would sound much more effective – that the object of my life was attained. That would be romancing rather too bare-facedly. I had better be honest and admit straight out that I have never known any man to be placed in such a diametrically opposite position to the goal of his desires as I was at that moment. The regions around the North Pole – well, yes, the North Pole itself – had attracted me from childhood, and here I was at the South Pole. Can anything more topsy-turvy be imagined?

CHAPTER 8

'TRAGEDY ALL ALONG THE LINE'

from *Scott's Last Expedition* (1913)

Robert Falcon Scott

Robert Scott perceived the Pole very differently than Amundsen when his party of five arrived there a month later, already exhausted and hungry, already suffering from weaknesses which would be exacerbated by the extreme cold they would encounter on the long trek back towards safety. What followed was a slow-motion calamity, which generations have been able to enter into, imaginatively, by reading Scott's own chronicle of it in his journal – each time hoping, as one reader put it, that this time the terrible tale may come out differently. This is Antarctica's passion story, its famous founding tragedy. Even if you blame Scott himself for what happened, it isn't easy to look away.

Wednesday, January 17. – Camp 69. T. –22° at start. Night –21°. The Pole. Yes, but under very different circumstances from those expected. We have had a horrible day – add to our disappointment a head wind 4 to 5, with a temperature –22°, and companions labouring on with cold feet and hands.

We started at 7.30, none of us having slept much after the shock of our discovery. We followed the Norwegian sledge tracks for some way; as far as we make out there are only two men. In about three miles we passed two small cairns. Then the weather overcast, and the tracks being increasingly drifted up and obviously going too far to the west, we decided to make straight for the Pole according to our calculations. At 12.30 Evans had such cold hands we camped for lunch – an excellent 'week-end one.' We had marched 7.4 miles. Lat. sight gave 89° 53′ 37″. We started out and did 6½ miles due south. To-night little Bowers is laying himself out to get sights in terrible difficult circumstances; the wind is blowing hard, T. –21°, and there is that curious damp, cold feeling in the air which chills one to the bone in no time. We have been descending again, I think, but there looks to be a rise ahead; otherwise there is very little that is different from the awful monotony of past days. Great God! this is an awful place and terrible enough for us to have laboured to it without the reward of priority. Well, it is something to have got here, and the wind may be our friend to-morrow. We have had a fat Polar hoosh in spite of our chagrin, and feel comfortable inside – added a small stick of chocolate and the queer taste of a cigarette brought by Wilson. Now for the run home and a desperate struggle. I wonder if we can do it.

Wednesday, January 24. – Lunch Temp. –8°. Things beginning to look a little serious. A strong wind at the start has developed into a full blizzard at lunch, and we have had to get into our sleeping-bags. It was a bad march, but we covered 7 miles. At first Evans, and then Wilson went ahead to scout for tracks. Bowers guided the sledge alone for the first hour, then both Oates and he remained alongside it; they had a fearful time trying to make the pace between the soft patches. At 12.30 the sun coming ahead made it impossible to see the tracks further, and we had to stop. By this time the gale was at its height and we had the dickens of a time getting up the tent, cold fingers all round. We are only 7 miles from our depot, but I made sure we should be there to-night. This is the second full gale since we left the Pole. I don't like the look of it. Is the weather breaking up? If so, God help us, with the tremendous summit journey and scant food. Wilson and Bowers are my standby. I don't like the easy way in which Oates and Evans get frostbitten.

Saturday, January 27. – R. 10. Temp. –16° (lunch), –14.3° (evening). Minimum –19°. Height 9900. Barometer low? Called the hands half an hour late, but we got away in good time. The forenoon march was over the belt of storm-tossed sastrugi; it looked like a rough sea. Wilson and I pulled in front on ski, the remainder on foot. It was very tricky work following the track, which pretty constantly disappeared, and in fact only showed itself by faint signs anywhere – a foot or two of raised sledge-track, a dozen yards of the trail of the sledge-meter wheel, or a spatter of hard snow-flicks where feet had trodden. Sometimes none of these were distinct, but one got an impression of lines which guided. The trouble was that on the outward track one had to shape course constantly to avoid the heaviest mounds, and consequently there were many zig-zags. We lost a good deal over a mile by these halts, in which we unharnessed and went on the search for signs. However, by hook or crook, we managed to stick on the old track. Came on the cairn quite suddenly, marched past it, and camped for lunch at 7 miles. In the afternoon the sastrugi gradually diminished in size and now we are on fairly level ground to-day, the obstruction practically at an end, and, to our joy, the tracks showing up much plainer again. For the last two hours we had no difficulty at all in following them. There has been a nice helpful southerly breeze all day, a clear sky and comparatively warm temperature. The air is dry again, so that tents and equipment are gradually losing their icy condition imposed by the blizzard conditions of the past week.

Our sleeping-bags are slowly but surely getting wetter and I'm afraid it will take a lot of this weather to put them right. However, we all sleep well enough in them, the hours allowed being now on the short side. We are slowly getting more hungry, and it would be an advantage to have a little more food, especially for lunch. If we get to the next depôt in a few marches (it is now less than 60 miles and we have a full week's food) we ought to be able to open out a little, but we can't look for a real feed till we get to the pony food depot. A long way to go, and, by Jove, this is tremendous labour.

Tuesday, January 30. – R. 13. 9860. Lunch Temp. –25°, Supper Temp. –24.5°. Thank the Lord, another fine march – 19 miles. We have passed the last cairn before the depôt, the track is clear ahead, the weather fair, the wind helpful, the gradient down – with any luck we should pick up our depôt in the middle of the morning march. This is the bright side; the reverse of the medal is serious. Wilson has strained a tendon in his leg; it has given pain all day and is swollen to-night. Of course, he is full of pluck over it, but I don't like the idea of such an accident here. To add to the trouble Evans has dislodged two finger-nails to-night; his hands are really bad, and to my surprise he shows signs of losing heart over it. He hasn't been cheerful since the accident. The wind shifted from S.E. to S. and back again all day, but luckily it keeps strong. We can get along with bad fingers, but it (will be) a mighty serious thing if Wilson's leg doesn't improve.

Tuesday, February 6. – Lunch 7900; Supper 7210. Temp. –15°. We've had a horrid day and not covered good mileage. On turning out found sky overcast; a beastly position amidst crevasses. Luckily it cleared just before we started. We went straight for Mt. Darwin, but in half an hour found ourselves amongst huge open chasms, unbridged, but not very deep, I think. We turned to the north between two, but to our chagrin they converged into chaotic disturbance. We had to retrace our steps for a mile or so, then struck to the west and got on to a confused sea of sastrugi, pulling very hard; we put up the sail, Evans' nose suffered, Wilson very cold, everything horrid. Camped for lunch in the sastrugi; the only comfort, things looked clearer to the west and we were obviously going downhill. In the afternoon we struggled on, got out of sastrugi and turned over on glazed surface, crossing many crevasses – very easy work on ski. Towards the end of the march we realised the certainty of maintaining a more or less straight course to the depot, and estimate distance 10 to 15 miles.

Food is low and weather uncertain, so that many hours of the day were anxious; but this evening, though we are not as far advanced as I expected, the outlook is much more promising. Evans is the chief anxiety now; his cuts and wounds suppurate, his nose looks very bad, and altogether he shows considerable signs of being played out. Things may mend for him on the glacier, and his wounds get some respite under warmer conditions. I am indeed glad to think we shall so soon have done with plateau conditions. It took us 27 days to reach the Pole and 21 days back – in all 48 days – nearly 7 weeks in low temperature with almost incessant wind.

Thursday, February 8. – R. 22. Height 6260. Start Temp. –11°; Lunch Temp. –5°; Supper, zero. 9.2 miles. Started from the depot rather late owing to weighing biscuit, &c., and rearranging matters. Had a beastly morning. Wind very strong and cold. Steered in for Mt. Darwin to visit rock. Sent Bowers on, on ski, as Wilson can't wear his at present. He obtained several specimens, all of much the same type, a close-grained granite rock which weathers red. Hence the pink limestone. After he rejoined we skidded downhill pretty fast, leaders on ski, Oates and Wilson on foot alongside sledge – Evans detached. We lunched at 2 well down towards Mt. Buckley, the wind half a gale and everybody very cold and cheerless. However, better things were to follow. We decided to steer for the moraine under Mt. Buckley and, pulling with crampons, we crossed some very irregular steep slopes with big crevasses and slid down towards the rocks. The moraine was obviously so interesting that when we had advanced some miles and got out of the wind, I decided to camp and spend the rest of the day geologising. It has been extremely interesting. We found ourselves under perpendicular cliffs of Beacon sandstone, weathering rapidly and carrying veritable coal seams. From the last Wilson, with his sharp eyes, has picked several plant impressions, the last a piece of coal with beautifully traced leaves in layers, also some excellently preserved impressions of thick stems, showing cellular structure. In one place we saw the cast of small waves on the sand. To-night Bill has got a specimen of limestone with archeo-cyathus – the trouble is one cannot imagine where the stone comes from; it is evidently rare, as few specimens occur in the moraine. There is a good deal of pure white quartz. Altogether we have had a most interesting afternoon, and the relief of being out of the wind and in a warmer temperature is inexpressible. I hope and trust we shall all buck up again now that the conditions are more favourable. We have been in shadow all the afternoon, but the sun has just reached us, a little obscured by night haze. A lot could be written on the delight of setting foot on rock after 14 weeks of snow and ice and nearly 7 out of sight of aught else. It is like going ashore after a sea voyage. We deserve a little good bright weather after all our trials, and hope to get a chance to dry our sleeping-bags and generally make our gear more comfortable.

Wednesday, February 14. – Lunch Temp. 0°; Supper Temp. –1°. A fine day with wind on and off down the glacier, and we have done a fairly good march. We started a little late and pulled on down the moraine. At first I thought of going right, but soon, luckily, changed my mind and decided to follow the curving lines of the moraines. This course has brought us well out on the glacier.

Started on crampons; one hour after, hoisted sail; the combined efforts produced only slow speed, partly due to the sandy snow-drifts similar to those on summit, partly to our torn sledge runners. At lunch these were scraped and sand-papered. After lunch we got on snow, with ice only occasionally showing through. A poor start, but the gradient and wind improving, we did 6½ miles before night camp.

There is no getting away from the fact that we are not going strong. Probably none of us: Wilson's leg still troubles him and he doesn't like to trust himself on ski; but the worst case is Evans, who is giving us serious anxiety. This morning he suddenly disclosed a huge blister on his foot. It delayed us on the march, when he had to have his crampon readjusted. Sometimes I fear he is going from bad to worse, but I trust he will pick up again when we come to steady work on ski like this afternoon. He is hungry and so is Wilson. We can't risk opening out our food again, and as cook at present I am serving something under full allowance. We are inclined to get slack and slow with our camping arrangements, and small delays increase. I have talked of the matter to-night and hope for improvement. We cannot do distance without the ponies. The next depot some 30 miles away and nearly 3 days' food in hand.

Friday, February 16. – 12.5 m. Lunch Temp. –6.1°; Supper Temp. –7°. A rather trying position. Evans has nearly broken down in brain, we think. He is absolutely changed from his normal self-reliant self. This morning and this afternoon he stopped the march on some trivial excuse. We are on short rations with not very short food; spin out till to-morrow night. We cannot be more than 10 or 12 miles from the depot, but the weather is all against us. After lunch we were enveloped in a snow sheet, land just looming. Memory should hold the events of a very troublesome march with more troubles ahead. Perhaps all will be well if we can get to our depot to-morrow fairly early, but it is anxious work with the sick man. But it's no use meeting troubles half way, and our sleep is all too short to write more.

Saturday, February 17. — A very terrible day. Evans looked a little better after a good sleep, and declared, as he always did, that he was quite well. He started in his place on the traces, but half an hour later worked his ski shoes adrift, and had to leave the sledge. The surface was awful, the soft recently fallen snow clogging the ski and runners at every step, the sledge groaning, the sky overcast, and the land hazy. We stopped after about one hour, and Evans came up again, but very slowly. Half an hour later he dropped out again on the same plea. He asked Bowers to lend him a piece of string. I cautioned him to come on as quickly as he could, and he answered cheerfully as I thought. We had to push on, and the remainder of us were forced to pull very hard, sweating heavily. Abreast the Monument Rock we stopped, and seeing Evans a long way astern, I camped for lunch. There was no alarm at first, and we prepared tea and our own meal, consuming the latter. After lunch, and Evans still not appearing, we looked out, to see him still afar off. By this time we were alarmed, and all four started back on ski. I was first to reach the poor man and shocked at his appearance; he was on his knees with clothing disarranged, hands uncovered and frostbitten, and a wild look in his eyes. Asked what was the matter, he replied with a slow speech that he didn't know, but thought he must have fainted. We got him on his feet, but after two or three steps he sank down again. He showed every sign of complete collapse. Wilson, Bowers, and I went back for the sledge, whilst Oates remained with him. When we returned he was practically unconscious, and when we got him into the tent quite comatose. He died quietly at 12.30 A.M. On discussing the symptoms we think he began to get weaker just before we reached the Pole, and that his downward path was accelerated first by the shock of his frostbitten fingers, and later by falls during rough travelling on the glacier, further by his loss of all confidence in himself. Wilson thinks it certain he must have injured his brain by a fall. It is a terrible thing to lose a companion in this way, but calm reflection shows that there could not have been a better ending to the terrible anxieties of the past week. Discussion of the situation at lunch yesterday shows us what a desperate pass we were in with a sick man on our hands at such a distance from home.

At 1 A.M. we packed up and came down over the pressure ridges, finding our depôt easily.

Sunday, February 18. – R. 32. Temp. –5.5°. At Shambles Camp. We gave ourselves 5 hours' sleep at the lower glacier depot after the horrible night, and came on at about 3 to-day to this camp, coming fairly easily over the divide. Here with plenty of horsemeat we have had a fine supper, to be followed by others such, and so continue a more plentiful era if we can keep good marches up. New life seems to come with greater food almost immediately, but I am anxious about the Barrier surfaces.

Tuesday, February 28. – Lunch. Thermometer went below –40° last night; it was desperately cold for us, but we had a fair night. I decided to slightly increase food; the effect is undoubtedly good. Started marching in –32° with a slight north-westerly breeze – blighting. Many cold feet this morning; long time over foot gear, but we are earlier. Shall camp earlier and get the chance of a good night, if not the reality. Things must be critical till we reach the depot, and the more I think of matters, the more I anticipate their remaining so after that event. Only 24½ miles from the depot. The sun shines brightly, but there is little warmth in it. There is no doubt the middle of the Barrier is a pretty awful locality.

Friday, March 2. – Lunch. Misfortunes rarely come singly. We marched to the (Middle Barrier) depot fairly easily yesterday afternoon, and since that have suffered three distinct blows which have placed us in a bad position. First we found a shortage of oil; with most rigid economy it can scarce carry us to the next depot on this surface (71 miles away). Second, Titus Oates disclosed his feet, the toes showing very bad indeed, evidently bitten by the late temperatures. The third blow came in the night, when the wind, which we had hailed with some joy, brought dark overcast weather. It fell below –40° in the night, and this morning it took 1½ hours to get our foot gear on, but we got away before eight. We lost cairn and tracks together and made as steady as we could N. by W., but have seen nothing. Worse was to come – the surface is simply awful. In spite of strong wind and full sail we have only done 5½ miles. We are in a very queer street since there is no doubt we cannot do the extra marches and feel the cold horribly.

Monday, March 5. – Lunch. Regret to say going from bad to worse. We got a slant of wind yesterday afternoon, and going on 5 hours we converted our wretched morning run of 3½ miles into something over 9. We went to bed on a cup of cocoa and pemmican solid with the chill off. (R. 47.) The result is telling on all, but mainly on Oates, whose feet are in a wretched condition. One swelled up tremendously last night and he is very lame this morning. We started march on tea and pemmican as last night – we pretend to prefer the pemmican this way. Marched for 5 hours this morning over a slightly better surface covered with high moundy sastrugi. Sledge capsized twice; we pulled on foot, covering about 5½ miles. We are two pony marches and 4 miles about from our depot. Our fuel dreadfully low and the poor Soldier nearly done. It is pathetic enough because we can do nothing for him; more hot food might do a little, but only a little,

I fear. We none of us expected these terribly low temperatures, and of the rest of us Wilson is feeling them most; mainly, I fear, from his self-sacrificing devotion in doctoring Oates' feet. We cannot help each other, each has enough to do to take care of himself. We get cold on the march when the trudging is heavy, and the wind pierces our warm garments. The others, all of them, are unendingly cheerful when in the tent. We mean to see the game through with a proper spirit, but it's tough work to be pulling harder than we ever pulled in our lives for long hours, and to feel that the progress is so slow. One can only say 'God help us!' and plod on our weary way, cold and very miserable, though outwardly cheerful. We talk of all sorts of subjects in the tent, not much of food now, since we decided to take the risk of running a full ration. We simply couldn't go hungry at this time.

Wednesday, March 7. – A little worse I fear. One of Oates' feet very bad this morning; he is wonderfully brave. We still talk of what we will do together at home.

We only made 6½ miles yesterday. (R. 49.) This morning in 4½ hours we did just over 4 miles. We are 16 from our depot. If we only find the correct proportion of food there and this surface continues, we may get to the next depot [Mt. Hooper, 72 miles farther] but not to One Ton Camp. We hope against hope that the dogs have been to Mt. Hooper; then we might pull through. If there is a shortage of oil again we can have little hope. One feels that for poor Oates the crisis is near, but none of us are improving, though we are wonderfully fit considering the really excessive work we are doing. We are only kept going by good food. No wind this morning till a chill northerly air came ahead. Sun bright and cairns showing up well. I should like to keep the track to the end.

Saturday, March 10. – Things steadily downhill. Oates' foot worse. He has rare pluck and must know that he can never get through. He asked Wilson if he had a chance this morning, and of course Bill had to say he didn't know. In point of fact he has none. Apart from him, if he went under now, I doubt whether we could get through. With great care we might have a dog's chance, but no more. The weather conditions are awful, and our gear gets steadily more icy and difficult to manage. At the same time of course poor Titus is the greatest handicap. He keeps us waiting in the morning until we have partly lost the warming effect of our good breakfast, when the only wise policy is to be up and away at once; again at lunch. Poor chap! it is too pathetic to watch him; one cannot but try to cheer him up.

Sunday, March 11. – Titus Oates is very near the end, one feels. What we or he will do, God only knows. We discussed the matter after breakfast; he is a brave fine fellow and understands the situation, but he practically asked for advice. Nothing could be said but to urge him to march as long as he could. One satisfactory result to the discussion; I practically ordered Wilson to hand over the means of ending our troubles to us, so that any one of us may know how to do so. Wilson had no choice between doing so and our ransacking the medicine case. We have 30 opium tabloids apiece and he is left with a tube of morphine. So far the tragical side of our story. (R. 53.)

Friday, March 16 or Saturday 17. – Lost track of dates, but think the last correct. Tragedy all along the line. At lunch, the day before yesterday, poor Titus Oates said he couldn't go on; he proposed we should leave him in his sleeping-bag. That we could not do, and induced him to come on, on the afternoon march. In spite of its awful nature for him he struggled on and we made a few miles. At night he was worse and we knew the end had come.

Should this be found I want these facts recorded. Oates' last thoughts were of his Mother, but immediately before he took pride in thinking that his regiment would be pleased with the bold way in which he met his death. We can testify to his bravery. He has borne intense suffering for weeks without complaint, and to the very last was able and willing to discuss outside subjects. He did not – would not – give up hope to the very end. He was a brave soul. This was the end. He slept through the night before last, hoping not to wake; but he woke in the morning – yesterday. It was blowing a blizzard. He said, 'I am just going outside and may be some time.' He went out into the blizzard and we have not seen him since.

I take this opportunity of saying that we have stuck to our sick companions to the last. In case of Edgar Evans, when absolutely out of food and he lay insensible, the safety of the remainder seemed to demand his abandonment, but Providence mercifully removed him at this critical moment. He died a natural death, and we did not leave him till two hours after his death. We knew that poor Oates was walking to his death, but though we tried to dissuade him, we knew it was the act of a brave man and an English gentleman. We all hope to meet the end with a similar spirit, and assuredly the end is not far.

I can only write at lunch and then only occasionally. The cold is intense, –40° at midday. My companions are unendingly cheerful, but we are all on the verge of serious frostbites, and though we constantly talk of fetching through I don't think anyone of us believes it in his heart.

We are cold on the march now, and at all times except meals. Yesterday we had to lay up for a blizzard and to-day we move dreadfully slowly. We are at No. 14 pony camp, only two pony marches from One Ton Depôt. We leave here our theodolite, a camera, and Oates' sleeping-bags. Diaries, &c., and geological specimens carried at Wilson's special request, will be found with us or on our sledge.

Monday, March 19. – Lunch. We camped with difficulty last night, and were dreadfully cold till after our supper of cold pemmican and biscuit and a half a pannikin of cocoa cooked over the spirit. Then, contrary to expectation, we got warm and all slept well. To-day we started in the usual dragging manner. Sledge dreadfully heavy. We are 15½ miles from the depot and ought to get there in three days. What progress! We have two days' food but barely a day's fuel. All our feet are getting bad – Wilson's best, my right foot worst, left all right. There is no chance to nurse one's feet till we can get hot food into us. Amputation is the least I can hope for now, but will the trouble spread? That is the serious question. The weather doesn't give us a chance – the wind from N. to N.W. and –40° temp, to-day.

Wednesday, March 21. – Got within 11 miles of depôt Monday night; had to lay up all yesterday in severe blizzard. To-day forlorn hope, Wilson and Bowers going to depot for fuel.

Thursday, March 22 and 23. – Blizzard bad as ever – Wilson and Bowers unable to start – to-morrow last chance – no fuel and only one or two of food left – must be near the end. Have decided it shall be natural – we shall march for the depot with or without our effects and die in our tracks.

Thursday, March 29. – Since the 21st we have had a continuous gale from W.S.W. and S.W. We had fuel to make two cups of tea apiece and bare food for two days on the 20th. Every day we have been ready to start for our depot 11 miles away, but outside the door of the tent it remains a scene of whirling drift. I do not think we can hope for any better things now. We shall stick it out to the end, but we are getting weaker, of course, and the end cannot be far.

It seems a pity, but I do not think I can write more.

R. SCOTT.

For God's sake look after our people.

CHAPTER 9

'SCOTT DIES'

from *I May Be Some Time* (1996)

Francis Spufford

In contrast to Roald Amundsen, Scott was a very literary explorer. Some might say that he put altogether too much of his effort into his sentences, and not nearly enough into his practical skills. Writing almost to the last, he was able, to an astonishing extent, to set the scene of his own extinction. But a point must have come when the words ran out for him; a point, of course, after which there could also be no more documentary evidence. This is a recent attempt to imagine the very last hours, the ones Scott couldn't put on paper. It is fiction, not fact.

Sometimes you wake from a dream of guilt or horror that has filled your whole sleeping mind, a dream that feels final, as if it held a truth about you that you cannot hope to evade, and the kind day dislodges it bit by bit, showing you exits where you had thought there were none, reminding you of a world where you still move among choices. Day has always done this for you. It seems unfair that it should not, today. Scott's eyes open. Green canvas wall of tent, rush of snow outside seen only as a tireless spatter of dark. The canvas rustles. He has not been sleeping. He has been trying to drift, but the habit of self-command cuts him off, calls him back over and over to the realisation that it is all true. This irrevocable position *is* the whole, waking truth, and the tent is his life's last scene, beyond any possibility of alteration. He can make no effort that would change anything. If he had taken Oates' advice last autumn and pushed One Ton Depot further south, he might not be lying eleven miles short of it now. If he had left different instructions about the dog-teams, even now help might be on its way, rather than receding through the Barrier blizzard as Cherry-Garrard, unknowing, drives for Cape Evans. But these are ironies that have lost their power to torment, through many repetitions. Edgar Evans is dead under a shallow mound of snow on the Beardmore: brain haemorrhage, Wilson thought. Oates 'left us the other day', as it says in Birdie's letter to his mother, neatly folded on the groundsheet. Oates is a white hummock now somewhere a little to the side of the line of march. And Wilson and Bowers lie one each side of Scott in the tent, their sleeping bags pulled over their faces. How many hours ago he does not know, the breathing first of one and then of the other turned briefly ragged and then stopped. The breath sighed out and never drew in again. Except for the silence they might be sleeping. Scott has a terrible desire that he must keep quelling, to reach and shake them, to try and summon again their company. He can imagine all too well the way the illusion of sleep would break if he did; and the moment when he asked for an answer and got none would be beyond bearing. So he must not break down and ask. He must not touch them at all. He is entirely alone, beyond all hope. For who knows what scoured and whirling distance all about, he is the only living thing. There is nothing left to do but die. But he is still here. He composes himself as best he can (it is difficult to want to stop, your mind is not adjusted to it) but nothing happens. The greater nothing which he supposes will replace this tiny green space when he goes – still unimaginable – does not arrive. His heart beats in his chest with stupid strength.

It was better when he was writing. Twelve days ago Scott's feet froze at last and crippled him. Eleven days ago, the immobilising blizzard began. Ten days ago they ran out of fuel. Eight days ago they ate the last of the food, and soon the thing became absolutely certain. Everyone wrote, though the pencil was hard to hold, and the paper glazed over with ice if you exhaled on it. Wilson wrote a letter to Oriana, a letter to his parents in Cheltenham (carefully adding the address anew on the second page in case it should be separated) and a note to his friends the Smiths. Bowers apologised to his mother that his letter should be 'such a short scribble', and for other things. 'It will be splendid however to pass with such companions as I have . . . Oh how I do feel for you when you hear all, you will know that for me the end was peaceful as it is only sleep in the cold. Your ever loving son to the end of this life and the next when God shall wipe away all tears from our eyes – H. R. Bowers.' But Scott wrote and wrote and wrote. He paid his professional debts. He told Mrs Bowers that her son had been magnificent to the end, and Mrs Wilson that her husband had the 'comfortable blue look of hope' in his eyes. He told his mother that 'the Great God has called me'. There are twelve letters by him in the tent, besides his diary and a Message to the Public. His teeth are loose in his gums from scurvy, his feet would be gangrenous if the cold were not slowing up the bacteria, his face is cracked with snow-burn and marked with unhealed red and purple sores where the frost bit at the points of the bones; but while he wrote he commanded the kingdom of words. He was *making*. He could see the story of the expedition as a parabola that descended to earth at its completion, and might be made to do so with a power and a grace that justified the whole; that gave the whole an inevitable fall, like any good story whose end is latent in its middle and beginning. He knew exactly what to do. A century and more of expectations were to hand, anonymous and virtually instinctive to him: he shaped them.

Scarcely a word needed crossing out. One, inside the cover of his diary: 'Send this diary to my wife.' Correction: 'widow'. With the authority of death he insisted 'The causes of the disaster are not due to faulty organisation but to misfortune in all risks which had to be undertaken.' Into the syntax of his best sentences, he wove appeals to the practical charity of the nation, so that – like a politician on television taking care his soundbite cannot be edited into smaller units – the emotion and the appeal should be indivisible. 'These rough notes and our dead bodies must tell the tale, but surely, surely, a great rich country like ours will see that those who are dependent on us are properly provided for.' Grand sombre cadences, funeral music in words, came to him; long sentences running parallel in sound to each other, inviting a voice to work its way through the scored heights and depths of the phrasing.

> We are weak, writing is difficult, but for my own sake I do not regret this journey, which has shown that Englishmen can endure hardships, help one another, and meet death with as great a fortitude as ever in the past. We took risks, we knew we took them; things have come out against us, and therefore we have no cause for complaint, but bow to the will of Providence, determined still to do our best to the last.

But he had to stop. 'It seems a pity but I do not think I can write more.' When the writing stopped, so did all that words can do to give this situation meaning. His words are exhausted. The tale is told; but he is still here, in the silence afterwards, waiting. Some people wear their roles so closely they become their skin. There is nothing left of them besides, no residue that does not fit the proper emotions of a judge, or a salesman, or an explorer. Scott is wonderfully good at his role, but he is not one of these; he has always been self-conscious. Tucked beneath him, 'I have taken my place throughout, haven't I?' says the letter to Kathleen – whether with pride, or anxiety, or final bitterness at the explorer's place and its mortal demands, he hardly knows. 'What tales you would have had for the boy, but oh, what a price to pay.' After the storied death it seems there remains all of you to die that you had only glimpsed sidelong as you subdued yourself to the part. You cannot die in a story; you have to die in your body. He wonders if the other two travelled, invisibly to him, sometime in the night hours, past the end of their belief, their belief not quite stretching all the way to the fact of death, and faced this horrible vacancy. He thinks not, and is glad. They were certain enough, so far as he could judge, that the eyes they closed here would open again elsewhere. They still looked forward, 'slept' only to wake. Sleep, sleep: all at once he hates this lulling metaphor for the disappearance of every slightest speck of forty-three years of thinking and feeling. Such a lie. It is not sleep, this formless prospect from which his mind recoils helplessly though it is imminent.

But whatever he thinks, whatever he wants, here he is still, both holding death at bay, he cannot *help* it, and wishing it would hurry. He wants to see Kathleen again. He wants the world to expand again from this narrow trap to the proportions you learn to trust, living. He thinks that he would very much like to go indoors. The tent is a feeble cone perched beneath a huge sky on a bed of ice sustained by black, black water. He left Cape Evans five months ago: for almost a hundred and fifty nights he's been in the open, or within this portable fiction of shelter. You never realise until you come out here that the world divides so absolutely into outdoors and indoors. It is almost metaphysical. It seems marvellous to him now that people take open space, and floor it and wall it and roof it, and transform it utterly. He thinks of doors opening, and himself passing through. The door at Cape Evans, of course; but also he stands on the steps by the railings in Buckingham Palace Road knocking at the coloured front door of his own house. He waits at the bigger door of the Geographical Society, and through the glass panes he can see the porter in the vestibule coming to let him in, quite unflustered by the balaclava and the drip of melting frost off his windproof smock. Thresholds: the thick metal door in the corridor of a destroyer, whose rivets are cool bulges in a skin of paint, whose foot-high sill is shiny steel in the centre where feet touch it. A screen-door in the verandah of an American house on a hot day, which has an aquarium cool you are glad of on the inside of it, and a remote buzz of insects and traffic. Doors squeaking, grating, gliding ajar with huge solidity. He thumps for entry at the doors of St Paul's, not on the little gateway inset in the greater but on the vast sculpted panels of the great door itself, which swing wide on a chessboard floor where his footsteps fall echoey yet distinct. The gates of ivory and of horn in the *Odyssey*, from whose parted leaves stream out true visions and false dreams . . . *Have the gates of death been opened unto thee? or hast thou seen the doors of the shadow of death? Hast thou perceived the breadth of the earth? declare if thou knowest it all. Where is the way where light dwelleth? and as for darkness, where is the place thereof, that thou shouldest take it to the bound thereof, and that thou shouldest know the paths to the house thereof? . . . Hast thou entered into the treasures of the snow? or hast thou seen the treasures of the hail . . . Out of whose womb came the ice? and the hoary frost of heaven who hath gendered it? The waters are hid as with a stone, and the face of the deep is frozen. Canst thou bind the sweet influences of Pleiades, or loose the bands of Orion?* Drift . . . Drift . . . Stop! Get a grip, man. Or, no, he supposes perhaps he ought not to take hold again. But it is already done. He has tightened whatever it is in him that lashes a crumbly fear together into a block strong enough to face things. And the tent returns. The tent, the place, the two corpses, the bottle of opium tablets that would dissolve him away irresistibly if he once chose to swallow them. He is still here.

Scott kicks out suddenly, like an insomniac angry with the bed-clothes. Yes, alright, but *quickly* then, without thinking. He pulls open the sleeping bag as far down as he can reach, wrenches his coat right open too, lays his arm deliberately around the cold lump of the body of his friend Edward Wilson (who is not sleeping, no, but dead) and holds tight. It is forty below in the tent. The cold comes into him. Oh how it hurts. His skin, which was the frontier of him this whole long time past, is breached: he is no longer whole: the ice is inside his chest, a spearing and dreadful presence turning the cavities of him to blue glass. His lips pull back from his teeth in an enormous snarl; but Scott has left the surface of his face, and does not know. At its tip the cold moves inside him like a key searching for a lock. An impersonal tenderness seems to be watching as it finds the latch of a box, a box of memories, and spills them out, the most private images, one by one, some that would never have been expected because they were scarcely remembered and it was never known that they had been diligently stored here all the time; one by one, each seen complete and without passion, until the last of them is reached, and flutters away, and is gone.

CHAPTER 10

'MAWSON LIVES'

from *Home of the Blizzard* (1915; 1930)

Douglas Mawson

At the same time as the race for the Pole was dominating the Ross Sea sector, an Australian expedition was at work far away on the other side of Antarctica, led by Douglas Mawson, a scientific veteran of Shackleton's 1907 crew. The Australians were based on a shore of Wilkes Land so steadily wind-scoured that, around their hut, they learned to walk tilted right over to the diagonal. Inland, as ice streams from the interior poured down to the coast, the terrain was heavily crevassed. Mawson was out on a survey mission with two companions when one, Ninnis, abruptly fell down a crevasse, never to be seen again: most of the food went with him. Then his other sledgemate, Xavier Mertz, died of food poisoning. Mawson was alone, virtually without supplies or equipment, and seriously ill himself, 200 miles and more from base. His death was the overwhelmingly likely outcome. Instead, step by tottering step, he walked home.

Outside the bowl of chaos was brimming with drift-snow and as I lay in the sleeping-bag beside my dead companion I wondered how, in such conditions, I would manage to break and pitch camp single-handed. There appeared to be little hope of reaching the Hut, still one hundred miles away. It was easy to sleep in the bag, and the weather was cruel outside. But inaction is hard to bear and I braced myself together determined to put up a good fight.

Failing to reach the Hut it would be something done if I managed to get to some prominent point likely to catch the eye of a search-party, where a cairn might be erected and our diaries cached. So I commenced to modify the sledge and camping gear to meet fresh requirements.

The sky remained clouded, but the wind fell off to a calm which lasted several hours. I took the opportunity to set to work on the sledge, sawing it in halves with a pocket tool and discarding the rear section. A mast was made out of one of the rails no longer required, and a spar was cut from the other. Finally, the load was cut down to a minimum by the elimination of all but the barest necessities, the abandoned articles including, sad to relate, all that remained of the exposed photographic films.

Late that evening, the 8th, I took the body of Mertz, still toggled up in his bag, outside the tent, piled snow blocks around it and raised a rough cross made of the two discarded halves of the sledge runners.

On January 9 the weather was overcast and fairly thick drift was flying in a gale of wind, reaching about fifty miles an hour. As certain matters still required attention and my chances of re-erecting the tent were rather doubtful, if I decided to move on, the start was delayed.

Part of the time that day was occupied with cutting up a waterproof clothes-bag and Mertz's burberry jacket and sewing them together to form a sail. Before retiring to rest in the evening I read through the burial service and put the finishing touches on the grave.

January 10 arrived in a turmoil of wind and thick drift. The start was still further delayed. I spent part of the time in reckoning up the food remaining and in cooking the rest of the dog meat, this latter operation serving the good object of lightening the load, in that the kerosene for the purpose was consumed there and then and had not to be dragged forward for subsequent use. Late in the afternoon the wind fell and the sun peered amongst the clouds just as I was in the middle of a long job riveting and lashing the broken shovel.

The next day, January 11, a beautiful, calm day of sunshine, I set out over a good surface with a slight down grade.

From the start my feet felt curiously lumpy and sore. They had become so painful after a mile of walking that I decided to examine them on the spot, sitting in the lee of the sledge in brilliant sunshine. I had not had my socks off for some days for, while lying in camp, it had not seemed necessary. On taking off the third and inner pair of socks the sight of my feet gave me quite a shock, for the thickened skin of the soles had separated in each case as a complete layer, and abundant watery fluid had escaped saturating the sock. The new skin beneath was very much abraded and raw. Several of my toes had commenced to blacken and fester near the tips and the nails were puffed and loose.

I began to wonder if there was ever to be a day without some special disappointment. However, there was nothing to be done but make the best of it. I smeared the new skin and the raw surfaces with lanoline, of which there was fortunately a good store, and then with the aid of bandages bound the old skin casts back in place, for these were comfortable and soft in contact with the abraded surface. Over the bandages were slipped six pairs of thick woollen socks, then fur boots and finally crampon over-shoes. The latter, having large stiff soles, spread the weight nicely and saved my feet from the jagged ice encountered shortly afterwards.

So glorious was it to feel the sun on one's skin after being without it for so long that I next removed most of my clothing and bathed my body in the rays until my flesh fairly tingled – a wonderful sensation which spread throughout my whole person, and made me feel stronger and happier.

Then on I went, treading rather like a cat on wet ground endeavouring to save my feet from pain. By 5.30 p.m. I was quite worn out – nerve-worn – though having covered but six and a quarter miles. Had it not been a delightful evening I should not have found strength to erect the tent.

The day following passed in a howling blizzard and I could do nothing but attend to my feet and other raw patches, festering finger-nails and inflamed frost-bitten nose. Fortunately there was a good supply of bandages and antiseptic. The tent, spread about with dressings and the meagre surgical appliances at hand, was suggestive of a casualty hospital.

Towards noon the following day, January 13, the wind subsided and the snow cleared off. It turned out a beautifully fine afternoon. Soon after I had got moving the slope increased, unfolding a fine view of the Mertz Glacier ahead. My heart leapt with joy, for all was like a map before me and I knew that over the hazy blue ice ridge in the far distance lay the Hut. I was heading to traverse the depression of the glacier ahead at a point many miles above our crossing of the outward journey and some few miles below gigantic ice cascades. My first impulse was to turn away to the west and avoid crossing the fifteen miles of hideously broken ice that choked the valley before me, but on second thought, in view of the very limited quantity of food left, the right thing seemed to be to make an air-line for the Hut and chance what lay between. Accordingly, having taken an observation of the sun for position and selected what appeared to be the clearest route across the valley, I started downhill. The névé gave way to rough blue ice and even wide crevasses made their appearance. The rough ice jarred my feet terribly and altogether it was a most painful march.

So unendurable did it become that, finding a bridged crevasse extending my way, I decided to march along the snow bridge and risk an accident. It was from fifteen to twenty feet wide and well packed with winter snow. The march continued along it down slopes for over a mile with great satisfaction as far as my feet were concerned. Eventually it became irregular and broke up, but others took its place and served as well; in this way the march was made possible. At 8 P.M. after covering a distance of nearly six miles a final halt for the day was made.

About 11 P.M. as the sun skimmed behind the ice slopes to the south I was startled by loud reports like heavy gun shots. They commenced up the valley to the south and trailed away down the southern side of the glacier towards the sea. The fusillade of shots rang out without interruption for about half an hour, then all was silent. It was hard to believe it was not caused by some human agency, but I learnt that it was due to the cracking of the glacier ice.

A high wind which blew on the morning of the 14th diminished in strength by noon and allowed me to get away. The sun came out so warm that the rough ice surface underfoot was covered with a film of water and in some places small trickles ran away to disappear into crevasses.

Though the course was downhill, the sledge required a good deal of pulling owing to the wet runners. At 9 P.M., after travelling five miles, I pitched camp in the bed of the glacier. From about 9.30 P.M. until 11 P.M. 'cannonading' continued like that heard the previous evening.

January 15 – the date on which all the sledging parties were due at the Hut! It was overcast and snowing early in the day, but in a few hours the sun broke out and shone warmly. The travelling was so heavy over a soft snowy surface, partly melting, that I gave up, after one mile, and camped.

At 7 P.M. the surface had not improved, the sky was thickly obscured and snow fell. At 10 P.M. a heavy snowstorm was in progress, and, since there were many crevasses in the vicinity, I resolved to wait.

On the 16th at 2 A.M. the snow was falling as thick as ever, but at 5 A.M. the atmosphere lightened and the sun appeared. Camp was broken without delay. A favourable breeze sprang up, and with sail set I managed to proceed in short stages through the deep newly-fallen blanket of snow. It clung in lumps to the runners, which had to be scraped frequently. Riven ice ridges as much as eighty feet in height passed on either hand. Occasionally I got a start as a foot or a leg sank through into space, but, on the whole, all went unexpectedly well for several miles. Then the sun disappeared and the disabilities of a snow-blind light had to be faced.

After laboriously toiling up one long slope, I had just taken a few paces over the crest, with the sledge running freely behind, when it dawned on me that the surface fell away unusually steeply. A glance ahead, even in that uncertain light, flashed the truth upon me – I was on a snow cornice, rimming the brink of a great blue chasm like a quarry, the yawning mouth of an immense and partly filled crevasse. Already the sledge was gaining speed as it slid past me towards the gaping hole below. Mechanically, I bedded my feet firmly in the snow and, exerting every effort, was just able to take the weight and hold up the sledge as it reached the very brink of the abyss. There must have been an interval of quite a minute during which I held my ground without being able to make it budge. It seemed an interminable time; I found myself reckoning the odds as to who would win, the sledge or I. Then it slowly came my way, and the imminent danger was passed.

The day's march was an extremely heavy five miles; so before turning in I treated myself to an extra supper of jelly soup made from dog sinews. I thought at the time that the acute enjoyment of eating compensated in some measure for the sufferings of starvation.

January 17 was another day of overcast sky and steady falling snow. Everything from below one's feet to the sky above was one uniform ghostly glare. The irregularities in the surfaces not obliterated by the deep soft snow blended harmoniously in colour and in the absence of shadows faded into invisibility. These were most unsuitable conditions for the crossing of such a dangerous crevassed valley, but delay meant a reduction of the ration and that was out of the question, so nothing remained but to go on.

A start was made at 8 a.m. and the pulling proved more easy than on the previous day. Some two miles had been negotiated in safety when an event occurred which, but for a miracle, would have terminated the story then and there. Never have I come so near to an end; never has anyone more miraculously escaped.

I was hauling the sledge through deep snow up a fairly steep sloop when my feet broke through into a crevasse. Fortunately as I fell I caught my weight with my arms on the edge and did not plunge in further than the thighs. The outline of the crevasse did not show through the blanket of snow on the surface, but an idea of the trend was obtained with a stick. I decided to try a crossing about fifty yards further along, hoping that there it would be better bridged. Alas! it took an unexpected turn catching me unawares. This time I shot through the centre of the bridge in a flash, but the latter part of the fall was decelerated by the friction of the harness ropes which, as the sledge ran up, sawed back into the thick compact snow forming the margin of the lid. Having seen my comrades perish in diverse ways and having lost hope of ever reaching the Hut, I had already many times speculated on what the end would be like. So it happened that as I fell through into the crevasse the thought 'so this is the end' blazed up in my mind, for it was to be expected that the next moment the sledge would follow through, crash on my head and all go to the unseen bottom. But the unexpected happened and the sledge held, the deep snow acting as a brake.

In the moment that elapsed before the rope ceased to descend, delaying the issue, a great regret swept through my mind, namely, that after having stinted myself so assiduously in order to save food, I should pass on now to eternity without the satisfaction of what remained – to such an extent does food take possession of one under such circumstances. Realizing that the sledge was holding I began to look around. The crevasse was somewhat over six feet wide and sheer walled, descending into blue depths below. My clothes, which, with a view to ventilation, had been but loosely secured, were now stuffed with snow broken from the roof, and very chilly it was. Above at the other end of the fourteen-foot rope, was the daylight seen through the hole in the lid.

In my weak condition, the prospect of climbing out seemed very poor indeed, but in a few moments the struggle was begun. A great effort brought a knot in the rope within my grasp, and, after a moment's rest, I was able to draw myself up and reach another, and, at length, hauled my body on to the overhanging snow-lid. Then, when all appeared to be well and before I could get to quite solid ground, a further section of the lid gave way, precipitating me once more to the full length of the rope.

There, exhausted, weak and chilled, hanging freely in space and slowly turning round as the rope twisted one way and the other, I felt that I had done my utmost and failed, that I had no more strength to try again and that all was over except the passing. Below was a black chasm; it would be but the work of a moment to slip from the harness, then all the pain and toil would be over. It was a rare situation – a chance to quit small things for great – to pass from the petty exploration of a planet to the contemplation of vaster worlds beyond. But there was all eternity for the last and, at its longest, the present would be but short. I felt better for the thought.

My strength was fast ebbing; in a few minutes it would be too late. It was the occasion for a supreme attempt. Fired by the passion that burns the blood in the act of strife, new power seemed to come as I applied myself to one last tremendous effort. The struggle occupied some time, but I slowly worked upward to the surface. This time emerging feet first, still clinging to the rope, I pushed myself out extended at full length on the lid and then shuffled safely on to the solid ground at the side. Then came the reaction from the great nerve strain and lying there alongside the sledge my mind faded into a blank.

When consciousness returned it was a full hour or two later, for I was partly covered with newly fallen snow and numb with the cold. I took at least three hours to erect the tent, get things snugly inside and clear the snow from my clothes. Between each movement, almost, I had to rest. Then reclining in luxury in the sleeping-bag I ate a little food and thought matters over. It was a time when the mood of the Persian philosopher appealed to me:

> Unborn To-morrow and dead Yesterday,
> Why fret about them if To-day be sweet?

CHAPTER 11

'THE BLOW'

from *Alone* (1938)

Richard Byrd

Midway between the Antarctica of the Heroic Age and the modern continent, the US explorer who pioneered Antarctic aviation here experiences the continent at ground level; at its most icebound and solitary, in fact. In an experiment that would not have been safe without recently invented technologies, Richard Byrd overwintered solo in 1934 in an isolated weather station on the Ross Ice Shelf. It was not so very safe even so: shortly after the passage excerpted here, his heater would start pumping carbon monoxide into the air, giving him for two grim months a daily choice between heat and life and hallucinations, on the one hand, and cold and clarity of mind and death on the other. At this point, though, the inside of his shelter is still a safe haven – if he can just find his way back in.

May was a round boulder sinking before a tide. Time sloughed off the last implication of urgency, and the days moved imperceptibly one into the other. The few world news items which Dyer read to me from time to time seemed almost as meaningless and blurred as they might to a Martian. My world was insulated against the shocks running through distant economies. Advance Base was geared to different laws. On getting up in the morning, it was enough for me to say to myself: To-day is the day to change the barograph sheet, or, To-day is the day to fill the stove tank. The night was settling down in earnest. By May 17th, one month after the sun had sunk below the horizon, the noon twilight was dwindling to a mere chink in the darkness, lit by a cold reddish glow. Days when the wind brooded in the north or east, the Barrier became a vast stagnant shadow surmounted by swollen masses of clouds, one layer of darkness piled on top of the other. This was the polar night, the morbid countenance of the Ice Age. Nothing moved; nothing was visible. This was the soul of inertness. One could almost hear a distant creaking as if a great weight were settling.

Out of the deepening darkness came the cold. On May 19th, when I took the usual walk, the temperature was 65° below zero. For the first time the canvas boots failed to protect my feet. One heel was nipped, and I was forced to return to the hut and change to reindeer mukluks. That day I felt miserable; my body was racked by shooting pains – exactly as if I had been gassed. Very likely I was; in inspecting the ventilator pipes next morning I discovered that the intake pipe was completely clogged with rime and that the outlet pipe was two-thirds full. Next day – Sunday the 20th – was the coldest yet. The minimum thermometer dropped to 72° below zero; the inside thermograph, which always read a bit lower than the instruments in the shelter, stood at −74°; and the thermograph in the shelter was stopped dead – the ink, though well laced with glycerine, and the lubricant were both frozen. So violently did the air in the fuel tank expand after the stove was lit that oil went shooting all over the place; to insulate the tank against similar temperature spreads I wrapped around it the rubber air cushion which by some lucky error had been included among my gear. In the glow of a flashlight the vapour rising from the stovepipe and the outlet ventilator looked like the discharge from two steam engines. My fingers agonized over the thermograph, and I was hours putting it to rights. The fuel wouldn't flow from the drums; I had to take one inside and heat it near the stove. All day long I kept two primus stoves burning in the tunnel.

Sunday the 20th also brought a radio schedule; I had the devil's own time trying to meet it. The engine balked for an hour; my fingers were so brittle and frostbitten from tinkering with the carburetor that, when I actually made contact with Little America, I could scarcely work the key. 'Ask Haines come on,' was my first request. While Hutcheson searched the tunnels of Little America for the Senior Meteorologist, I chatted briefly with Charlie Murphy. Little America claimed only –60°. 'But we're moving the brass monkeys below,' Charlie advised. 'Seventy-one below here now,' I said. 'You can have it,' was the closing comment from the north.

Then Bill Haines's merry voice sounded in the earphones. I explained the difficulty with the thermograph. 'Same trouble we've had,' Bill said. 'It's probably due to frozen oil. I'd suggest you bring the instrument inside, and try soaking it in gasoline, to cut whatever oil traces remain. Then rinse it in ether. As for the ink's freezing, you might try adding more glycerine.' Bill was in a jovial mood. 'Look at me, Admiral,' he boomed. 'I never have any trouble with the instruments. The trick is in having an ambitious and docile assistant.' I really chuckled over that because I knew, from the first expedition, what Grimminger, the Junior Meteorologist, was going through; Bill, with his back to the fire and blandishment on his tongue, persuading the recruit that duty and the opportunity for self-improvement required him to go up into the blizzard to fix a balky trace; Bill humming to himself in the warmth of a shack while the assistant in an open pit kept a theodolite trained on the sounding balloon soaring into the night, and stuttered into a telephone the different vernier readings from which Bill was calculating the velocities and directions of the upper air currents. That day I rather wished that I, too, had an assistant. He would have taken his turn on the anemometer pole, no mistake. The frost in the iron cleats went through the fur soles of the mukluks, and froze the balls of my feet. My breath made little explosive sounds on the wind; my lungs, already sore, seemed to shrivel when I breathed.

Seldom had the aurora flamed more brilliantly. For hours the night danced to its frenetic excitement. And at times the sound of Barrier quakes was like that of heavy guns. My tongue was swollen and sore from drinking scalding hot tea, and the tip of my nose ached from frostbite. A big wind, I guessed, would come out of this still cold; it behoved me to look at my roof. I carried gallons of water topside, and poured it around the edges of the shack. It froze almost as soon as it hit. The ice was an armour plating over the packed drift.

At midnight, when I clambered topside for an auroral 'ob,' a wild sense of suffocation came over me the instant I pushed my shoulders through the trapdoor. My lungs gasped, but no air reached them. Bewildered and perhaps a little frightened, I slid down the ladder and lunged into the shack. In the warm air the feeling passed as quickly as it had come. Curious but cautious, I again made my way up the ladder. And again the same thing happened; I lost my breath, but I perceived why. A light air was moving down from eastward; and its bitter touch, when I faced into it, was constricting the breathing passages. So I turned my face away from it, breathing into my glove; and in that attitude finished the 'ob.' Before going below, I made an interesting experiment. I put a thermometer on the snow, let it lie there awhile, and discovered that the temperature at the surface was actually 5° colder than at the level of the instrument shelter, four feet higher. Reading in the sleeping bag afterwards, I froze one finger, although I shifted the book steadily from one hand to the other, slipping the unoccupied hand into the warmth of the bag.

Out of the cold and out of the east came the wind. It came on gradually, as if the sheer weight of the cold were almost too much to be
moved. On the night of the 21st the barometer started down. The
night was black as a thunderhead when I made my first trip topside;
and a tension in the wind, a bulking of shadows in the night indicated that a new storm centre was forming. Next morning, glad of
an excuse to stay underground, I worked a long time on the Escape
Tunnel by the light of a red candle standing in a snow recess. That
day I pushed the emergency exit to a distance of twenty-two feet,
the farthest it was ever to go. My stint done, I sat down on a box,
thinking how beautiful was the red of the candle, how white the
rough-hewn snow. Soon I became aware of an increasing clatter of
the anemometer cups. Realizing that the wind was picking up, I
went topside to make sure that everything was secured. It is a queer
experience to watch a blizzard rise. First there is the wind, rising out
of nowhere. Then the Barrier unwrenches itself from quietude; and
the surface, which just before had seemed as hard and polished as
metal, begins to run like a making sea. Sometimes, if the wind
strikes hard, the drift comes across the Barrier like a hurrying white
cloud, tossed hundreds of feet in the air. Other times the growth is
gradual. You become conscious of a general slithering movement
on all sides. The air fills with tiny scraping and sliding and rustling
sounds as the first loose crystals stir. In a little while they are
moving as solidly as an incoming tide, which creams over the
ankles, then surges to the waist, and finally is at the throat. I have
walked in drift so thick as not to be able to see a foot ahead of me;
yet, when I glanced up, I could see the stars shining through the
thin layer just overhead.

Smoking tendrils were creeping up the anemometer pole when
I finished my inspection. I hurriedly made the trapdoor fast, as a

sailor might batten down a hatch; and knowing that my ship was well secured, I retired to the cabin to ride out the storm. It could not reach me, hidden deep in the Barrier crust; nevertheless the sounds came down. The gale sobbed in the ventilators, shook the stovepipe until I thought it would be jerked out by the roots, pounded the roof with sledge-hammer blows. I could actually feel the suction effect through the pervious snow. A breeze flickered in the room and the tunnels. The candles wavered and went out. My only light was the feeble storm lantern.

Even so, I didn't have any idea how really bad it was until I went aloft for an observation. As I pushed back the trapdoor, the drift met me like a moving wall. It was only a few steps from the ladder to the instrument shelter, but it seemed more like a mile. The air came at me in snowy rushes; I breasted it as I might a heavy surf. No night had ever seemed so dark. The beam from the flashlight was choked in its throat; I could not see my hand before my face.

My windproofs were caked with drift by the time I got below. I had a vague feeling that something had changed while I was gone, but what, I couldn't tell. Presently I noticed that the shack was appreciably colder. Raising the stove lid, I was surprised to find that the fire was out, though the tank was half full. I decided that I must have turned off the valve unconsciously before going aloft; but, when I put a match to the burner, the draught down the pipe blew out the flame. The wind, then, must have killed the fire. I got it going again, and watched it carefully.

The blizzard vaulted to gale force. Above the roar the deep, taut thrumming note of the radio antenna and the anemometer guy wires reminded me of wind in a ship's rigging. The wind direction trace turned scratchy on the sheet; no doubt drift had short-circuited the electric contacts, I decided. Realizing that it was hopeless to attempt to try to keep them clear, I let the instrument be. There were other ways of getting the wind direction. I tied a handkerchief to a bamboo pole and ran it through the outlet ventilator; with a flashlight I could tell which way the cloth was whipped. I did this at hourly intervals, noting any change of direction on the sheet. But by 2 o'clock in the morning I had had enough of this periscope sighting. If I expected to sleep and at the same time maintain the continuity of the records, I had no choice but to clean the contact points.

The wind was blowing hard then. The Barrier shook from the concussions overhead; and the noise was as if the entire physical world were tearing itself to pieces. I could scarcely heave the trapdoor open. The instant it came clear I was plunged into a blinding smother. I came out crawling, clinging to the handle of the door until I made sure of my bearings. Then I let the door fall shut, not wanting the tunnel filled with drift. To see was impossible. Millions of tiny pellets exploded in my eyes, stinging like BB shot. It was even hard to breathe, because snow instantly clogged the mouth and nostrils. I made my way toward the anemometer pole on hands and knees, scared that I might be bowled off my feet if I stood erect; one false step and I should be lost forever.

I found the pole all right; but not until my head collided with a cleat. I managed to climb it, too, though ten million ghosts were tearing at me, ramming their thumbs into my eyes. But the errand was useless. Drift as thick as this would mess up the contact points as quickly as they were cleared; besides, the wind cups were spinning so fast that I stood a good chance of losing a couple of fingers in the process. Coming down the pole, I had a sense of being whirled violently through the air, with no control over my movements. The trapdoor was completely buried when I found it again, after scraping around for some time with my mittens. I pulled at the handle, first with one hand, then with both. It did not give. It's a tight fit, anyway, I mumbled to myself. The drift has probably wedged the corners. Standing astride the hatch, I braced myself and heaved with all my strength. I might just as well have tried hoisting the Barrier.

Panic took me then, I must confess. Reason fled. I clawed at the three-foot square of timber like a madman. I beat on it with my fists, trying to shake the snow loose; and, when that did no good, I lay flat on my belly and pulled until my hands went weak from cold and weariness. Then I crooked my elbow, put my face down, and said over and over again, You damn fool, you damn fool. Here for weeks I had been defending myself against the danger of being penned inside the shack; instead, I was now locked out; and nothing could be worse, especially since I had only a wool parka and pants under my windproofs. Just two feet below was sanctuary — warmth, food, tools, all the means of survival. All these things were an arm's length away, but I was powerless to reach them.

There is something extravagantly insensate about an Antarctic blizzard at night. Its vindictiveness cannot be measured on an anemometer sheet. It is more than just wind; it is a solid wall of snow moving at gale force, pounding like surf.* The whole malevolent rush is concentrated upon you as upon a personal enemy. In the senseless explosion of sound you are reduced to a crawling thing on the margin of a disintegrating world; you can't see, you can't hear, you can hardly move. The lungs gasp after the air sucked out of them, and the brain is shaken. Nothing in the world will so quickly isolate a man.

Half-frozen, I stabbed toward one of the ventilators, a few feet away. My mittens touched something round and cold. Cupping it in my hands, I pulled myself up. This was the outlet ventilator. Just why, I don't know — but instinct made me kneel and press my face against the opening. Nothing in the room was visible, but a dim patch of light illuminated the floor, and warmth rose up to my face. That steadied me.

---

* Because of this blinding, suffocating drift, in the Antarctic winds of only moderate velocity have the punishing force of full-fledged hurricanes elsewhere.

Still kneeling, I turned my back to the blizzard and considered what might be done. I thought of breaking in the windows in the roof, but they lay two feet down in hard crust, and were reinforced with wire besides. If I only had something to dig with, I could break the crust and stamp the windows in with my feet. The pipe cupped between my hands supplied the first inspiration; maybe I could use that to dig with. It, too, was wedged tight; I pulled until my arms ached, without budging it; I had lost all track of time, and the despairing thought came to me that I was lost in a task without an end. Then I remembered the shovel. A week before, after levelling drift from the last light blow, I had stabbed a shovel handle up in the crust somewhere to leeward. That shovel would save me. But how to find it in the avalanche of the blizzard?

I lay down and stretched out full length. Still holding the pipe, I thrashed around with my feet, but pummeled only empty air. Then I worked back to the hatch. The hard edges at the opening provided another grip, and again I stretched out and kicked. Again no luck. I dared not let go until I had something else familiar to cling to. My foot came up against the other ventilator pipe. I edged back to that, and from the new anchorage repeated the manoeuvre. This time my ankle struck something hard. When I felt it and recognized the handle, I wanted to caress it.

Embracing this thrice-blessed tool, I inched back to the trapdoor. The handle of the shovel was just small enough to pass under the little wooden bridge which served as a grip. I got both hands on the shovel and tried to wrench the door up; my strength was not enough, however. So I lay down flat on my belly and worked my shoulders under the shovel. Then I heaved, the door sprang open, and I rolled down the shaft. When I tumbled into the light and warmth of the room, I kept thinking, How wonderful, how perfectly wonderful.

CHAPTER 12

'THE BLASPHEMOUS CITY'

from *At the Mountains of Madness* (1936)

H.P. Lovecraft

Richard Byrd had a fervent reader in the horror novelist H. P. Lovecraft, who saw that the plane journeys across titanic landscapes, and even the sense of a terrain quivering with some not-quite-sayable message, could be recruited into his private cosmos. With purple gusto At the Mountains of Madness *expands the Transantarctic Range into something truly outsized, a fit location for another of the secrets which – as ever in Lovecraft – make the sanity of the beholder snap like overstretched elastic. Here, Lovecraft's use of Antarctica can stand in for the whole vein of paranoid fantasy in which the continent hides away lost tribes, mysterious temples and swastika-painted UFOs popping out of holes in the icecap like Nazi party-favours.*

In spite of all the prevailing horrors, we were left with enough sheer scientific zeal and adventurousness to wonder about the unknown realm beyond those mysterious mountains. As our guarded messages stated, we rested at midnight after our day of terror and bafflement – but not without a tentative plan for one or more range-crossing altitude flights in a lightened plane with aerial camera and geologist's outfit, beginning the following morning. It was decided that Danforth and I try it first, and we awaked at 7 A.M.

intending an early flight; however, heavy winds – mentioned in our brief bulletin to the outside world – delayed our start till nearly nine o'clock.

I have already repeated the noncommittal story we told the men at camp – and relayed outside – after our return sixteen hours later. It is now my terrible duty to amplify this account by filling in the merciful blanks with hints of what we really saw in the hidden transmontane world – hints of the revelations which have finally driven Danforth to a nervous collapse. I wish he would add a really frank word about the thing which he thinks he alone saw – even though it was probably a nervous delusion – and which was perhaps the last straw that put him where he is; but he is firm against that. All I can do is to repeat his later disjointed whispers about what set him shrieking as the plane soared back through the wind-tortured mountain pass after that real and tangible shock which I shared. This will form my last word. If the plain signs of surviving elder horrors in what I disclose be not enough to keep others from meddling with the inner antarctic – or at least from prying too deeply beneath the surface of that ultimate waste of forbidden secrets and inhuman, aeon-cursed desolation – the responsibility for unnamable and perhaps immeasurable evils will not be mine.

Danforth and I, studying the notes made by Pabodie in his afternoon flight and checking up with a sextant, had calculated that the lowest available pass in the range lay somewhat to the right of us, within sight of camp, and about twenty-three thousand or twenty-four thousand feet above sea level. For this point, then, we first headed in the lightened plane as we embarked on our flight of discovery. The camp itself, on foothills which sprang from a high continental plateau, was some twelve thousand feet in altitude; hence the actual height increase necessary was not so vast as it might seem. Nevertheless we were acutely conscious of the rarefied air and intense cold as we rose; for, on account of visibility conditions, we had to leave the cabin windows open. We were dressed, of course, in our heaviest furs.

As we drew near the forbidding peaks, dark and sinister above the line of crevasse-riven snow and interstitial glaciers, we noticed more and more the curiously regular formations clinging to the slopes; and thought again of the strange Asian paintings of Nicholas Roerich. The ancient and wind-weathered rock strata fully verified all of Lake's bulletins, and proved that these pinnacles had been towering up in exactly the same way since a surprisingly early time in earth's history — perhaps over fifty million years. How much higher they had once been, it was futile to guess; but everything about this strange region pointed to obscure atmospheric influences unfavorable to change, and calculated to retard the usual climatic processes of rock disintegration.

But it was the mountainside tangle of regular cubes, ramparts, and cave mouths which fascinated and disturbed us most. I studied them with a field glass and took aerial photographs while Danforth drove; and at times I relieved him at the controls — though my aviation knowledge was purely an amateur's — in order to let him use the binoculars. We could easily see that much of the material of the things was a lightish Archaean quartzite, unlike any formation visible over broad areas of the general surface; and that their regularity was extreme and uncanny to an extent which poor Lake had scarcely hinted.

As he had said, their edges were crumbled and rounded from untold aeons of savage weathering; but their preternatural solidity and tough material had saved them from obliteration. Many parts, especially those closest to the slopes, seemed identical in substance with the surrounding rock surface. The whole arrangement looked like the ruins of Macchu Picchu in the Andes, or the primal foundation walls of Kish as dug up by the Oxford Field Museum

Expedition in 1929; and both Danforth and I obtained that occasional impression of separate Cyclopean blocks which Lake had attributed to his flight-companion Carroll. How to account for such things in this place was frankly beyond me, and I felt queerly humbled as a geologist. Igneous formations often have strange regularities – like the famous Giants' Causeway in Ireland – but this stupendous range, despite Lake's original suspicion of smoking cones, was above all else nonvolcanic in evident structure.

The curious cave mouths, near which the odd formations seemed most abundant, presented another albeit a lesser puzzle because of their regularity of outline. They were, as Lake's bulletin had said, often approximately square or semicircular; as if the natural orifices had been shaped to greater symmetry by some magic hand. Their numerousness and wide distribution were remarkable, and suggested that the whole region was honeycombed with tunnels dissolved out of limestone strata. Such glimpses as we secured did not extend far within the caverns, but we saw that they were apparently clear of stalactites and stalagmites. Outside, those parts of the mountain slopes adjoining the apertures seemed invariably smooth and regular; and Danforth thought that the slight cracks and pittings of the weathering tended toward unusual patterns. Filled as he was with the horrors and strangenesses discovered at the camp, he hinted that the pittings vaguely resembled those baffling groups of dots sprinkled over the primeval greenish soapstones, so hideously duplicated on the madly conceived snow mounds above those six buried monstrosities.

We had risen gradually in flying over the higher foothills and along toward the relatively low pass we had selected. As we advanced we occasionally looked down at the snow and ice of the land route, wondering whether we could have attempted the trip with the simpler equipment of earlier days. Somewhat to our surprise we saw that the terrain was far from difficult as such things go;

and that despite the crevasses and other bad spots it would not have been likely to deter the sledges of a Scott, a Shackleton, or an Amundsen. Some of the glaciers appeared to lead up to wind-bared passes with unusual continuity, and upon reaching our chosen pass we found that its case formed no exception.

Our sensations of tense expectancy as we prepared to round the crest and peer out over an untrodden world can hardly be described on paper; even though we had no cause to think the regions beyond the range essentially different from those already seen and traversed. The touch of evil mystery in these barrier mountains, and in the beckoning sea of opalescent sky glimpsed betwixt their summits, was a highly subtle and attenuated matter not to be explained in literal words. Rather was it an affair of vague psychological symbolism and aesthetic association – a thing mixed up with exotic poetry and paintings, and with archaic myths lurking in shunned and forbidden volumes. Even the wind's burden held a peculiar strain of conscious malignity; and for a second it seemed that the composite sound included a bizarre musical whistling or piping over a wide range as the blast swept in and out of the omnipresent and resonant cave mouths. There was a cloudy note of reminiscent repulsion in this sound, as complex and unplaceable as any of the other dark impressions.

We were now, after a slow ascent, at a height of twenty-three thousand, five hundred and seventy feet according to the aneroid; and had left the region of clinging snow definitely below us. Up here were only dark, bare rock slopes and the start of rough-ribbed glaciers – but with those provocative cubes, ramparts, and echoing cave mouths to add a portent of the unnatural, the fantastic, and the dreamlike. Looking along the line of high peaks, I thought I could see the one mentioned by poor Lake, with a rampart exactly on top. It seemed to be half lost in a queer antarctic haze – such a haze, perhaps, as had been responsible for Lake's early notion of volcanism.

The pass loomed directly before us, smooth and windswept between its jagged and malignly frowning pylons. Beyond it was a sky fretted with swirling vapors and lighted by the low polar sun – the sky of that mysterious farther realm upon which we felt no human eye had ever gazed.

A few more feet of altitude and we would behold that realm. Danforth and I, unable to speak except in shouts amidst the howling, piping wind that raced through the pass and added to the noise of the unmuffled engines, exchanged eloquent glances. And then, having gained those last few feet, we did indeed stare across the momentous divide and over the unsampled secrets of an elder and utterly alien earth.

I think that both of us simultaneously cried out in mixed awe, wonder, terror, and disbelief in our own senses as we finally cleared the pass and saw what lay beyond. Of course, we must have had some natural theory in the back of our heads to steady our faculties for the moment. Probably we thought of such things as the grotesquely weathered stones of the Garden of the Gods in Colorado, or the fantastically symmetrical wind-carved rocks of the Arizona desert. Perhaps we even half thought the sight a mirage like that we had seen the morning before on first approaching those mountains of madness. We must have had some such normal notions to fall back upon as our eyes swept that limitless, tempest-scarred plateau and grasped the almost endless labyrinth of colossal, regular, and geometrically eurythmic stone masses which reared their crumbled and pitted crests above a glacial sheet not more than forty or fifty feet deep at its thickest, and in places obviously thinner.

The effect of the monstrous sight was indescribable, for some fiendish violation of known natural law seemed certain at the outset. Here, on a hellishly ancient table-land fully twenty thousand feet high, and in a climate deadly to habitation since a prehuman age not less than five hundred thousand years ago, there stretched nearly to the vision's limit a tangle of orderly stone which only the desperation of mental self-defense could possibly attribute to any but conscious and artificial cause. We had previously dismissed, so far as serious thought was concerned, any theory that the cubes and ramparts of the mountainsides were other than natural in origin. How could they be otherwise, when man himself could scarcely have been differentiated from the great apes at the time when this region succumbed to the present unbroken reign of glacial death?

Yet now the sway of reason seemed irrefutably shaken, for this Cyclopean maze of squared, curved, and angled blocks had features which cut off all comfortable refuge. It was, very clearly, the blasphemous city of the mirage in stark, objective, and ineluctable reality. That damnable portent had had a material basis after all – there had been some horizontal stratum of ice dust in the upper air, and this shocking stone survival had projected its image across the mountains according to the simple laws of reflection. Of course, the phantom had been twisted and exaggerated, and had contained things which the real source did not contain; yet now, as we saw that real source, we thought it even more hideous and menacing than its distant image.

Only the incredible, unhuman massiveness of these vast stone towers and ramparts had saved the frightful things from utter annihilation in the hundreds of thousands – perhaps millions – of years it had brooded there amidst the blasts of a bleak upland. 'Corona Mundi – Roof of the World –' All sorts of fantastic phrases sprang to our lips as we looked dizzily down at the unbelievable spectacle. I thought again of the eldritch primal myths that had so persistently haunted me since my first sight of this dead antarctic world – of the demoniac plateau of Leng, of the Mi-Go, or abominable Snow Men of the Himalayas, of the Pnakotic Manuscripts with their prehuman implications, of the Cthulhu cult, of the Necronomicon, and of the Hyperborean legends of formless Tsathoggua and the worse than formless star spawn associated with that semientity.

For boundless miles in every direction the thing stretched off with very little thinning; indeed, as our eyes followed it to the right and left along the base of the low, gradual foothills which separated it from the actual mountain rim, we decided that we could see no thinning at all except for an interruption at the left of the pass through which we had come. We had merely struck, at random, a limited part of something of incalculable extent. The foothills were more sparsely sprinkled with grotesque stone structures, linking the terrible city to the already familiar cubes and ramparts which evidently formed its mountain outposts. These latter, as well as the queer cave mouths, were as thick on the inner as on the outer sides of the mountains.

The nameless stone labyrinth consisted, for the most part, of walls from ten to one hundred and fifty feet in ice-clear height, and of a thickness varying from five to ten feet. It was composed mostly of prodigious blocks of dark primordial slate, schist, and sandstone – blocks in many cases as large as 4 x 6 x 8 feet – though in several places it seemed to be carved out of a solid, uneven bed rock of pre-Cambrian slate. The buildings were far from equal in size, there being innumerable honeycomb arrangements of enormous extent as well as smaller separate structures. The general shape of these things tended to be conical, pyramidal, or terraced; though there were many perfect cylinders, perfect cubes, clusters of cubes, and other rectangular forms, and a peculiar sprinkling of angled edifices whose five-pointed ground plan roughly suggested modern fortifications. The builders had made constant and expert use of the principle of the arch, and domes had probably existed in the city's heyday.

The whole tangle was monstrously weathered, and the glacial

surface from which the towers projected was strewn with fallen blocks and immemorial debris. Where the glaciation was transparent we could see the lower parts of the gigantic piles, and we noticed the ice-preserved stone bridges which connected the different towers at varying distances above the ground. On the exposed walls we could detect the scarred places where other and higher bridges of the same sort had existed. Closer inspection revealed countless largish windows; some of which were closed with shutters of a petrified material originally wood, though most gaped open in a sinister and menacing fashion. Many of the ruins, of course, were roofless, and with uneven though wind-rounded upper edges; whilst others, of a more sharply conical or pyramidal model or else protected by higher surrounding structures, preserved intact outlines despite the omnipresent crumbling and pitting. With the field glass we could barely make out what seemed to be sculptural decorations in horizontal bands – decorations including those curious groups of dots whose presence on the ancient soapstones now assumed a vastly larger significance.

In many places the buildings were totally ruined and the ice sheet deeply riven from various geologic causes. In other places the stonework was worn down to the very level of the glaciation. One broad swath, extending from the plateau's interior to a cleft in the foothills about a mile to the left of the pass we had traversed, was wholly free from buildings. It probably represented, we concluded, the course of some great river which in Tertiary times – millions of years ago – had poured through the city and into some prodigious subterranean abyss of the great barrier range. Certainly, this was above all a region of caves, gulfs, and underground secrets beyond human penetration.

Looking back to our sensations, and recalling our dazedness at viewing this monstrous survival from aeons we had thought prehuman, I can only wonder that we preserved the semblance of equilibrium, which we did. Of course, we knew that something – chronology, scientific theory, or our own consciousness – was woefully awry; yet we kept enough poise to guide the plane, observe many things quite minutely, and take a careful series of photographs which may yet serve both us and the world in good stead. In my case, ingrained scientific habit may have helped; for above all my bewilderment and sense of menace, there burned a dominant curiosity to fathom more of this age-old secret – to know what sort of beings had built and lived in this incalculably gigantic place, and what relation to the general world of its time or of other times so unique a concentration of life could have had.

For this place could be no ordinary city. It must have formed the primary nucleus and center of some archaic and unbelievable chapter of earth's history whose outward ramifications, recalled only dimly in the most obscure and distorted myths, had vanished utterly amidst the chaos of terrene convulsions long before any human race we know had shambled out of apedom. Here sprawled a Palaeogaean megalopolis compared with which the fabled Atlantis and Lemuria, Commoriom and Uzuldaroum, and Olathoc in the land of Lomar, are recent things of today – not even of yesterday; a megalopolis ranking with such whispered prehuman blasphemies as Valusia, R'lyeh, Ib in the land of Mnar, and the Nameless city of Arabia Deserta. As we flew above that tangle of stark titan towers my imagination sometimes escaped all bounds and roved aimlessly in realms of fantastic associations – even weaving links betwixt this lost world and some of my own wildest dreams concerning the mad horror at the camp.

The plane's fuel tank, in the interest of greater lightness, had been only partly filled; hence we now had to exert caution in our explorations. Even so, however, we covered an enormous extent of ground – or, rather, air – after swooping down to a level where the wind became virtually negligible. There seemed to be no limit to the mountain range, or to the length of the frightful stone city which bordered its inner foothills. Fifty miles of flight in each direction showed no major change in the labyrinth of rock and masonry that clawed up corpselike through the eternal ice. There were, though, some highly absorbing diversifications; such as the carvings on the canyon where that broad river had once pierced the foothills and approached its sinking place in the great range. The headlands at the stream's entrance had been boldly carved into Cyclopean pylons; and something about the ridgy, barrel-shaped designs stirred up oddly vague, hateful, and confusing semi-remembrances in both Danforth and me.

We also came upon several star-shaped open spaces, evidently public squares, and noted various undulations in the terrain. Where a sharp hill rose, it was generally hollowed out into some sort of rambling-stone edifice; but there were at least two exceptions. Of these latter, one was too badly weathered to disclose what had been on the jutting eminence, while the other still bore a fantastic conical monument carved out of the solid rock and roughly resembling such things as the well-known Snake Tomb in the ancient valley of Petra.

Flying inland from the mountains, we discovered that the city was not of infinite width, even though its length along the foothills seemed endless. After about thirty miles the grotesque stone buildings began to thin out, and in ten more miles we came to an unbroken waste virtually without signs of sentient artifice. The course of the river beyond the city seemed marked by a broad, depressed line, while the land assumed a somewhat greater ruggedness, seeming to slope slightly upward as it receded in the mist-hazed west.

So far we had made no landing, yet to leave the plateau without an attempt at entering some of the monstrous structures would have been inconceivable. Accordingly, we decided to find a smooth place on the foothills near our navigable pass, there grounding the plane and preparing to do some exploration on foot. Though these gradual slopes were partly covered with a scattering of ruins, low flying soon disclosed an ampler number of possible landing places. Selecting that nearest to the pass, since our flight would be across the great range and back to camp, we succeeded about 12:30 P.M. in effecting a landing on a smooth, hard snow field wholly devoid of obstacles and well adapted to a swift and favorable take-off later on.

It did not seem necessary to protect the plane with a snow banking for so brief a time and in so comfortable an absence of high winds at this level; hence we merely saw that the landing skis were safely lodged, and that the vital parts of the mechanism were guarded against the cold. For our foot journey we discarded the heaviest of our flying furs, and took with us a small outfit consisting of pocket compass, hand camera, light provisions, voluminous notebooks and paper, geologist's hammer and chisel, specimen bags, coil of climbing rope, and powerful electric torches with extra batteries; this equipment having been carried in the plane on the chance that we might be able to effect a landing, take ground pictures, make drawings and topographical sketches, and obtain rock specimens from some bare slope, outcropping, or mountain cave. Fortunately we had a supply of extra paper to tear up, place in a spare specimen bag, and use on the ancient principle of hare and hounds for marking our course in any interior mazes we might be able to penetrate. This had been brought in case we found some cave system with air quiet enough to allow such a rapid and easy method in place of the usual rock-chipping method of trail blazing.

Walking cautiously downhill over the crusted snow toward the stupendous stone labyrinth that loomed against the opalescent west, we felt almost as keen a sense of imminent marvels as we had felt on approaching the unfathomed mountain pass four hours previously. True, we had become visually familiar with the incredible secret concealed by the barrier peaks; yet the prospect of actually entering primordial walls reared by conscious beings perhaps millions of years ago – before any known race of men could have existed – was none the less awesome and potentially terrible in its implications of cosmic abnormality. Though the thinness of the air at this prodigious altitude made exertion somewhat more difficult than usual, both Danforth and I found ourselves bearing up very well, and felt equal to almost any task which might fall to our lot. It took only a few steps to bring us to a shapeless ruin worn level with the snow, while ten or fifteen rods farther on there was a huge, roofless rampart still complete in its gigantic five-pointed outline and rising to an irregular height of ten or eleven feet. For this latter we headed; and when at last we were actually able to touch its weathered Cyclopean blocks, we felt that we had established an unprecedented and almost blasphemous link with forgotten aeons normally closed to our species.

This rampart, shaped like a star and perhaps three hundred feet from point to point, was built of Jurassic sandstone blocks of irregular size, averaging 6 x 8 feet in surface. There was a row of arched loopholes or windows about four feet wide and five feet high, spaced quite symmetrically along the points of the star and at its inner angles, and with the bottoms about four feet from the glaciated surface. Looking through these, we could see that the masonry was fully five feet thick, that there were no partitions remaining within, and that there were traces of banded carvings or bas-reliefs on the interior walls – facts we had indeed guessed before, when flying low over this rampart and others like it. Though lower parts must have originally existed, all traces of such things were now wholly obscured by the deep layer of ice and snow at this point.

We crawled through one of the windows and vainly tried to decipher the nearly effaced mural designs, but did not attempt to disturb the glaciated floor. Our orientation flights had indicated that many buildings in the city proper were less ice-choked, and that we might perhaps find wholly clear interiors leading down to the true ground level if we entered those structures still roofed at the top. Before we left the rampart we photographed it carefully, and studied its mortar-less Cyclopean masonry with complete bewilderment. We wished that Pabodie were present, for his engineering knowledge might have helped us guess how such titanic blocks could have been handled in that unbelievably remote age when the city and its outskirts were built up.

The half-mile walk downhill to the actual city, with the upper wind shrieking vainly and savagely through the skyward peaks in the background, was something of which the smallest details will always remain engraved on my mind. Only in fantastic nightmares could any human beings but Danforth and me conceive such optical effects. Between us and the churning vapors of the west lay that monstrous tangle of dark stone towers, its outré and incredible forms impressing us afresh at every new angle of vision. It was a mirage in solid stone, and were it not for the photographs, I would still doubt that such a thing could be. The general type of masonry was identical with that of the rampart we had examined; but the extravagant shapes which this masonry took in its urban manifestations were past all description.

Even the pictures illustrate only one or two phases of its endless variety, preternatural massiveness, and utterly alien exoticism. There were geometrical forms for which an Euclid would scarcely find a name – cones of all degrees of irregularity and truncation, terraces of every sort of provocative disproportion, shafts with odd bulbous enlargements, broken columns in curious groups, and five-pointed or five-ridged arrangements of mad grotesqueness. As we drew nearer we could see beneath certain transparent parts of the ice sheet, and detect some of the tubular stone bridges that connected the crazily sprinkled structures at various heights. Of orderly streets there seemed to be none, the only broad open swath being a mile to the left, where the ancient river had doubtless flowed through the town into the mountains.

Our field glasses showed the external, horizontal bands of nearly effaced sculptures and dot groups to be very prevalent, and we could half imagine what the city must once have looked like – even though most of the roofs and tower tops had necessarily perished. As a whole, it had been a complex tangle of twisted lanes and alleys, all of them deep canyons, and some little better than tunnels because of the overhanging masonry or overarching bridges. Now, outspread below us, it loomed like a dream fantasy against a west-ward mist through whose northern end the low, reddish antarctic sun of early afternoon was struggling to shine; and when, for a moment, that sun encountered a denser obstruction and plunged the scene into temporary shadow, the effect was subtly menacing in a way I can never hope to depict. Even the faint howling and piping of the unfelt wind in the great mountain passes behind us took on a wilder note of purposeful malignity. The last stage of our descent to the town was unusually steep and abrupt, and a rock outcropping at the edge where the grade changed led us to think that an artificial terrace had once existed there. Under the glaciation, we believed, there must be a flight of steps or its equivalent.

When at last we plunged into the town itself, clambering over fallen masonry and shrinking from the oppressive nearness and dwarfing height of omnipresent crumbling and pitted walls, our sensations again became such that I marvel at the amount of self-control we retained. Danforth was frankly jumpy, and began making some offensively irrelevant speculations about the horror at the camp – which I resented all the more because I could not help sharing certain conclusions forced upon us by many features of this morbid survival from nightmare antiquity. The speculations worked on his imagination, too; for in one place – where a debris-littered alley turned a sharp corner – he insisted that he saw faint traces of ground markings which he did not like; whilst elsewhere he stopped to listen to a subtle, imaginary sound from some unde-fined point – a muffled musical piping, he said, not unlike that of the wind in the mountain caves, yet somehow disturbingly differ-ent. The ceaseless five-pointedness of the surrounding architecture and of the few distinguishable mural arabesques had a dimly sin-ister suggestiveness we could not escape, and gave us a touch of terrible subconscious certainty concerning the primal entities which had reared and dwelt in this unhallowed place.

CHAPTER 13

'SEA DADDY, STORMALONG JOHN AND MINUTE MAID'

from *Life at the Bottom* (1977)

John Langone

John Langone was a journalist who set out to capture the timbre of daily life in American Antarctica, just as the phase of military dominance was drawing to a close. Here, three US Navy SeaBees talk about overwintering at a South Pole which is no longer an abstract spot on the map, or a goal of heroic struggle, but a posting; one place, exceptionally cold and weird and sex-deprived, in the roster of places a guy might be sent to work construction and maintenance under difficult circumstances. Blue-collar Antarctica would remain, but it would never again be this purely male, or this much a pure extension of military culture.

'The hard part about it,' says Minute Maid, sipping his coffee, 'is when you come back to the world, to the hustle and bustle. Down here, once you get into the winter, you just get into a routine and it's nice and slow. Comin' off the ice can be rougher, to my way of thinkin', than goin' on. Like, you know what one of the first things that just hits at you is when you get off here? It's the shrill sounds that a woman makes. You get to really notice her voice, that shrill kind of piercing voice. And you notice the hardness of the pavements, and the different smells, and the traffic noises.'

'Yeah,' says Sea Daddy, 'there's no red lights here, no traffic like that, no nothin', and you're on your own, that's why I like it, it's real fine.'

'Different at Palmer than here, though,' says Minute Maid. 'This here place's a metropolis; down at Palmer we had ten, eleven of us.'

'Whooee, beach party place, man,' laughs Sea Daddy, showing white teeth through his black beard. 'How'd you guys stand the fuckin' heat?'

'Buried myself in my work,' says Minute Maid. 'Mechanic and equipment operator, but you wouldn't know nothin' about that shit, Daddy; I do more accidentally than you do on purpose. Let me tell you, there was only but four Seabees in the whole place, so you sort of did just about everything that came up, like a lot of projects. We got a little bit of everything from building to utilities, which is plumbing. And I didn't volunteer for it, neither, not like that asshole, Daddy over there, and I just came up for orders. When they came in they had the words "Deep Freeze" on there, you know? I called the detailer, which is the mechanic chief, Buddy Dew, and I talked to him and he says, well, he's been down there and he says he thinks it's a good thing for me, and I ought to go down one time anyway. I says, thanks a lot, you fat fuck, I could really care what you think of the place, I don't want to go, no way. But they shipped my ass down anyway.'

'I had thirteen seasons down and three winters-over,' Sea Daddy says proudly, thumping the table three times. 'I own the fuckin' place. Pole, Byrd, McMurdo, name it, men. I was there when Crazy Charlie was down.'

Stormalong John comes alive at Charlie's name, smiles wistfully, shakes his head. 'Oh Jesus, Crazy Charlie. Used to get a little drunk down there, paint a face on the back of his head, didn't know whether he was comin' or goin'. Pasted a battleship on the top of his head and went to sleep like that at night. Crazy stuff like that to get morale goin', that's why they called him Crazy Charlie.'

'Yeah, lots of laughs in those days,' says Sea Daddy. 'It's changed now. Place is becomin' Skirt City. Used to get lots of things in the old days. It's all over now, Navy's gettin' out in a couple years once we get Pole built, I'm gettin' out. Used to be like when you wintered over you got a promotion, sometimes got a first duty choice, sometimes got somethin' named after you. Now they're siftin' so many people in and out, it's like a Ford plant down here, not what they call . . . used to call, exotic duty, you know.'

'I'll say one thing, though,' says Minute Maid. 'Everyone who asked for their first choice while down there this year got it. Palmer is good that way. Only thing is I didn't ask to go there in the first place, and I didn't think it was so great, duty or not. One year, right? Nine months before that I got Vietnam. Separated from my wife for a year then, right? I really didn't care that much for it. Now I'm down here. This time, all the guys were tellin' me that when I get the screenin', you know, all I got to do is run in there and kiss the first guy I see, and they'll let me out. Well, I didn't exactly do that, but when the shrink asks me how I felt about goin' onto the ice, I tell him anybody goes to the Antarctic and winters over is a nut. And you know what he says? He says, you're all right, get your gear together, buddy. Well, I got down there, and I didn't think too much about it until my ship, *Hero*, pulls out. Last one to leave, you know, pulls out in April and that's it, no more for a long time.

'Well, I hated it, but it really wasn't too bad, lowest it got was ten below, highest was fifty-five. But you still got all your Antarctic differences, changing winds that blow in circles, the isolation. They kept us busy, just busy. Only thing was I got tired of seeing the same guys all the time. Only two buildings at Palmer. To get away from the guys you had to go on a hike or some such. Like this one guy and I we went out onto a glacier with our sleeping bags and slept up there, just to break the monotony. But you know, I wouldn't winter over again. This is fine for a few months here at McMurdo, but I wouldn't winter over again. I've asked for summer support and I'll be goin' down a few more times, and there is an advantage of sorts, you know. You get to meet different people from other countries and you never find any hostility. Everybody is human down here. And there's somethin' about the Antarctic that you just can't describe. It has its own . . . environment or somethin'. I can't get the right words . . . But it's just . . . somethin' . . .'

Stormalong John says, 'Let me say something about that. Last year I was out in the Dry Valleys at Vanda, and there was nobody around, nobody. I couldn't see a soul. The helo left and went over to somewhere else for a few hours and I couldn't see a soul. In my whole life, I never been in a situation like that, where you feel like it's the cleanest, nicest place in the world. But I think I've had enough, too; I've put in four times, given 'em three winters. And I put in for twenty choices of duty, too, and I got none of 'em. Last time, before this one, I got orders for Cape Hatteras, and I just had left one year of isolated duty at Pole, so they sent me to Cape Hatteras, must have figured I needed a rest. But that place. Nearest dime store is fifty miles away and that's in the so-called States. Base was fallin' apart, they wanted it repaired, and there I was with a ulcer tour starin' me in the face, and I just got done with one ulcer tour in the Antarctic. Finished up the Cape Hatteras tour, and come back here, and figured that was the least of two evils. I don't really mind it, though. The wintering over is really the best part of it. Once you get the summer support people and most of the scientists the hell out, then it's good duty. During the winter you don't have fifteen, twenty bosses trying to tell you how to run a job, from the skipper on down.'

'Yeah,' says Sea Daddy. 'More damned tourists comin' down, plus scientists, tellin' you what to do, tryin' to do five hundred things when they should be doin' one, or maybe none, lookin' at some of these ding-dongs.'

'It's better, like I say, in the winter. But, about halfway through, things start to happen, like you may be topside throwin' snow, and one time I turned out the lights and started lookin' out there, just standin' and lookin' and it's so pitch black, and I thought, why you dumb sonofabitch, what are you doin' here anyway? You got to be crazy. Periodically, you'll do that. Everybody'll sit there and all of a sudden someone will say, hey, what the hell am I doin' here? I must be fuckin' nuts. But all in all, I liked it. It ain't such a bad place. You're more or less your own boss, particularly at the outlying stations, and if you want to try something new they'll let you, build somethin' or try an experiment. If it works, great, if it doesn't, well, WTF. There's just no place in the service that you have that except on the ice. There's no place to go, but there's freedom.

'You either like it or you don't. And if you're winterin' in and you don't like it, well, man, you're in trouble.

'I was up at Pole when they locked up the first guy they ever locked up in the Antarctic. We built a brig and shoved his ass in it. He was with the weather people, an ex-Air Force guy, and he seemed like a real nice fella during the summer. Well, the day the last plane left he did a one-eight. He became a problem. Drinking, liar, a thief. Finally, one night they put him on medication, and he stayed on it and he seemed to do pretty good. Well, then he said the hell with it and he went bananas. When he first started up like that, the OIC says we're going to build a brig, and this guy got the message, he knew it was for him. They held that over him for a while, and he stuck straight. But, just when we got to where we had six to eight weeks left before we got relieved, he flipped again, and he got hold of some booze and some medicine, and he just went snaky. He decked the medical officer, and he decked me when I jumped in, and he run out and got a fire ax and started heavin' that around.

Well, we finally got hold of him and quieted him down, and I told the watch that if anything happened don't mess around with this dude, just hit the fire bell. Well, I'm in the sack and this alarm goes off, and it was him, out on a rampage again. We finally found him hidin' out in the club, and there were twenty of us, and we gave him a choice, beat his ass off or he goes into the brig peacefully. Well, he says he's going to call his lawyer in New York, going to sue the OIC, me, the whole fuckin' Navy, goin' to contact his lawyer with a ham radio, he says.

'Well, we canned him for three days, and we sent a message out when we locked this dude up, and this was the first word, our message, that the admiral back in Christchurch had that we had a problem. He gets this message that we done locked up a civilian at Pole Station, and he went right up through the overhead. Well, he sent a message to McMurdo, told 'em to tell us to unlock this dude, we don't confine nobody, but nobody, much less a civilian, turn him loose or it's our asses. Well, the OIC, he starts sweatin', he's got twenty years in, and he says to me, hey, what do you make for base pay 'cause I think I'm goin' to be busted to chief after this is over.

'So, we let his ass out and put locks on all our doors, and he's out, roaming around the corridors night and mornin', and we stayed away from him as far as we could. We put up with that six weeks, scared shitless. Nothin' came of it that I know; they yanked six weeks off his pay. I think we would have killed him if he started in on us again during that six weeks. There was also this other civilian at Byrd Station, just started walkin' and just took off one night.'

'That guy was so depressed,' says Sea Daddy, 'we never found a trace of him. Found the dog, but not him. We had some guys like that fella up at Pole, but after a while they straightened out. You do get a little downhearted when the planes go out, and I missed all the football. But the funny part of it was when the reliefs come in, and that's somethin' to see, when they come in. Scared, don't know where they're at, in a state of shock, they are. Well, you're so glad to see these guys you start a party. The admiral come out this one time on the first plane and stayed overnight, and we're in the club havin' our party. These new guys have altitude sickness, you know, and they're tired and not climatized and they're just sittin' around sort of stunned lookin' at these here animals. Well, the admiral is out there talkin' to the OIC, and our cook, Herbie, has got a beanie on. We built him this propeller on top, and he's really blowed out of his mind on them vodka freezes he used to whip up; he did that with snow and a eggbeater and they'll send you higher than helium. Well, Herbie walks over to the admiral and he says, hey admiral, have a drink. The admiral says, no thanks. And you know what that crazy-ass Herbie does? He pours one right over the admiral's head, right over the rear admiral's head, it's dripping right down his parka. Well, the admiral, he's a good shit, no one like him that I know, and he says to the OIC, ah, doctor, I uh think you ought to secure this here little party. And the OIC says, admiral, I ain't never secured one of their parties and I can't start now.'

Stormalong John laughs hard, and Minute Maid asks him about the time they built this cage, for the benefit of the relief party, and they put this guy in it, and when the plane comes in there it is waiting for them.

'Oh Jesus, we used to do that shit all the time for the reliefs, scared the piss out of 'em. One time in sixty-nine our foreman came dressed as Mickey Mouse, made this plaster of paris Mickey Mouse suit, a beautiful thing. When the first plane drops down, there's the reliefs on board, eyes buggin' out, and there's ol' Myron standin' out there with this suit on, wavin' the plane to the fuel pit. Another year we ran up weather balloons, up about two hundred feet, strung a big sign between 'em, WATCH YOUR ASS. The best thing we did, though, was get out there with nothin' on, just your bunny boots, and you'd stand there, wavin' bottles of booze, and they'd just about shit, think we'd all gone Asiatic.'

Stormalong John pulls out a card and waves it. It reads, 'This is to certify that Stormalong John Wheeler, being of sufficient courage and questionable sanity, is a member of South Pole 200 Degree Club. Temperature: − 108 F. Nutus Extremis.'

'We started this club, and we built the first steam bath out there in sixty-four. The OIC, being a doctor, he's not familiar with Seabees, and they'll do anything. So we decided we're goin' to build a steam bath. Took a fifty-five-gallon drum, cut two-thirds of it off, stuck some holes in her, welded in some fittings, put in some electric hot water tank heating elements, and a float valve in there with a water line comin' into it so it maintained its own level, and we wired that up to a thermostat and took a piece of sheet metal and cut a hole out of it and set that on top of this, and we run a pipe out into this room we built under the ice at Pole. In July, we decided to commission her, and we called the OIC up and said, doc, we goin' to fire up the steam bath. By this time, he's ready for anything, but all he says – he's shakin' his head and stayin' in his quarters a lot – he says, it won't work. So we told him, oh yeah, that's what they told Orville, and we set the thermostat at one hundred eighteen, and we're in there in our skivvies, about twenty minutes. Somebody says, let's go out and roll in the snow. So we opened the door and run upstairs, and that night at Pole it was a record cold, one hundred twelve point five below. And that ain't includin' any wind-chill factor, either, like they do at McMurdo in them familygrams to let the folks back home figure it's a lot colder than it is. That's straight cold, I don't know what it is with wind. Well, we rolled around out there for a few minutes, and it wasn't too bad; you couldn't feel it at the beginning. When they took our pictures, you couldn't see nothin', only this blob of steam your body's throwin' off. Breaks the monotony. It's entertainment.'

CHAPTER 14

'WHITE LANTERNS'

from *The Moon by Whale Light* (1991)

Diane Ackerman

The New Yorker *writer Diane Ackerman travelled to the Antarctic Peninsula as a tourist, which had become possible for the first time a few years earlier, and which provided a whole, new, shipboard social setting from which to experience the continent. She went to write about penguins, to explore the science of the zone of intense marine life which rings the dead interior of the continent. But she found herself reflecting, too, on the intensity with which a traveller to Antarctica feels alive, when cold air touches warm skin and the summer light glows on 24 hours a day.*

At first light, on calmer seas, I opened the two porthole covers like a second pair of eyes and looked out onto Antarctica for the first time. White upon white with white borders was all I expected to see; instead, colossal icebergs of palest blue and mint-green floated across the vista. Beyond them, long chalky cliffs stretched out of view. Throwing on a parka, I raced upstairs to the deck and looked all around. As far as I could see in any direction, icebergs meandered against a backdrop of tall, crumbly Antarctic glaciers, which were still pure and unexplored. Human feet had not touched the glaciers I saw; nor had many pairs of eyes beheld them. In many ways, the

Antarctic is a world of suspended animation. Suspended between outer space and the fertile continents. Suspended in time – without a local civilization to make history. Civilization has been brought to it; it has never sustained any of its own. It sits suspended in a hanging nest of world politics. When things die in the Antarctic, they decay slowly. What has been is still there and will always be, unless we interfere. *Interfere* is such a simple word for what is happening: the ozone hole, the greenhouse effect, disputes over territory, pollution, mining. Who discovered Antarctica we may never know. We remember the Shackletons and the Scotts, but it was the whalers and sealers who opened up the Antarctic, not the explorers. Because the whalers and sealers didn't talk much about their good hunting grounds, they have sifted between the seams of history.

Soon we dropped anchor at Harmony Cove, Nelson Island, in the South Shetland Islands, whose ice cliffs are layered with volcanic ash from the Deception Island eruption of 1970. Piling into the Zodiacs, we dashed toward a cobble beach, where one of the crew, who had gone ashore early, had teased the other Zodiac drivers by spelling out LANDING in stones against the snow. A blue odalisque of ice floated offshore. Hundred-foot white glacial cliffs stood next to huge rooms of pure aquamarine ice. Ah-hah! A small welcoming party of gentoo penguins, ashore to feed their waiting chicks, waddled close to look us over. One penguin tilted its head one way, then the other, as it stared at me. This made the bird look like an art dealer, quietly thinking and appraising. Penguins don't have binocular vision as humans do, so they turn one eye to an object, then the other, to see it. Although they can see well underwater, they don't need long vision when they're on land. The last time I saw a look quite like that gentoo's was in the Penguin House at the Central Park Zoo. There, in a shower of artificial Antarctic light, in a display created by a theatrical-lighting designer, gentoos and chinstraps had eyed the crowd of people watching them –

including some of the homeless of Manhattan, who used the Penguin House as a favorite warming-up spot.

According to one saying, 'There are two kinds of penguins in the Antarctic, the white ones coming toward you, and the black ones going away from you.' All penguins are essentially black and white on their bodies, a feature known as countershading. Their white bellies and chins blend in with the shimmery light filtering through the water, so they're less likely to be spotted from below when they're in the ocean. That makes hunting fish easier, as well as escaping leopard seals. Their black backs also make them less visible from above as they fly through the murky waters. To the krill, the white belly of the penguin looks like a pale orb, harmless as the sky. To the leopard seal, the black back of the penguin looks like a shadow on the ocean bottom, unpalatable. Researchers found that if they marked penguins with aluminum bands, the tags flashed and leopard seals could spot them too easily. A lot of their study birds were killed, and they switched to black tags. Another advantage of being black and white: If they're too hot, they can turn their white parts to the sun and reflect heat; if too cold, they can turn their black parts to the sun and absorb heat. Because most of a penguin's body is below water, it's the head that has developed so many interesting designs and colors. A field guide to penguins would only need to show you the heads. Adélie penguins (named after Adélie Land, a stretch of Antarctic coast below Australia that was itself named after Adélie Dumont d'Urville, the wife of the nineteenth-century French explorer Jules-Sébastian-César Dumont d'Urville, who first sighted it; among Captain d'Urville's other accomplishments was sending the Venus de Milo to the Louvre) have black heads, with chalk-white eye rings. They are the little men in the tuxedo suits we see in cartoons. Rock-hoppers have lively red eyes, long yellow and black head feathers resembling a crewcut that's been allowed to grow out, and thick yellow satanic eyebrows that slant up and away from their eyes, giving their face an expression that says, *I dare you!* Chinstraps get their name from the helmet of black feathers that seems to be attached by a thin black 'strap' across their white throats. Their amber eyes, outlined in thick black, look Egyptian, like a hieroglyph for some as-yet-undecipherable verb. Emperors have black heads, a tawny stripe on the bill, and a bib of egg-yolk yellow around their neck and cheeks. The most flamboyant of all, king penguins display a large, velvety-orange comma on each cheek, as if always in the act of being quoted about something. A throbbing orange at their neck melts into radiant yellow. And, on either side of their bills, a comet of apricot or lavender flies toward their mouth. Fairy penguins are tiny and blue-headed. Each of the seventeen different species of penguins, though essentially black-and-white, differs from all others in head pattern.

On shore, of course, a mass of penguins with predominantly black-and-white bodies looks a bit like linoleum in a cheap diner. Human beings tend to be obsessed with black-and-white animals, like killer whales, giant pandas, and penguins. 'We live in a world of grays, could be's, ambiguities,' Frank Todd once observed. 'Maybe it's just nice to see something that's cut-and-dried. It's black-and-white. It's there, and that's the way it is.'

Gentoos feed their chicks every eighteen to twenty-four hours, and the adults that had just arrived were fat-bellied, crammed with fish and krill. Native to the Antarctic and sub-Antarctic, the gentoos were white-breasted and black-backed like all penguins, but they had a white bonnet on their heads. Though quiet and friendly, they drifted just out of reach. Along with Adélies and chinstraps, the gentoos belong to the genus *Pygoscelis* ('brush-tailed'), because of their short, paintbrush-shaped tail, and they are shy penguins, whose chicks grow slowly, staying close to a parent's warm body for weeks after hatching. The gentle gentoos are docile and may not have to pair-bond as vigorously as other penguins; otherwise they would need to declare their territory and mate more stridently and become more aggressive about intruders. The name gentoo is from the deceit of a British Museum man, who received a gentoo skin from an Antarctic explorer, thought it was a new species of bird, and decided to hide the information for a while. Later, he went off to Papua New Guinea, and when he returned, he described the bird as if it were one of the local species, naming it after the Gentoo, a religious sect on Papua New Guinea.

As we straggled along the shore toward granite outcroppings where penguins nest, two large brown birds began forays, dive-bombing. This was our first close encounter with the skua, nemesis of the baby penguin, and I held an arm above my head because, like lightning, skuas strike at the highest spot. They can pick an animal's eyes out before it knows what has happened. Hawklike, cunning, and bold, they are the ace predators of sick, young, or abandoned penguins. Some claim that skuas divide up a penguin colony into thousand-pair lots and that if you want a quick population estimate of a penguin colony, count the skuas and multiply by two thousand. A skua will carefully monitor a rookery, find a deserted chick, knock the bird senseless on the back of the head to kill it, then consume almost every scrap. When it devours an adult, it eats the viscera first, turning the carcass inside out like a sleeve, leaving only the head, skin, and bones. A big skua landed in front of us, spread its wings, and noisily proclaimed its territory. Then we saw why it was so anxious: A fluffy skua chick, head tucked into its shoulders, scurried away in the other direction and crouched. Another skua arrived, and both parents tried to draw our attention away. A little farther on, we found a small rookery of chinstraps, one with its flipper out straight, as if it were signaling a left turn, all looking like a gathering of crosswalk guards. Another was lying on its stomach and turned the soles of its feet up to cool off. Moving its flippers, it revealed an underside that had gone pink in the penguin equivalent of a blush. It was a warm day for them in Antarctica. A group of gentoo penguins ambled by, going anywhere, going nowhere. Penguins are born followers. If one begins to move with purpose, the others fall in behind it.

'Those poor penguins, living in this awful cold!' one woman lamented in a Southern drawl as she pulled her red parka tight around her neck and dragged a knitted cap down almost over her eyes. In fact, penguins rarely mind the cold. Quite the opposite. More often, they overheat. Like mammals, penguins are warm-blooded, which means that they're able to make their own heat and carry it with them wherever they go, instead of taking on the temperature of their environment. This allows them to migrate and to live in otherwise inhospitable regions of the earth. Of course, keeping warm can become something of a problem in the Antarctic. Penguins have evolved thick layers of blubber, which their bodies make from krill and planktonic oils, and because blubber conducts heat poorly, a layer of it below the skin acts as an excellent insulator. It is also a place to store fuel for the long, cold breeding season. The farther south you go, the bigger the penguins get, since big animals find it easier to stay warm. About one third of the weight of the emperor penguin, which lives in the coldest regions, is blubber. In addition, as anyone who skis or spends much time outdoors in the winter knows, air makes one of the best insulators. Travelers to the Antarctic are advised to dress in many layers of clothing with plenty of air in between them. Penguins do that with tightly overlapping feathers, which don't ruffle very easily and, as a result, trap a layer of warm air against the skin. Also, each feather develops a fluffy down at the base of its shaft, and that downy layer adds even more insulation. Penguins are watertight and airtight and thought to have more feathers than any other bird. The feathers are shiny, long, and curved, arranged like carefully laid roof shingles. Dipping into the oil gland at the base of the tail, a penguin spreads a layer of oil on the feathers to keep them slick and tight. Of course, feathers do get tattered after a year or so, and then the bird must molt, to slough off the old feathers and grow new ones. If it molted gradually, it wouldn't be waterproof any longer, so it goes through all the steps of molting at the same time, a process that takes about thirty days. New feathers grow in underneath the ones that are molting and push the old ones out. It makes the penguin look scruffy and slightly crazed, as if it were ripping its feathers out in some avian delirium. What is worse, since they're not waterproof while they're molting, they can't go hunting food in the ocean. *Fasting* is what it's called by scientists, although that word suggests choice on the part of the penguin, which loses about 30 percent of its body weight and is bound to be hungry and is not exactly a volunteer.

But heat is a problem. There are few things as ridiculous as a penguin suffering the equivalent of heat stroke in the middle of the coldest place on earth. All around the rookery, overheated penguins resort to what look like vaudeville moves: Ruffling their feathers, they release some of the hot insulating air next to the skin. They hold one arm out, as if parking a 747, then they pirouette and signal a turn in the other direction. They flush pink under the wings, where capillaries swell with blood. Baby penguins like to lie down on their bellies and stick their feet up behind them, so that they can lose heat through the soles of their feet. They radiate heat through the few featherless zones on their bodies (usually around the eyes, flippers, and feet). A large adult suddenly ruffles up all over and extends its flippers at the same time, as if someone had scraped a fingernail across a blackboard.

The cold, on the other hand, isn't really a problem. If the temperature drops too low (around 15° F. with a strong wind), thousands of birds will huddle together to stay warm in what the French researchers call *tortues* (turtles). Using one another for insulation, they don't burn up their fat stores quickly. Huddling birds lose only half as much weight as birds braving the winds solo, because only a small portion of their bodies are exposed to the wind. It is akin to the protection apartment dwellers get, surrounded by apartments on either side that act as insulation.

'Come and look at this krill poop,' Harrison said, bending down to consider some guano. 'It's not very fresh. See those black spots in it?' He held up a handful and smudged it between his fingers. 'That's the eyes of krill, which are indigestible, like tomato seeds to us. When you see the ground stained red like this, it's probably a chinstrap or an Adélie rookery rather than a gentoo, because the chinstraps eat krill and poop red. White poop comes from a diet of fish or squid. And green poop means they're not eating at all; what you're seeing is bile.' Across the hillside and around the large slabs of rock, the ground was stained pink. Even if the rookery had been deserted, we could tell chinstraps or Adélies lived there. Most of the zoologists I know are, by necessity, coprophiles. A living system leaves its imprint on what passes through it. So I'm no longer surprised to find a naturalist sifting through bat, alligator, or penguin excrement. Some even study petrified dinosaur excrement, or coprolites, as they're called.

Beyond the rookery, molting elephant seals snoozed on the shore like overgrown salamis. They rolled around the sand together and against each other, to rub off the old fur, which wears out and has to be replaced each year. Pieces of molted fur and skin littered the beach. One often finds elephant seals with penguins, lying on the beach like so many old cast-off horsehair couches. It takes seven or eight years for the long nose of the bulls to develop. These pug-nosed ones were young males, which would grow larger, although they were already around twelve feet long and weighed about three thousand pounds. A gang of penguins strolled among them, seemingly without care. One in the center scratched his neck with a five-clawed flipper. Sluggish as they may look, elephant seals can dive to more than three thousand feet to feed on squid and fish.

On a rise, three fur seals sat up and stared aggressively as we passed. If they wanted to, they could gallop across the sand at great speed, tucking their pelvic girdles and undulating like fast worms. Fur seals will attack human beings. The previous year, a fur seal had grabbed a lecturer as he was getting into a Zodiac and punctured his lung. The man needed thirty-six stitches, and it took many months for the wounds to heal, since, to add to their armament, fur seals have an enzyme in their mucus that keeps their bites from healing properly. 'I hate these,' one of the guides said under his breath. 'I have nothing whatsoever against fur-seal coats. I tell you, I'm sincere about this.' As a territorial male started toward him, Stonehouse clapped his gloved hands, shouted, and kicked black volcanic sand up at its face. The seal stopped, huffed loudly, and sidled back to its original spot.

Between two rock knobs, a chinstrap-penguin colony sat on red krill-stained rocks. The gentoos choose a flat shelf area to nest and breed on; chinstraps prefer rocks, and gentoos a flatter terrain, so even though living in close quarters, they don't compete with one another for nesting sites. A baby gentoo put its head up and made a metallic gargling sound. The babies, forming little crèches with their flippers wrapped around each other, achieved a look of intense mateyness. (Other animals, like young flamingos, eider ducklings, and baby bats, form crèches, too.) While the parents are away hunting food, the babies are open to attack from skuas and other birds and are a lot safer in a nursery of chicks. Not only is there strength in numbers, but adults wandering through to feed their young can help ward off attacks by skuas. King penguins feed their chicks for nine or ten months, so their young spend a long time in crèches. Returning from the sea, adult gentoos easily recognize their babies by voice. The pattern of white dots, bar over the eyes, and other characteristics also varies slightly from one individual to another.

A chick flapped rubbery flippers. It takes time for the bones to set into the strong, hard flight-muscles of the adult. As immature birds, gentoos have a great tendency to wander and may migrate as much as two hundred miles. But in the second year they will return to the rookery, ready to breed. Because they're a mated pair, the gentoo couple doesn't have to go back to the same site each year to nest. Like all other penguins, they take two to three weeks to build a nest and copulate, but they're mobile and can change their nests. Because they don't split up when the breeding season is over, they probably remain together as mates year-round. Gentoos are the most passive penguins, and perhaps that has been their undoing. There are only about forty thousand gentoos left in the world, but at least their numbers are not declining.

In some areas, the ground was streaked with beautiful white star-bursts – squirted guano – so that it looked like a moonscape. And it was pungent! Sailors have been known to use the smell of a well-known rookery as a navigation aid, especially when fog is too thick for them to see any of the birds. A pink tinge of algae glowed from beneath the snow, which acted as a greenhouse. Frost polygons had turned the sod into a six-sided design. A chinstrap raised its bill into the air, its air sacs puffed up, and it worked the bellows of its chest. Just offshore, a row of giant petrels waited for the chicks. The range of light was so wide it was taxing for the eye to take every-thing in – the round, dark, wet, sullen rocks, the brilliant white snow reflecting against low clouds in a visual echo chamber of white.

On the ground were the remains of that morning's breakfast for a skua: a pair of orange penguin feet, a head, a skeleton. Stonehouse picked up the half-eaten chinstrap, showed me the flight muscles, the thick red ribbons that were the salt glands, and the concertina ribs. He handed me a small white feather, revealing the main shaft, and then, at its base, a second feather of silky down.

'Why would *this* one have died?' I said. 'Why would a skua have singled it out?'

Turning the skeleton over, he discovered its eccentric bottom bill, bent at a ninety-degree angle. 'You occasionally see penguins like this, with deformed bills. There's no way they can feed correctly, but even if they did manage to feed, they still wouldn't be able to preen themselves. So they would get heavily infested with lice. It's very sad, like seeing a deformed and neglected child. That's a simple, small thing to go wrong, when you think about it – just a misshapen bottom bill. But the chick would lead a difficult life for about nine months and then die of starvation. Before that happens, a skua usually identifies it as a weakling. Chicks running around without parents in this colony soon die, and they eventually form the debris on the floor of the colony that you see.'

Looking more closely at the ground, I saw the long scatter of bones for the first time and was stunned. We were standing in an ancient cemetery. This penguin colony lived on top of a graveyard that may have been thousands of years old. Under the feet and nests of the birds lay all the frozen, partially mummified remains of their ancestors. The cold had preserved their carcasses for as long as three thousand years. Most adult penguins die in the ocean, but babies die right on land, and no one removes their skeletons. The bones gradually sink into the permafreeze like designs into some fantastic paperweight. The chicks are born astride a grave. A wind gust sent feathers blowing into the air as if in a pillow fight. Penguins molt each year, some even shedding parts of their bills. The ground litter included not just corpses, but also pungent guano, spilled krill, blood, feathers, molted elephant-seal skin and hair, and miscellaneous bits of animal too dismembered for an amateur to identify.

Seeing Stonehouse with the chinstrap skeleton in his hands, his wife, Sally, walked up and smiled. Her lovely English complexion had gone ruddy in the brisk Antarctic air and a few wisps of brown hair strayed from under her knitted hat. 'We're so used to Daddy bringing home dead finnies,' she said cheerfully. 'When we were in New Zealand, if we could find a dead penguin, he was always so pleased.'

Just then a lone male chinstrap tossed its helmeted head to the sky, arched its flippers back, and trumpeted an 'ecstatic display' loud enough to stop a train. Its chest and throat rippled rhythmically as it called, as if with all its soul it hoped to lure a willing female by telling her that he was available and ready with a lovely little nesting site. Penguins are not profound thinkers, but their instincts guide them through all the demands of the landscape and of their hormones. An ecstatic display sounds both desperate and automatic. It may happen at any time, sometimes with good reason, sometimes by mistake, sometimes in a chorus of tens of thousands of voices screaming at the top of their lungs the equivalent of *Tell me you love me! I said, Tell me you love me!* It is a little like overhearing thousands of actors auditioning simultaneously for a Sam Shepard play. All summer, their frantic ecstasy fills the Antarctic air. Plighting their troth, an Adélie pair will do an ecstatic display, then the male will give her a precious and, to her eye, perfect stone. The actual copulation takes only seconds, and has been termed a cloacal kiss. Foreplay is everything – a complex drama of eye contact and body language. Courting males repeatedly bow to females, and the female has her own balletic gestures to use in reply.

'Well, he *is* eager, isn't he?' Sally said good-naturedly. We laughed. Life goes on, having nowhere else to go.

❃

Somewhere along the way, we had lost the nighttime. Where did we lose it? In the deserted whaling station, in whose smoky hall we ate a barbecue of reindeer meat and danced to Glenn Miller? At the Polish station, whose greenhouses grew snapdragons and tomatoes? In the volcanic ring of Deception Island? Watching rippling terraces of Adélie penguins go about their lapidary business, obsessed with nesting stones? At the small British base, Signy, whose young men had not seen strangers, or women, for nearly two years? (Visiting with us in the lounge, some of them were trembling; and we sent them away with handshakes, good wishes, and sacks of potatoes, onions, and other fresh food.) At the Valentine's Day dance, on seas so rough that dancers held on to the ceiling? On Elephant Island, a forbidding snag of mountain but a thriving chinstrap rookery, where Shackleton and his men landed after their trials on the pack ice? At the eerie, deserted penguin rookery, where watching a lone penguin chick face the death machine of a rampaging skua, which played out its instincts blow by blow, tortured our hearts? Among the guano-thick beaches, where waves of hungry penguins bobbed in the sea and babies clamored to be fed? Listening to the assistant cruise director, a fine pianist, give recitals of Debussy, Haydn, Bach, and Beethoven against a backdrop of sunstruck glaciers?

Now we lived only in a late summer twilight. Icebergs clustered around us like statuary as the ship sailed through the Gerlache Strait, which separates the Antarctic Peninsula from Brabant and Anvers islands. Each narrow waterway seemed to lead into another one, until finally we sailed through the Lemaire Channel, which narrows to a mere sixteen hundred feet wide at its southern end. This too was the penguins' world. On either side of the ship, glaciers spilled into the sea, jagged mountain peaks rose into the clouds, and icebergs roamed freely. In the channel, the water was like lucid tar, with icebergs of all sizes drifting through it, their white tops a thin reflection of mortality – their blue bases pale and inscrutable. The blazing white of an iceberg lay on a thick wide base of blue ancient as the earth, older than all of the people who had ever seen it or who had ever visited the Antarctic combined. The icebergs took all sorts of shapes, and some had fissures through which a searing blue light shone. In the wake of an iceberg the water looked like oiled silk because the surface of the water had been smoothed by the ice's palm. On both sides of the boat, black, jagged, ice-drizzled mountains reflected in the mirror surface. On a small berg, five gentoo penguins sat, their white bonnets sparkling in the sun. On another small berg sat their death – a leopard seal, sprawling on one side, idly scratching its flank with a five-fingered paw.

'*Seehund*,' a woman from Frankfurt said solemnly. We were all on the side of the penguins, though nature should have no partisans, no sides, no center, except the center that is forever shifting, as Emerson said, a center that moves within circles and circles that move.

Great tongues of ice stretch out from the continent and speak in a language like music, with no words but with undeniable meaning. And like music, the vista is a language we don't have to learn to be profoundly moved – we who do not just use our environment but also appreciate, admire, even worship it. True, we kill other lifeforms to survive, but we feel a kinship to them, we apologize for stealing their life from them. We are the most vital creatures ever to inhabit the earth, and the one truth we live by is that life loves life. Still, nature proceeds 'red in tooth and claw,' as Tennyson said. This becomes simpler to see in a simpler environment. When you walk through a penguin rookery, where the underweight chicks stand doomed and the skuas maneuver like custodians of death, pages of Darwin's *Origin of Species* spring to life in front of you. All the cozy denials we use as shields fall aside.

The sky that day was clear, and the air as astringent as ammonia vapor. The sun poured down but had no heat, and the ice mountains occasionally revealed weavings of blue and green. After the darkness of winter, the five months of summer sun did not warm things up much. Because the sun rode so low on the horizon, it seemed to have little warmth. The ice reflected the heat back into the sky. Most people on board had greatly dilated pupils by then, a side effect of the scopolamine patch they wore behind one ear to ward off seasickness. It made them look a little like zombies, but it also allowed their eyes to take in big gulps of light. In Zodiacs, we drifted along the peninsula, through an ice-sculpture garden. Heraclitus said you never step in the same stream twice. The Antarctic version of that is that you never see the same iceberg twice. Because each iceberg is always changing, one sees a personal and unique iceberg that no one else has ever seen or will ever see. They are not always smooth. Many had textures, waffle patterns, pockmarks, and some looked pounded by Persian metalsmiths. A newly calved iceberg lay like a chunk of glass honeycomb, spongy from being underwater. (At some point it was other-side-up.) Another had beautiful blue ridges like muscles running along one side. So many icelets thickened the water, each one quivering with sparkle, that the sea looked like aluminum foil shaken in the sun. There were baths of ice with blue lotion, ice grottos, ice curved round the fleecy pelt of a lamb, razor-backed ice, sixteen ice swans on an ice merry-go-round, ice pedestals, ice combs, ice dragons with wings spread, an ice garden where icebergs grew and died, ice tongs with blue ice between their claws, an ice egret stretching its wings and a long rippling neck out of the water. Apricot light spilled over the distant snow-tipped mountains. Chunky wedges of peppermint-blue ice drifted past us. Behind us, the Zodiac left a frothy white petticoat. And farther beyond, shapes arched out of the water – penguins feeding, oblivious to what we call beauty.

We paused at Paradise Bay, where blue-eyed shags nested along the cliffs, a whale maneuvered at a distance, penguins porpoised to feed, and crabeater seals lazed on small icebergs, red krill juice dripping down their chins. Through pale green water, clear and calm, a gray rocky bottom was shining, along with red and brown seaweeds and patches of yellow-blooming phytoplankton. A loud explosion startled us and, turning, we saw ice breaking off a glacier to become an iceberg, which would float for four years or so before it succumbed to the sea. I looked down through the fathoms of crystal water to the smooth rocks on the bottom. Suddenly an eight-foot leopard seal swiveled below the boat, surfaced to breathe, cut a fast turn, and began circling the Zodiac, around and around, underneath it and alongside. Each time it spun underwater, large blue air bubbles rose to the surface like jellyfish. Mouth open, baring its sharp yellow teeth, it lunged up through the water and bit a pontoon on the Zodiac. 'Back away from the edge!' David Kaplan, our driver, said with contained urgency, and the twelve passengers leaned inward, away from the attacking seal, which could leap out of the water and seize an arm, pulling a person under. Circling, fast, handsome, wild, ferocious, it spun below again, dove, and leapt to the surface. It was attacking us as it would penguins on an ice floe. We who live at the top of our food chain rarely get the chance to feel like prey, to watch a predator maneuver around us with a deftness that's instinctive, cunning, and persistent – and live to tell about it.

'Just an average day in Paradise,' Kaplan said, brightening the motor and heading for shore. We climbed out at an abandoned Argentinian base. As the clouds drifted behind the peninsula, the continent itself appeared to be moving, as of course it was. On a rock ledge, an Antarctic tern – a small white bird with black cap and startling red beak and matching red feet – thrilled the sky with song. A teal vein of copper ore cascaded down the rocks among patches of fiery orange lichen and green moss. As the rest of our party climbed up a steep slope of glacier to the top of a mountain where a wooden cross had been planted, I stood like a sentinel, still as a penguin, watching my kind struggle up the hill from the sea. Across the bay, the snow mountains were glazed in a dusky pink light and the water was cerulean blue. Gray clouds hung in front of and below the powdered tops of the mountains. The air was so pure that the clouds looked cut-out and solid, suspended by a sleight of hand, a magician's trick. Mirrors lay scattered on the surface of the water, where there was no ice to disrupt the flowing light. A blue iceberg shaped like open jaws a hundred feet high floated near shore. Corrugated-metal buildings shot off hot orange. A long hem of brash ice undulated across the south end of the bay. Somewhere the leopard seal sat looking for less elusive quarry, and would find it.

The birders were up early as we approached Coronation Island, in the South Orkneys; they were desperate to spot an Antarctic petrel, a bird that resembles but is slightly larger than the many pintados, or painted petrels, swirling in small tornadoes behind the boat. Most Antarctic petrels are in their rookeries as much as a hundred miles inland from the ice shelf. When one finally winged across the water, the birders went berserk.

'Oh! There it is! Beautiful!' a woman cried.

'Wow! The nape is almost buff!' said an enraptured man.

All the Antarctic petrels we saw that day were pale. They were in molt, a wonderful coffee-tan color, and flapped stiffly because their new feathers weren't in yet. To see one or two at this time of year so far out was a bonus. However, many of us were not looking for petrels but for a rarer sight: the emperor penguin. Largest of all penguins, emperors can dive to nearly nine hundred feet to feed on squid and stay submerged for nearly twenty minutes or more. When they stand in the snow like vigilant UFO watchers, they have the usual black-and-white coloring, but also a spill of honey at their throats and cheeks. Emperor penguins are such altruistic parents – or fanatical, depending on your point of view – that they will even pick up a frozen or ruined egg and try to incubate it, or try to incubate stones or an old dead chick. An abandoned or wayward chick will immediately be adopted. Sometimes adults even squabble so much over a chick that the chick gets hurt or killed in the process. Emperors rarely, if ever, touch bare ground. They live out their whole lives standing sentry on shelf ice or swimming in the ocean. Unfortunately, their rookeries were too far south for us to see them.

A small flock of Antarctic prions hydroplaned over the water, plowing a furrow through it, using their tongues to sift krill into a feeding pouch under the jaw, feeding the way baleen whales do.

'Bird alert! Bird alert!' sounded over the intercom, waking passengers from their slumber and early diners from drowsy breakfasts. 'EP alert! EP alert! A juvenile emperor penguin has been spotted off the stern of the boat!' I ran to the stern, colliding with people frantically running up the stairs from the cabins below. HOLD THESE RAILS it said on brass plates at each stairway on every deck, as if in rebuke to excited birders who had been turning the ship into an aviary. The stampede ended with a clash of bodies on the stern deck. And there it was: porpoising out of the water, looking like part of an inner tube with a flash of yellow showing every now and again. Then it vanished, and we were left standing quietly with our amazement. To glimpse an emperor penguin in the wild, feeding this far from its home, was a benediction.

Stowing my binoculars, I went downstairs to breakfast, which I barely touched. Despite the elaborate meals, I'd been losing weight at a reckless pace. It was as if I was being nourished so thoroughly through my senses that I felt too full to eat. Before coming to the Antarctic, I had thought that penguins lived in a world of extreme sensory deprivation. But I had found just the opposite – a landscape of the greatest sensuality. For one thing, there was so much life, great herds of animal life to rival those in East Africa. Many people have compared Antarctica to a wasteland; instead, it is robust with life. For another, the range of colors was breathtaking; though subtle, it had changing depths and illuminations, like flesh tones. The many colors were in the ever-bluing sky, in the cloud formations, the muted light, the midnight sun, the auroras dancing over still waters with icebergs and crash ice, and in areas that dazzled like small hand mirrors, through which black-and-white penguins dove. Who would have imagined the depth of blue in the icebergs, appearing as sugar-frosted cakes with muted sunlight bursting off them?

Or the scale, the massiveness – sitting alongside an iceberg, you couldn't see around it in either direction. One day the water was so smooth that you could use it as a mirror, and four hours later the wind was howling at ninety knots. And was as beautiful at ninety knots as when crystal-calm. Huge ice caverns formed arches of pastel ice. *Glare* had so many moods that it seemed another pure color. The mountains, glaciers, and fiords bulged and rolled through endless displays of inter-flowing shapes. The continent kept turning its shimmery hips, and jutting up hard pinnacles of ice, in a sensuality of rolling, sifting, cascading landscapes. There was such a liquefaction to its limbs. And yet it could also be blindingly abstract, harrowing and remote, the closest thing to being on another planet, so far from human life that its desolation and iciness made you want to do impetuous, life-affirming things: commit acts of love, skip Zodiacs at reckless speeds over the bays, touch voices with a loved one by way of satellite, work out in the gym on thrones of steel until your muscles quit, drink all night, be passionate and daring, renew the outlines of your humanity.

CHAPTER 15

'PARTICLES'

from *Water, Ice and Stone* (1995)

Bill Green

Here a specialist in the science of lakes meditates on the connection between the small, slow, subtle mystery he is trying to solve in the Dry Valleys of Antarctica, and the globe's biggest processes. For Bill Green, scientific procedures are forms of questioning which naturally belong alongside poetry and mythology; and as one of its scientific inheritors, he takes the continent of Antarctica to be the richest possible playground, somewhere whose layers of system and meaning deserve lifetimes of attention.

When I tell people there are lakes in Antarctica, they think surely I am joking. 'Lakes there?' they ask. 'How can that be? It's all ice and snow. Penguins running around.' Then, when I assure them that it's true, they ask, in a more assertive tone, 'But they're frozen, of course?' And I say, 'Well, yes, there's ice on the surface, but below there's liquid water, sometimes as deep as two hundred feet.' Then they ask – and this is inevitable – 'Are there fish?' I say, 'No, not a single one.' 'Hmmm,' they respond, incredulous, 'a lake without fish. Does anything live in them, at all?' And they emphasize 'at all.' 'Only algae and bacteria,' I say. 'Nothing you can actually see with your eyes. Except for the mats of algae, which are tiny columns and pinnacles on the bottom, far below the ice.'

But then it is precisely what is not there, what has never been there, that makes the lakes – indeed, the whole continent on which they lie – so strange and so important.

For me these absences, and the simplicity to which they give rise, were the key. The lakes are the most isolated inland waters in the world. Landlocked, they are without spillage or outflow; each has only a few streams, and these hold water for only a few weeks out of the year. They are ice-covered, so that very little in the form of dust or snow enters them from the air. And, of course, there is never rain. That in itself makes them magic. How can you have a lake without rain? A lake without fish, maybe, but a lake without rain? A land without rain. A whole continent. Such living things as there are are mostly microscopic – algae, bacteria, yeast, a mini-malist's tableau. And into this setting, stark and largely inorganic, Martian almost, the elements come – nitrogen, phosphorus, the metals – unheralded, but replete with possibilities, with lives to be lived.

It would be no exaggeration to say that I was obsessed with the lakes, and especially with the metals that coursed through them like bits and pieces of an invisible wind. In this seemingly fantastical concern, I was not unlike Borges, who once wrote of a silver coin he had dropped into the sea. The coin had become, in consequence, a kind of persona in the drama of the world, its destiny unfolding alongside that of the poet Borges himself. I had my coins, too, by the countless billions.

I knew, for example, that the Onyx River in Wright Valley had brought tons of cobalt and lead and copper into Lake Vanda over its long history. Yet there were virtually no metals in the lake. I knew this. But where had they gone? What was removing them? What thin veil of purity had caught them in its mesh? And whatever veil it was, did it fall elsewhere across the Earth and its seas, purifying as it went? Did the Earth, or this tiny piece of it, regenerate itself? At what speeds? By what agencies? Last year I had set particle 'traps' in the lakes, had left them there for a whole year. They were nothing more than clear plastic tubes, capped at one end and suspended below the ice. But in time, if all went well, I would get them back and I would know the answers.

We took two sleds. Into each we threw a trap catcher and a bunch of plastic caps so that we could stopper the traps if we were lucky enough to retrieve them. Dr. Yu and I headed off toward the deep hole; Mike and Tim headed east toward the center of the lake. We had the sled tethered to a long rope that opened up into a skinny isosceles triangle – the sled at one corner, Dr. Yu and I at the other two. The sled pulled easily and I held the rope near my shoulder with just one hand. We were moving toward a huge glacial erratic that lay among much finer debris on the lower slopes of the Olympus Range. The boulder was a landmark. The line between it and our Scott tent ran through the point on the ice where we had placed our most important trap. This was the same boulder that Canfield had mentioned in his note, the stone behind which he had secured the bamboo pole. 'Thought you might need this, guys,' he had written in that casual voice. It was pure Canfield.

As we approached the site, I began to feel apprehensive. The traps had been suspended for twelve months. In that much time, anything can go wrong. Even here, where we knew no one had been. We were certain, and yet there was the question: What if something had been here? What if the rope had been severed, been eaten through? In the distance I was beginning to make out the rock cairn we had left as a marker. As I drew closer, I could see that a curious separation had occurred. The dark basalts, warmed by the sun, had melted deep into the lake ice. They were looking up at me as if from a crystal sarcophagus. The white granites had hardly melted through at all. They lay in smooth hollows on the surface of the ice. I was not expecting this. But I should have been.

Dr. Yu stood there with his hands on his hips. He was turning in a slow circle, looking over the valley from beneath his parka hood. 'It is like Qaidam Basin,' he said in his clipped English, which was a kind of poetry. 'In Qaidam,' he said, 'No birds fly in sky. No green grass on land. Stones run before wind. Mountains are knives. I must climb icy mountain, go down fiery sea. People say this of Qaidam, of salt lake. What say of this place?' He was facing down valley, looking over the length of the lake, down toward the dry Onyx. Tim and Mike were still moving across the ice, although I could no longer hear their sled. But I was not thinking of the valley. I was not thinking of China. I only wanted the traps back.

We had laid the traps where we had to, up and down the lake: near the Onyx, about half a mile from the debouchment; by the peninsula, where the lake constricts before it opens into its major basin; and a mile or so west of the peninsula. In the deep lake, we suspended three sets of traps from a single line. The first hung at forty-eight meters, just at the top of the calcium chloride brine layer; the second was at sixty meters, where the oxygen-rich region met the oxygen-starved region of the lake; the third was at sixty-five meters, deep within the sulfide brine. We placed the traps where the lake's long history foreordained.

It was twelve hundred years ago, near the close of the first Christian millennium, while the young Charlemagne was uniting Europe, that an epochal event occurred in the Wright Valley. At that time, in the years of the Crusades, Vanda had evaporated to become little more than a salt flat, a glistening whiteness in the center of which lay a shallow circle of water. Then the change came, and it came rapidly. The climate warmed and the Lower Wright Glacier began to discharge water, not the springtime trickle that had gone before, but whole sheets of water. The lake level rose. The fresh waters from the glacier overlaid the dense brine. There was little or no mixing, only diffusion, the slow transfer of matter. Now it was as though there were two lakes: one large and made of fresh water that had rolled suddenly down the Onyx like a deluge; the other a dense brine, the sweating evaporite remains of the ancient lake.

It was this single medieval event that had set the structure of Lake Vanda, that had ensured that the upper waters would be light and clear and oxygen-filled, and that the depths would be heavy and dark and rife with decay. Knowing these things, we had set the traps.

As I lowered the new trap catcher hand over hand, the bottom folded at the hinge, twelve feet of bamboo slowly disappeared through the opaque slurry that clogged the hole. I was holding my breath. Then I felt the horizontal arm fall open when it cleared the bottom of the ice. I lay on my stomach, spread my legs, wrapped my gloves around the pole, and slowly turned it, first clockwise, then counterclockwise, in small, gentle arcs, fishing for the line that I knew was hanging parallel, just a foot away. After a few minutes I thought I touched it. I began to twist the pole. It was resisting, as though something were being wound on it, as though something were coming in. I could hear the bamboo creak below the ice and I thought it might splinter. I bent my head around to look at Dr. Yu. 'I think I have something,' I said. 'But it feels like it's going to snap. It's very heavy.'

He lay on the ice across from me, his head only a few inches from mine. He took hold of the pole just above where my hands were placed. We both began to turn the bamboo. The sounds were becoming louder, like the creaking of a wooden ship at the docks.

I could hear nothing else. We were looking at each other, talking with our eyes: I imagined Dr. Yu thinking, *Maybe a little more, just a little, it's okay; bamboo, bamboo strong.* Then we were looking at the slurry and at the pole turning through it. There was a cloud of fog over the hole from my breath and his. I could feel the weight of the line in my fingers. It seemed too much. I wanted to just hold it there in place, for a few seconds, not risk anything. We were touching the traps. The particles were down there at the end of the line. I wanted to pretend we already had them.

Sometimes the geochemists made it sound like a riddle. 'Why isn't the sea a copper blue?' they would ask. Not the blue of the sky, but the deep blue of a copper solution. After all, the rivers have been bringing copper to the sea from the beginning of time. And yet the seas are not full. Why?

To convince yourself of this truth, you could do the calculation on the back of an envelope. Each year the rivers pour into the oceans about seven thousand tons of copper. Over the last sixty million years, just since the demise of dinosaurs, the rivers have excavated and deposited whole mountain ranges of copper. But there is virtually none in the sea – a few nanomoles per liter, a few million tons in all.

Where has it gone? Why are the seas not absolutely deadly with copper? In just the last two decades, the geochemists have found the answer: particles.

It was one of those things you knew and didn't know. Science was full of them. Democritus knew there were atoms, little flicks of cold that pricked your skin, that made your nostrils flare. And Lucretius knew this too. You can look at *De Rerum Natura* and hear the wind as it shakes the mountains and rolls the seas and wracks the vessels that go there. And in Lucretius you think you 'see' the wind, not as something insubstantial but as a maelstrom of tiny bodies, of corporeal beings, of atoms. And so on up through history, through Boyle and Newton and Descartes. But did they really know, know in the same keen predictive sense that Dalton knew, or that Rutherford and Bohr and Schroedinger knew? Or was *atom* just a convenient name you gave to things, to causes you could not fathom, to whatever invisible mystery it was that could hollow a rock or float a tree or sweep the sky clean of clouds? The Greeks knew that light was particulate, but did they really *know*? Did anyone really know about light until Newton and Young, or perhaps until Einstein?

So it is sometimes said that the Danish oceanographer, Forschhammer, in one of the most eloquent and condensed passages about the chemistry of the sea, knew about particles. For what Forschammer saw was that the amounts of the elements found in the seas were not so much dependent on the rivers that poured them in, but on what happened to them once they arrived. Applied to the problem of copper, this seems to suggest that despite the burnished mountains of metal that come, dissolved, to the sea each year, we have no reason to expect the oceans to be awash in it. What is really important is what the sea is doing. And the sea is not passive. The sea, here, is Borges's sea, 'violent and ancient, who gnaws the foundations of earth.' It is the site of chemical and organochemical action, the place in which elements are rendered, in various ways and at various rates, insoluble. Where ions are transformed into particles. Where particles sink and are carried away. Where things, for a time, are lost.

In the oceanography of Karl Turekian and Wallace Broecker and Edward Goldberg, the shadowy particles of Forschhammer have been given flesh and identity. So abundant are they in the rivers and oceans of the world, and so varied and pervasive in their influence –

these clays, these oxides of iron and manganese, these cool flakes and platelets of calcite and cells of sinking plankton, and these circling desert dusts – that Turekian has referred to them as agents in a 'great particle conspiracy.' It is this 'conspiracy,' this great passage of grain and spore and flocculi, this pulverant earth-wide storm, that has in great measure removed metals from the sea. It is this simple process that has cleansed the sea of its most toxic bodies, leaving behind only traces of copper and zinc and cadmium and lead.

What particles exactly? There were thousands of them. Which ones were the most effective 'scavengers' – the cells of sinking organisms, the surfaces of calcite, the microscopic umber of the manganese and iron oxides? And did what happened in the sea happen also in lakes? And to what extent, and how fast? As Keith had said, 'the proof is in the particles.' I couldn't wait to see what particles our traps held.

❋

The sounds coming from below had gotten sharper. The cold bamboo, as it strained, made noises that rang out like shots. We were still winding the rope around the pole, inching the trap line up. Dr. Yu and I got to our feet. We bent over the bamboo that stood a foot or so above the surface of the ice. I was breathing hard, knowing that it was time to bring it up, but not wanting to, afraid that the leg of the L would break off. We were standing in a cloud of condensate from our own breath, delaying what we had to do.

I began to raise the pole. I felt the leg touch the bottom of the ice sheet. I could almost sense the texture of the ice, its smoothness, twelve feet below. It was as though the organic fibers of the bamboo were feeding into the circuitry of my own arm. It was as though my fingers were tracing along the underside of the sheet.

The hole was only ten inches in diameter – the width of the drill bit. The leg of the trap catcher was two feet long, long enough to allow us to snag the line. Tim had designed a hinge that would allow the leg of the L to straighten when it hit the ice – on the way up it would become an I. That way it could be pulled through the hole. If everything worked.

It resisted. Maybe we had wound the rope around the hinge. I pulled a little harder, but it still wouldn't budge. The leg was down. It would not come through the hole. I got on my knees again. I removed my gloves and began to scoop out the netting of ice crystals and slush that lay in the hole, that obscured what was happening below. As I pulled the ice from the surface, new rime from the drilling floated up. Five minutes, ten minutes, I don't know how long it took. It seemed I would never clear the hole. Then the last crystal bobbed to the surface. I lifted it with my thumb and forefinger and put it on the ice.

There was blue light coming off the hole. Its sides were gently corrugated. You could see how the drill had cut. The water was so clear it seemed invisible. I could see to the bottom of the ice sheet and below. Far below.

The rope had knotted around the hinge, but through the sparkling shaft of water it appeared that there was room for some play. We began to lift, slowly, so as not to ripple the surface. My head was down in the hole, as close to the waterline as I could get. I was almost breathing the water of the lake. The leg of the trap catcher began to bend. It was creaking. I could count the degrees as the angle opened up. Dr. Yu was above me. He was whispering as he pulled, as though he were repeating a mantra: 'Bamboo strong. No worry. Bamboo very strong. Very, very strong.' He repeated it over and over. 'I know this,' he said. 'I know this.'

It had opened to 150 or maybe 160 degrees when it cracked. I saw the leg detach from the long pole. I saw it wobble a bit and begin to sink under the weight of the traps. The rope was uncoiling, falling away. I felt my heart stop. Dr. Yu said 'Oooooooh,' his voice sinking with the traps.

Then I felt a tug on the line. The rope had thrown a coil over the catcher. Suddenly nothing was moving. There was no sound. The bamboo leg hung limp in the water. The traps were attached.

We were both on our feet now. We were bringing the pole up through the water. It was high above our heads, a line of bamboo against the mountains and the sky. As it rose, there was a length of rope and then the leg and then the hook and the coil wound around it. I grabbed the rope with both hands, held it tightly. I could feel the weight of the traps. For the first time in a year I knew we would get them back. Dr. Yu was standing there grinning, saying 'Goooood, goooood, very gooooooood.' It sounded to me as if he was singing.

❄

'You will never believe me,' Pablo Neruda said, 'but it sings, the salt sings, the hide of the salt plains, it sings through a mouth smothered by earth.' It sings, but we cannot hear. A voice beneath things, but earthwise, and everywhere, not just in the hide of the salt plains or in the rounded grapeskin of water. The comings and goings, the small visitations, the nanosecond or millennial lingerings, the departures – there is music in all of these. Not the music of a few distant spheres, but the music of a million cycles, like hooped bracelets, fine-spun silver twirling and whispering.

In this valley and in this lake and in the sediments beneath, these cycles turned in miniature, in a space that was comprehensible, but that was tied nonetheless into the larger space of the world. The river came in the springtime. It was sound and it was light, but it was also the head-over-heels tumbling of each water molecule, the combined energies of those molecules, their separated charges like torch fires, burning at the tips. What sound did the loosening of cobalt make, the adsorbed ion wavering a little like a minnow at the surface of a rock, then heading off downstream? How long did it stay in the lake after it had glided there on the current, after it had moved faceup, eyeing the blue Antarctic sky through the prism of ice? Maybe a year, maybe five. Not as long as sodium or chloride; longer certainly than iron. Then what? Perhaps an encounter with the surface of clay, glazed with a few atom-thicknesses of manganese oxide. Then capture. The cobalt transferred from water to stone, perhaps oxidized even, an electron transferred in the wink of an eye – now you see it, now it's gone, over there! – from the cobalt to the manganese. The stone sinks, first swiftly through fresh water, then more slowly through salt, the cobalt all the while clinging, being basketed and woven in like Moses by the manganese.

And this is the way it goes. A downward journey of a few weeks. Transit out of light. Transit into darkness. Transit into the deep. And in the oxygen-poor waters the manganese is reduced, falls away, unravels like thread. The atom of cobalt is free again, water-bound. The dazzling little motions of the water molecules, like tiny boomerangs whizzing about it, coming close to its charge, then retreating, are familiar and welcome. So it stays. Perhaps a year. Then another encounter: Something that was once living, a few cells still clinging together drift by. To the cobalt it is as though the roots and branches of a great elm were being dragged by in a flood. The branches reach out, enfold it: chelation. It is on its way to the sediments. Possibly to a small eternity there. Until the next ice sheet comes. But even buried you can hear it, you can hear the cobalt. Like the salt plains, you can hear it sing.

This was only a hypothesis, of course. Possibly it was extravagantly wishful thinking. Who knew whether the cobalt's fate was linked to manganese? I wanted it to be, but the proof was in the particles. I wanted to imagine it drawn from the water to the oxide surface and then released. I wanted to imagine the sound, the susurrus of that exchange, repeated over and over and over in every lake and ocean and river on earth, and for every element, modulated and toned and hallowed and joined in a single lifting chant. I wanted to speak the name of every element, every zinc and copper and mercury and lead, every iron and manganese and every compound of these and of hydrogen and oxygen and carbon and millions and millions more, intertwined and twirling on the wrists of the world.

The hypothesis was not without foundation, however. One year, Canfield and I had sampled for manganese and the trace metals. We did the manganese right there on the lake, on our knees on the ice, as soon as the samples came up. As soon as we got the points off the spectrophotometer, we plotted them on a sheet of graph paper. At the same time we plotted a set of oxygen values. It was remarkable. The data sets were mirror images. Where the oxygen was high, the manganese was low. Where the oxygen was low, the manganese was high. The little decrease in oxygen below fifty meters was matched by an increase in manganese at the same depth. And when the oxygen disappeared at sixty meters, the manganese rose to its highest value.

When I saw the graph, I thought of Keith's party and of what he had said about manganese and oxygen, how they were like kids on a seesaw, how when one went up the other went down, how in nature they seemed poised like yin and yang. I thought of oxidation and reduction, of the oxygen minimum zone above the crusts of the Hawaiian Ridge; about the hypolimnion of Acton Lake.

At fifty-five meters, manganese was being reduced, it was gaining electrons from all of the decaying carbon down there; you could see that in the profile. It was as clear as anything. I began to construct a little story about the manganese. I didn't know whether it was true or not, but I knew eventually we could test it and find out. That was the way science worked. You wrote a story. It was pure imagination bounded by a few, usually weak, constraints. Then you tested it, saw whether the world out there could really abide your notions of what was so. Usually it could not. So you tried again and again until you got it. Until you had something that might actually be so.

It appeared for all the world that manganese – probably in the form of solid manganese oxide, probably clinging to the flat surfaces of clay particles that had been weathered by the Onyx – was sinking into the deep lake and was dissolving away there into manganese ions. The solid, with a sigh and an exhalation, was becoming mere charge in the reducing, electron-rich waters below fifty meters. But if that was so, shouldn't there be a great release of other things as the oxide fell apart and crumbled in upon itself? Shouldn't there be a great release of cobalt, for example, or nickel or other metals that might be riding upon the oxide surface? Shouldn't the profiles for these tell a similar story?

I remember how I had looked forward to the metal analyses. No sooner had the samples arrived back in Ohio, in their sturdy wooden boxes, than I was looking at them. When you study metals, you become obsessed with purity. You can't escape. I worried about every stray breeze, about whether it carried with it a scintilla of lead or cobalt. I worried overtime about the reagents. Every working hour – which is to say every hour I was awake. Was the Freon TF as clean as it could be? What about the DDDC and the APDC and the nitric acid? And the bottles in which the samples had been collected, and the separatory funnels of expensive Teflon? I began to dream of metals. They were everywhere, truckloads of them, and I was counting every atom. Just another of my counting dreams!

After treating them and going through all of the preparatory steps, I had only a tiny extract from each sample. I took the extracts and lined them along the bench in Boyd Hall. The windows let in the winter light from outside; the trees were bare, snow had fallen in the woods. I switched on the instrument, dialed in the wavelength for cobalt, turned on the argon tank and the cooling water, and programmed in the temperatures for the graphite furnace. Into the cups of the automatic sampler I put a few milliliters of extract from each depth, in exactly the same order in which we had collected them. For a second I imagined I was in the field, facing the lake.

Then I set the instrument going. The little arm of the autosampler began to twist. Then it came down and took a few microliters from the cup, barely a drop. It halted a second before it rose again and moved toward the graphite tube. It looked like the pitching machine my father had used for throwing batting practice. Just like that. When it reached the tube, it hung there, deposited its precious droplet, then came back and rested. The furnace kicked in. The temperature of the tube climbed to 110, stopped; climbed to 250, stopped; then shot instantly to 2,300 degrees. You could hear the controller work. There was a surge of current through the tube. Then a burst of white steam, as though a tiny volcano had just erupted right there in the lab. A trace of light shot across the face of the instrument. A number appeared on the screen. Then it appeared on the printer. There were little clicks as the paper moved into position for the next reading.

It was working, but I couldn't watch. I was too nervous. I went back to my office and let the instrument tack downward into the depths of the lake: five meters, ten meters, fifteen meters; it was moving slowly, doing triplicates on each sample. I had the instrument interfaced with the computer. After each analysis the point was placed on a graph whose vertical axis represented depth and whose horizontal axis was the concentration of cobalt. I waited. I thought about what Keith had said at the party. About how

manganese might be controlling everything in the oxygen minimum zone of the Pacific. How oxygen and manganese were linked,
'like this,' as Keith had said. And how the metals might be linked to
manganese.

When I finally summoned the courage to go into the lab, the
analysis was complete. On the blue computer screen there was a
curve connecting the points, from the ice surface down through the
water column to the sediments. The whole journey, a whole year,
was laid out there on the screen in a single trace. It was frightening
to look at. I wanted to shield my eyes.

But there it was. Point for point, the curve for cobalt analysis
matched the curve for manganese. Matched it to a T. Where the dissolved maganese was low, so too was the cobalt. Where the
manganese rose, in response to the disappearance of oxygen, so too
did the cobalt. Even the fine structure between fifty and sixty
meters matched up. It was perfect. The story was beginning to
write itself.

It was night when I left for home. The woods behind Boyd Hall
were filling up with snow. The drifts came nearly to my knees. At
times as I walked I thought I was floating.

But as Keith had said that evening, overlooking the flat darkness of
the Pacific, the proof is in the particles. If the manganese oxides
were really transporting cobalt and lead and the other metals, as the
overlapping profiles in Vanda had suggested, then we should see it
in the particles, in their composition, in the way the metals were distributed among the complex tangle of plankton cells and minerals
and bits of clay and organic ooze. Each particle was, indeed, a universe, a world more extraordinary than even Blake had imagined.
On every particle there was generation and decay, the comings and

goings of ions from a million knotted surfaces; breathing and exhalation conjoined on a sphere no larger than a pinhead. How many angels could dance on the skin of a sinking particle? Maybe a million. Maybe more. And how many manganese atoms and how much cobalt?

So we had put the traps in. We had left them there suspended. They had seen the coming of winter. They had seen the sun extinguished. They had seen the moon rise over Linneaus Terrace and cast shadows on the mountains. They had heard the fierce Antarctic wind, the wind of the early explorers, the wind of Scott's death. They had seen the lake scoured with sand. They had heard the ice crack like a bullwhip.

Before I saw anything else, I saw the rope. It had gone in white. But in the lake it had turned brown and dark green. Filaments of algae clung to it and wove about it. It had the hoary look of things brought up from the sea.

I had not been expecting this. Vanda was known for its ultra-oligotrophy: biologically, it was among the least productive lakes in the world. In all the water I had drawn from it, all the thousands of liters, I had not seen a single rotifer. Nothing. Even under the microscope, I might as well have been looking at a drop of liquid mercury. Thoreau had said that Walden was 'not fertile in fish.' Vanda was fertile in nothing. It would have made the waters of Concord look fecund and teeming by comparison.

I had done some rough calculations, before we put them in, on just how much sediment we might expect to find in the traps. There was very little to go on – a single estimate of sedimentation rate that Alex Wilson had made several decades ago. Taking into account the diameter of the traps, I calculated that there should be about a hundred milligrams. Mostly sand, I thought. Sand that had worked its way through the ice cover. But my estimate could be off by a factor of ten either way. Maybe out here, so far from the river, we wouldn't find anything. Maybe like the rotifers, there wouldn't be a single particle.

The first trap, the one we had suspended at forty-eight meters, brimmed with crystalline water. Nothing broke its transparent perfection. I raised it like a dry martini to the afternoon sun. There was nothing to scatter the light. It moved in unbroken rays through the trap chambers. Had we come all this way, I wondered, waited so long, thought so much about the particles, about the rain of manganese oxides cleansing the lake, only to find this?

'Empty,' Dr. Yu was saying. 'Empty. Only water.' He had removed his balaclava and was scratching his head, wiping his forehead.

I put the traps on the ice, stood the chambers upright. I reached into my parka and took out some orange plastic caps. I placed these over the top of the cylinders. Then I lifted the whole assembly over my head and began to shake it. I don't know what I was expecting. Maybe that the water would somehow transform itself into earth, the way the Greeks thought it did at the mouth of the Hellespont. Maybe that it would become air. Maybe that it would burn. Water could do anything. You just had to believe.

Dr. Yu was saying 'Ohhhhhh, careful. No break.' I shook the tubes for a full minute. A dry snow had begun to fall. The flakes were large. They clung to my skin without melting. I put the tubes down on the ice, lay on my stomach, and held them in front of my face. I couldn't tell what I was seeing. Something was drifting down inside. Maybe it was just the snow. Maybe the water *was* turning to earth.

Gradually I began to discern what was happening. There were tiny bits of clay suspended in the water. It was faint, but you could see it. It was settling, but very, very slowly, the way small particles settle. Stoke's beautiful law. It was the dust of the lake, the dust of the river, the dust of the valley. We had waited a year for it. I let out a whooop.

We were on the lake all evening and well into the morning. It continued to snow out of a gray sky. The whole valley was enveloped in cloud. The mountains folded in around us. A wan light spread up toward the sound. The glaciers seemed to be floating again. The parkas whispered against themselves as we moved.

We repaired the trap catcher, and each time it held. It folded tight against itself and went down the hole. It opened and groped its way through the lake. It touched the line, gathered it in, wound the traps to itself. Then it released at the ice edge and straightened again, just the way Tim and Dr. Yu had designed it. Bamboo could do anything.

We covered the whole length of the lake, all the way down valley to where the Onyx would soon begin to flow in. We turned the sleds to shore and pulled them along the smooth annual ice, five miles back to camp. You could hear the water sloshing in the traps as we moved.

Just where the ice meets the shore, you could see a thin band of open water. It was no more than a few inches wide. Dr. Yu was pointing toward it and saying 'Ahhhhh, water! In Qaidam Basin, we say maybe spring. Maybe not long.'

CHAPTER 16

'CABIN 532'

from *Skating to Antarctica* (1997)

Jenny Diski

Not everybody comes to the Antarctic wide-eyed, or with their psyche neatly tuned for enthusiasm. The British novelist Jenny Diski took herself south in a state of wisecracking, deadpan melancholy, looking for a landscape that would soothe her the same way the sight of an all-white bedroom did. She found one, and in the process created a small classic of Antarctic iconoclasm. This is Antarctica, the neurotic version; very nearly the indoor version.

The next morning around 6.15, I lay shivery in my bunk, with a sore throat. I had a streaming, screaming head cold and felt ghastly, but it was OK since it was a travelling day and I didn't have to do anything if I didn't want to. I had woken earlier, at four, to the unrelenting daylight with a small damp weight inside of me. A tiny blueness. Perhaps it was a moment of panic at being out of reach of anywhere, hundreds of miles out of sight of land. A kind of bleakness. I closed the beige curtains across the bed, making a soft half-light, enclosing myself, and dozed on and off.

Later, I got my achey self up to look out of my window. Birds: pintados, petrels, black-browed albatross (I was getting good at this) were wheeling around, dipping and diving on the wind to feast off Melville's 'effulgent Antarctic sea'. The surface of the water was dark, hardly lively, but active enough to create a gentle rocking motion in the boat that sent me back to bed to enjoy it. I carried on with *Moby Dick* and Ahab's search for the great white whale. Such a pleasure. Grand, huge and free. Taking all the freedom a novelist needs. I couldn't think of a circumstance that would improve my life – apart from not having a cold. Though soon I would have to get up to have breakfast – which meant other people, greeting, smiling and talking. That felt like a bit of a trial. My wish was to stay where I was, in my cabin, in bed. As I put my book down for a moment, I looked through the window and realized that it was snowing. The sky was dove grey with heavy snow-weighted cloud, and the snow was falling softly, making the windswept wilderness of the Antarctic sea as silent as any suburban winter garden. The horizon was a very long way away.

I skipped breakfast and both of the lectures designed to help fill our at-sea time, devoting the day to my cold, my bunk, my book and the view from my window. I was perfectly contented. Sleeping, reading and staring out at the snow and sea, I could have done this forever. No Sister Winniki to nag. Just left alone to take all the pleasure I wanted in indolence. What more could anyone want?

Then in the evening the first iceberg floated by.

The iceberg emerged before my lazy gaze at the window, like a mirage, a dream appearance, a matt white edifice ghostly in the misty grey light and falling snow. A sudden, smoothly gliding event in the great empty sea under the great empty sky. I blinked at it. There was none of the disappointing familiarity of something seen too often on TV or in picture books. This startled with its brand-new reality, with its quality of not-like-anything-else. Even the birds seemed to have hushed for our entrance into the land of ice. The tannoy squawked into life, and Butch announced:

'Ladies and gentlemen, we have icebergs.'

Time to get up. I pulled on a tracksuit and headed up to the bridge where I discovered that like a momentous theatrical production we were proceeding into real Antarctica through a corridor of icebergs. For as far as the eye could see, to either side of us, icebergs lined our route. We were journeying along iceberg alley. It was absurdly symmetrical, like a boulevard in space. The bergs were tabular; as their name suggests they are flat as a table on top, as if someone has planed away their peaks, too smooth to be real, too real to be true. It took about an hour before we had sailed the length of iceberg alley, and all the time I and many of the other passengers stood and watched in silence, broken only by gasped oohs and ahhs and the inevitable camera clicks and camcorder whirr. For a while after that we seemed to travel through debris, odd-shaped bergy bits, and the larger growlers – some just the dimension of buoys bobbing and rocking like corks in the waves, others the size of a dinghy or a small cottage. These were the remnants of big bergs, worn down by wind and water, breaking off and melting away eventually to nothing. Finally we sailed through cracked pieces of ice, chips and fragments, as if we were making our way through a bowl of granita.

Later, in the early hours of the morning, more big bergs appeared, not in formation any more, but dotted about on the sea in gatherings of two and three, some of them huge, the size of our ship and bigger. I watched one go past that, we were told the next morning, was four miles long, an island of ice that took an age to sail along.

I didn't get much sleep. Irma may not have been so pathological in her attitude towards the steak. I was feeling decidedly nauseous and having stomach cramps. The light-soaked night was spent divided between hovering over my toilet without quite throwing up (there is very little I hate more than vomiting), and leaning out of the open window with my chin on my folded arms watching the superlunary white mountains float by. Sometimes, as I watched one huge berg sailing towards us, it would shift shape, playing parallax games, and getting nearer, became two or three separate bergs at what I finally saw were a considerable distance apart. Then when we had left it behind, it returned again to its singular form.

As a matter of fact, in keeping with the interesting but not fatal disparity between my fantasies and rest of the trip so far, the icebergs close up, even quite far away, were not daydream white at all. Blue. Icebergs are blue. At their bluest, they are the colour of David Hockney swimming pools, Californian blue, neon blue, Daz blue-whiteness blue, sometimes even indigo. Blue is an odd colour: the signifier of good things to come ('blue skies, nothing but blue skies') and of dark thoughts ('Mood Indigo'). Different shades, different promises, same colour. It can be bright, clean, even cold; and it can be mysterious, deep, the colour of night and dreams. Like Melville's notion of whiteness, it makes clear and it obscures; it is purity and complexity. The colour blue does no violence to my hankering for white. It belonged with and in the ice, making it seem colder, emotionally empty, and yet more dense, layered beyond what could be observed. The bergs were deepest blue at sea level, and where cracks and crevices gave a view of the depths of the berg where the ice was the oldest and so compacted that all the air had been forced out. Why this should cause them to be aching blue is not a question that someone who spent physics lessons turning notes into poetry can answer. The blue tinge higher up was, I was told, because ice absorbs all wavelengths of light except the shorter blue ones. I told this proudly to Marjorie who pointed out that this account would cover the reason why anything looks any colour. Melville again: there is no colour, only an appearance of colour that conceals the universal negation of white light. The explanation

didn't after all explain anything much, and once again I wished I
hadn't dicked around during physics and deprived myself of
answers to most of the questions I now found myself asking.

These floating mountains of blue ice shaded with white, white
ice shaded blue, were not slick and shiny like ice-rink ice. They
were dense, matt islands of compressed icing sugar. Confections
that lit up the lead-coloured sea and sky. All night they floated
along, carved by wind and water into ancient shapes – ships, cas-
tles, monuments, mythic creatures. None of the explorers who
described them managed to avoid these descriptions. They are as
unavoidable as a sigh at the sight of the elephant seals having sex.
I passed great craggy faces in profile, ominous fingers pointing,
lions crouching, birds leaping. The mind couldn't help it. But sometimes, and most breathtakingly, they were simply vast walls of ice,
passing so near to my window that they cut out the rest of the
world. A great blank wall of ancient compacted snow that had travelled from the blank centre of the Antarctic continent for
centuries – the deepest ice is 10,000 years old – to its edges to
become a tongue of glacier or the very periphery of the ice cap, and
finally broken off – calved is the correct term – to sail away on its
own. They head north and west at a rate of five miles a day until
they reach the convergence where the Antarctic Ocean meets
warmer seas. Some of them last for ten years, until the sea erodes
and melts them away.

Antarctica has seventy per cent of the world's fresh water locked
up in the ice. In places the ice sheet is two and a half miles deep.
Over the centuries people have planned to utilize the bigger icebergs as a source of water in drought-stricken regions. The only
problem has been how to get the bergs from where they are to
where they're needed. Grandiose plans to tow them have come to
nothing: once they are into warmer water the chances of landing
more than enough ice to cool a gin and tonic are unreasonably

small. Icebergs are one resource that the human race has failed to find a way to make use of – apart from Daniel and my Manhattans. While the sea ice, pack-ice, frazil, nilas, pancake-ice are salt – though not as salt as sea water – the bergs that break off from the continent are pure fresh water – as pure and fresh as anything can be on the planet. Certainly, for all the pollution, purer than the stuff that comes out of our taps. And these mountains of frozen water I watched floating on the surface of the sea are, as everyone knows, just the tip of the iceberg. Nine-tenths of each berg is indeed below the waterline, and melts faster than the bit you can see, so that eventually they become top-heavy and turn turtle into the sea. The smaller, most rounded bergs are actually upside down, tip-turned and unstable. Growlers, they are called, and not loved by sailors; they are the ones that creep up and scuttle ships in the dark, being harder to see and often invisible to radar.

The scene from my cabin window was otherworldly, I am afraid there is no other really apposite description. In the early hours of the morning, the light was pale silver, slightly misty. Half-close my eyes and there was nothing but a spectrum of grey, blue and off-white. It could have been bluey grey, greyish blue, hues of blue. There were huge bergs coming now. I suppose they were related. They came in waves. Three, four, but no, they were two big bergs. They must have broken off at the same time, or it could have been one great berg that split. On the horizon the cloud seemed to have settled down on to the sea and turned into another iceberg. It was impossible to tell what was cloud and what was berg in the distance. It looked fluffy, the same colour as the clouds higher up, only distinct, and squat, flat on the sea, but still cloudlike for all that. But it wasn't a cloud. Soon it turned into one . . . two separate bergs. It was all clouds and bergs, bergs and clouds. And there, close by the ship, was a single penguin on an iceberg that looked like a lion. The bird was riding on the lion's mane, standing stark still, looking ahead in the direction in which it travelled. I'd never seen a penguin look heroic before. It was 3.20 a.m. and luminous, misty daylight.

We stopped off at Deception Island, making the approach after breakfast, in silvery light. The name alone was worth getting up for. Who would want to lie abed when they were sailing towards Deception? The sight from the bridge was immortal. Deception Island is a caldera, a volcano summit that has collapsed to form a crater. One section sank far enough to allow the sea water to flood into the interior of the caldera. As we approached 'Neptune's Bellows' at the entrance to the crater, fleets of penguins came out to see what we were and swam, ducking and diving, alongside the ship. The sea was veneered with a pattern of sea ice made up of perfectly sharp-edged rectangles that looked as thin as wafers and pure white, floating side by side with narrow channels of dark water in between. It was a chessboard of flat floating squares of ice, as strange and orderly as anything I'd ever seen. It was shocking when the ship broke through one of the bigger rectangles on its way to the narrow entrance to Deception. The bow of the ship split the ice floe into two pieces which grew jaggedly ever wider apart as we pressed on through. There was something terrible about this, about breaking up the pattern just because we wanted to get beyond it. No real damage was done, but something artful in nature was dislocated. The design was spoiled. And yet the further into the checkerboard we got the more we seemed to be part of it. Soon it was surrounding us, an abstract picture made with great but delicate four-cornered slabs of ice, floating in the hazy sunlight, with a small white ship slipping through. The Zodiacs went ashore but I remained on board, on the deck at the back of the boat, and stared all morning at the chequered ocean. Checkmate.

The following morning I woke, still feeling rotten. Everything ached, my head was thick and I still felt sick and crampy. I couldn't move, not even to take a pill, not even to check out the state of the icebergs. I'd been up and down all night, at the window, then dozing, until I finally went back to sleep at 6.30 and slept until late. It was 11 a.m. and as light as it had been in the early hours. It was always light now, we were so far south. The lack of alternating dark and light made it very easy for me to stay where I was. The call to breakfast, lunch and the time-passing lectures failed to intrude on the structureless nature of continual daylight and feeling ill.

What was going to happen to my Antarctic adventure if I sank for days into my bunk, I wondered? Unless, of course, this *was* my Antarctic adventure. I was quite suspicious of my malaise. Through the aches and the nausea, pleasure shone through, at escaping the timetable, the events, the socializing. I guessed it was probably my psyche, rather than my immune system, that had revolted against being snuggled in with so many people. Still, the psyche had effectively persuaded the body to produce some impressive symptoms – good enough to justify hermiting without having to accuse myself of being anti-social. Though I did, in fact, accuse myself.

We were coming into Admiralty Bay, where humpback whales were supposed to hang out. We hadn't sighted any whales so far. Well, I could look out of the window if there were any sightings. Though only if they happened to be on my side of the ship. But I didn't want to see whales with a whole bunch of people on the bridge or the deck. I didn't want to be in a crowd watching whales, even if it meant missing them. I wanted to see my own whale out of my own window, all by myself. Or not. I imagined explaining to friends on my return to England how I didn't manage to see a whale. Wrong side of the ship. Didn't get up. Oh dear.

The following morning we were due to land at Paulet Island. Outside it looked very weird and alien. I had to keep telling myself I was on the same planet. Not on the moon. Maybe this sickness or not-sickness (I'd managed to throw up some yellow bile that night, which made me feel a little more authentic) was panic at not escaping, at never escaping. Here we were at the end of the earth and still it's the same planet. I would have liked to get somewhere else. Further off. One morning I was alarmed at being out of sight of the world, the next I was blue about not being able to escape the world altogether. Not very consistent, I told myself. Myself shrugged. I wondered, at last, if I was going to prevent myself from landing on Antarctica. What an odd thing, to have come all this way and then not land on the peninsula. There was a small but unmistakable internal smile at the thought. I located a tight subterranean knot of unwillingness to set foot on the last continent just because I happened to be there. Though of course I didn't just happen to be there. This was a place where no one just happens to be. Which made it all the more pleasing and/or distressing (the two emotions were inextricable) to consider the possibility of not stepping on to the land. There was considerable satisfaction at the thought that I might not set foot on the continent that I had taken a good deal of trouble to get to. I considered further ventures: how I might fail to let the sand run through my fingers in the Gobi desert; how I could turn back twenty-five feet from the summit of Anapurna; how, gaining disguised entrance to a Masonic initiation ceremony, I would shrug my shoulders at the door and wander away. I could easily go to Agra and fail to clap eyes on the Taj Mahal – too easily. What about a trip to Brazil spent entirely in the air-conditioned confines of the Brasilia Sheraton? Or a visit to every airport in Africa without setting foot on the continent itself?

I could keep myself busy as the resistant traveller until my last gasp and then, at the gates of Heaven, make my excuses and turn away. It's not the arriving but the not-arriving . . . it's not the seeing of the whales, but the possibility of choosing not to see them. This was an aspect of me that I recognized from every period in my life. The Fuck-it Factor. *I don't have to if I don't want to.* Sometimes it has looked like a lack of persistence. 'What you lack, my girl, is stick-ability' my oh-so-resolute father would say to me. I didn't finish pictures, knitting, stamp collections. Lost interest two-thirds, or even nine-tenths of the way through. I got thrown out of school. I left school two weeks before my A-levels. I wandered away from relationships. Sometimes, even now, I turn off movies on TV min-utes before the end. Lots of people have nodded knowingly to each other, 'She just can't finish things'. But no one ever mentions the exhilaration of not finishing things. The rush of pleasure at not doing what is expected of you, of not doing what you expect of yourself. Of not doing. If it was originally about disappointing other people, it has become refined into a matter of pleasing myself. Of making choice less inevitable. But it's not a policy. Only some-thing I notice happening from time to time, and the genuine satisfaction that goes with it. This time I'd caught myself in the early stages. Unless, of course, I was just not well. You can't say, and I may not choose to say.

I became gripped by the idea of willingness. As I gazed out of the window, I imagined myself into the future: the trip over, me back in London. Did I or didn't I get to Antarctica? At that deli-cious moment I really didn't know what the answer would be. It wouldn't make an iota of difference to the world, or in reality to me, if I didn't actually stand on the Antarctic landmass. Been there, haven't done that. I liked the absurdity of it, and the privacy. It's a matter entirely between me and myself. Indeed, I could say, back home, that I did, when I didn't. What difference would it make? Or, come to think of it, I could say that I didn't, when I did. And once I'd had this thought, it didn't matter whether I actually did or I didn't. The quality of my life wouldn't alter one bit, and either way only I, and a handful of fellow travellers, would know, and none of us would care. The decision became entirely academic. I could toss a coin: heads I land, tails I stay in my bunk – and then not go if it comes up heads. Or contrariwise. I might not have been feeling well, but my spirit was soaring. There was no longer a choice that had to be made, or an effort of will (I should, I ought, I must), no moral quandary, but something quite arbitrary. A great sense of freedom settled gently over me like a pure white goose-down quilt, and freedom, from that angle, looked very like uncertainty, as Antarctica slipped into Schrödinger's box and closed the lid quietly on itself. I had no idea whether I would get up and land the next day or not. And no one else, save a few scattered US citizens, would know for sure what I eventually did. This, for reasons I don't choose to examine too closely, was a huge comfort. What was all this getting to Antarctica thing anyway?

The book I was going to write about the trip, and my mother, was to be my first full-length non-fiction, it had been agreed. I took this to mean that I would not be writing a novel about it. Obviously. Who would agree to write a novel about a real trip they hadn't yet been on? Novels aren't like that. But beyond that I reserved my judgement on what non-fiction is. There are infinite ways of telling the truth, including fiction, and infinite ways of evading the truth, including non-fiction. The truth or otherwise of a book about Antarctica and my mother, I saw from my swaying bunk in Cabin 532, didn't depend on arriving at a destination. Nor in failing to arrive. I found myself beginning to get a taste for non-fiction.

Another day, and the tannoy announced that we were as far south as we were going to get: 63.42S 55.57W. We had arrived in the early hours at the Antarctic Sound. My landing quandary was resolved for this morning at least. The pack-ice was too thick to get through to Paulet Island, and things weren't looking good for the landing on the Peninsula at Hope Bay, scheduled for the afternoon. It looked possible that no one would be landing on Antarctica, and my decision – as so often – would be no decision at all in the event. However, Butch was doing his best for us and had arranged, instead of a walkabout on Paulet, a Zodiac cruise around the great field of icebergs surrounding us. The sun was blazing beyond my window and the sea was glacially still. There wasn't a ripple to be seen on the turquoise surface, nothing but the sharp reflections of the bergs. Suddenly, I thought I might be feeling a bit better. Time to get up. I very much wanted to get close up to the icing sugar mountains, and down near the surface of the brilliant sea.

After my sullen, anti-social couple of days in my cabin, I found myself greeted in the corridors, in the mud-room and on deck by everyone I saw, welcoming me back and asking how I was. They had noticed I was not around and asked Marjorie and Phoenix John if I was OK. I felt a little ashamed at the concern people were show-ing for me. Part of my sense of shame was that I slightly resented their attention. I don't like the idea of being thought or wondered about if I have gone to ground. This was so ungenerous compared to people I hardly knew telling me they were glad to see me up and about, that I was not pleased with myself.

The only noise was the buzz of the Zodiac engine. There was no wind, no screaming penguins, and when the Zodiac stopped at the foot of an iceberg, no sound at all, except for water lapping against the wall of ice. The sun shone and the sea was a deep green with sparkling lights, twinkling like sequins. The surface was calm, just slightly wrinkled by the gentle breeze, almost syrupy. A Crimplene ocean. Between the bergs, so common now but never boring, were flat ice floes, slabs several feet thick, on which the odd crab-eater seal lolled soaking up the sun. So long as we didn't get too near they refused to be bothered by our pottering about. If we went too close they slithered unhurriedly into the sea and disappeared.

To be at the base of an iceberg, rocking on the sea, is a remarkable feeling. The cold radiated off the wall of the berg and I peered into secret crevices that went to the deepest blue heart of the ice. The world was flat and still except for the bergs ranged above us as we wove in and out between them. The ship at anchor, as white and still as another berg, belonged there, another mythic shape in the landscape and didn't seem to impose itself. It was uncanny and peaceful, a near oblivion, but deceptive. This was not a place, though it was a position on a navigation chart. Nothing about this region would be quite the same again, as the floes and bergs floated and melted, winds whipped up the presently calm sea, seals made temporary lodging, and flotillas of penguins porpoised around the ship in the distance like flying fish. Everything about this seascape would change, but it would also remain essentially the same, its elements merely rejigged. It was so untroubled by itself that the heart ached. Other landscapes fidget – rainforests full of plants and creatures clamouring for a living, moors troubled and ruffled by scathing, distorting winds, mountains trembling with the weight of snow – but this was truly a dream place where melting and movement seemed only to increase immutability. Nothing there stays the same, but nothing changes.

But what, I wondered, was the point of witnessing this sublime empty landscape and then passing on? That question was one reason, I suppose, for the rate at which the cameras clicked away. The photograph was evidence for oneself, not others really, that you'd been there. The only proof that anything had once happened beyond an attack of imagination and fallible memory. It also caused there to be an event during the moment of experiencing, as if the moment of experiencing doesn't feel like enough all by itself. If you merely looked and left, what, when you returned home, was the point of having been? It was not hard to imagine such a landscape, to build one in your head in the comfort of your own home, and spend unrestricted time there all alone. In real life, you look, you pass through, you leave – you take a photo to make the activity less absurd. It provides something to do with your hands while you are trying to experience yourself experiencing this experience. But how do you become, as I wanted to be, part of this landscape, to be of it, not making a quick tour through it? What I was doing was having a taster of something, watching the trailer of a movie I would never see. I would take this memory of a place in motionless flux back with me, and add it to the Antarctic in my mind. I wondered if it would be a useful addition once the experience was in the past.

But I had forgotten about Cabin 532. That *had* been a new experience, something I hadn't already dreamed up or dreamed of, somewhere I couldn't have visited through pictures taken by someone else. Cabin 532 was something really new to carry back to London and play with.

CHAPTER 17

'HEY, WOO'

from *Terra Incognita* (1996)

Sara Wheeler

Sara Wheeler went to Antarctica to do for it, for the first time, what a good travel writer does for a place: to cast a beady, evocative eye on the manners and behaviour of the inhabitants, and to knit that sociable human reality together with the sublime ice in the background. In bases run by the British Antarctic Survey, the perpetually boyish scientists put spoonfuls of sherry trifle in her snow boots. At McMurdo, the National Science Foundation put her on their Writers and Artists Program, and assigned her office W–002: hence the nickname 'Woo' that follows her, here, out to a seismology field camp in the continent's big, empty centre.

Resuming the quest for Seismic Man and his group, I wheedled my way on to a fuel flight to Central West Antarctica, and after a series of false starts I was transported to the skiway with four members of a science project staging at CWA en route to Ice Stream B. The West Antarctic ice streams – fast-flowing currents of ice up to 50 miles wide and 310 miles long – are cited as evidence of possible glacial retreat and the much-touted imminent rise in global sea levels. The project leader pulled out *The Road to Oxiana*, the greatest travel book ever written and one which lies so close to my heart that it gave me a shock to see it there, as if the paraphernalia of home had followed me. He was a beatific man in his mid-fifties with a round, mottled face like a moon, and his name was Hermann. Ten years previously, he had climbed out of a crashed plane in Antarctica.

Later, when we were airborne, the scientists retreated into the hoods of their parkas, jamming unwieldily booted feet among the trellis of rollers, survival bags and naked machinery. I loitered on the flight deck for a while, but I couldn't see much. It grew colder.

The previous evening, in the galley at McMurdo, I had run into a mountaineer from a science group which had recently pulled out of CWA.

'Hey!' he had said when I told him I was on my way there. 'You can sublease the igloo I built just outside camp. It's the coolest igloo on the West Antarctic ice sheet.'

When we landed at eighty-two degrees south, the back flap lifted and light flooded into the plane. Tornadoes of powder snow were careering over the blanched wasteland like spectral spinning tops. There were no topographical features, just an ice sheet, boundless and burnished. Lesser (or West) Antarctica is a hypothesised rift system – a jumble of unstable plates – separated from the stable shield of Greater (or East) Antarctica by the Transantarctic Mountains. On top, most of Lesser Antarctica consists of the world's only marine-based ice sheet. This means that the bottom of the ice is far below sea level, and if it all melted, the western half of Antarctica would consist of a group of islands. The assemblage of plates which make up Lesser Antarctica have been moving both relative to one another and to the east for something like 230 million years, whereas Greater Antarctica, home of the polar plateau, has existed relatively intact for many hundreds of millions of years. In Gondwanaland, the prehistoric supercontinent, what we now know as South America and the Antipodes were glued to Antarctica.

Gondwanaland started to break up early in the Jurassic Period – say 175 million years ago – and geologists like to speculate on the relationship of Antarctica to still earlier super-continents. Most exciting of all, Antarctica once had its own dinosaurs.

The crewmen began rolling pallets off the back of the plane. We walked down after them, and the wind stung our faces. The engines roared behind us as we struggled to pull our balaclavas down around our goggles.

In the sepulchral light ahead I could see a scattering of Jamesways, a row of sledges, half a dozen tents, and Lars, the shaggy-haired Norwegian-American from Survival School. He was looking even shaggier, and proffering a mug of cocoa. We hugged one another. Lars led the way into the first Jamesway, where half a dozen weatherbeaten individuals were slumped around folding formica tables.

'Welcome, Woo!' somebody shouted. I had brought them cookies and a stack of magazines, and as I handed these over we all talked at once; a lot seemed to have happened in two months.

'Guess what?' said Lars. 'We saw a bird.'

The CWA field camp was probably the largest on the continent. Fifty people were based here for most of the summer season, working on four separate geological projects. Often small groups temporarily left camp, travelled over the ice sheet on snowmobiles or tracked vehicles, pitched their tents for a few days and tried to find out what the earth looked like under that particular bit of ice. They were creating a relief map of Antarctica without its white blanket.

Seeing Seismic Man's lightweight parka hanging on a hook in the Jamesway, I suspected he was away working at one of these small satellite camps. I was thinking about this, just as Lars produced another round of cocoa, when a familiar figure flew through the door of the Jamesway and clattered to a standstill beside me. It was José, the diminutive Mexican-American biker who grinned like a satyr and with whom I had failed to get to CWA on my first attempt. He had made it here a week before me. In one long exhalation of breath he said that he had heard I'd come, that he and two others were about to set off to strike a satellite camp thirty miles away, that it would take about twenty-four hours and they wouldn't be sleeping, that I could go too if I wanted . . . and then he trailed off, like his bike running out of fuel.

Having trekked halfway across the continent to find Seismic Man, I left immediately without seeing him at all. It was the idea of the quest that had appealed to me. Feeling vaguely irritated about this, as if the whole expedition had been someone else's idea, I climbed into the back of a tracked vehicle and shook hands with a tall loose-limbed Alaskan in the driver's seat.

'They call me Too-Tall Dave,' he said as he pumped my hand, crushing a few unimportant bones. 'Pleased to meet you.'

The man next to him – a medical corpsman on loan from the Navy – looked as if he had just got up. His name was Chuck, and apparently he had forgotten the American president's name one day and asked Too-Tall Dave to remind him. José and I spread out over the two bench seats in the back of the vehicle. It was a temperamental Tucker which only liked travelling between eight and ten miles an hour, and we were towing a flat, open trailer and a sledge loaded with survival gear. As we were following a flagged route to the small camp you couldn't really call what Too Tall was doing driving: it was more a question of stabilising the steering wheel with his elbow and looking at the dash every so often to make sure he was maintaining the correct rpm to keep the water and oil at a stable temperature. It was very warm in the Tucker. The ice was dappled with watery sunlight, and the sky pale, streaky blue.

'This', said José, 'is what travelling in a covered wagon across the United States must have been like.'

After five hours, we reached a weatherhaven and a Scott tent.
'Is this it?' I asked.

'Yep,' said Too Tall, swinging nimbly out of the Tucker.

When I saw the tent, its flap still open, sunlit against the white
prairies, an image flashed across my mind, and after a moment I
recognised it as J. C. Dollman's painting of Captain Oates stag-
gering off to die, arms outstretched and wearing a blue bobble hat.
The lone tent in the background of the picture was identical to the
one I was looking at, except that Dollman hadn't painted something
which looked like a Land Rover parked outside.

I packed up the contents of the weatherhaven while José and Too
Tall set about dismantling it from the outside. Fortunately the wind
had dropped, but it was bitterly cold.

'Why didn't the beakers do this themselves?' asked Too Tall irritably. 'Next time they'll be asking us to wipe their butts.'

By the time we had finished loading the gear on to the trailer it
was six o'clock in the morning. We squatted in a banana sledge we
had forgotten to pack up, and opened three cartons of orange juice
and a large bag of trail-mix.

As we rearranged our own gear in the back of the Tucker afterwards I noticed that fuel had leaked all over my sleeping bag, not
for the first time or the last. I wasn't the only one in Antarctica who
smelt like an oil rig.

I drove for the first three hours on the way back to camp. It was
a mesmerising occupation, and as I wandered into a reverie or
stared blankly out at the ice sheet, the needle crept up on the rev.
counter dial.

'Less gas!' Too Tall would then say, delivering a karate chop on
my shoulder from the bench in the back. The monotony was

broken by the appearance of a bottle of bourbon. José set up a Walkman with a pair of speakers.

'We need tortured blues,' said Too Tall. He was right. It was the perfect accompaniment to the inescapable monotony of the landscape and the hypnotic rhythm of the Tucker.

I got accused of picking all the cashews out of the trail-mix, a crime of which I was indeed guilty. Everyone started talking.

'Are you married?' José asked me.

'No,' I said. 'Are you?'

'No.' There was a pause, which something was waiting to fill.

'Go on José, tell her!' said Chuck.

José cleared his throat.

'Actually, I married my Harley Davidson,' he said.

I choked on the last cashew.

'Oh, really?' I said, in an English kind of way. 'Who performed the, er – ceremony?'

'Owner of my local bike shop. He does it a lot.'

This information was almost more than the human spirit could bear. Fortunately an empty fuel drum chose that moment to fall off our trailer and roll over the ice sheet, and after we had dealt with that, the topic was forgotten.

A fresh one, however, was looming.

'You know that Captain Scott,' said Too Tall in my direction as the bourbon went round again. 'Was he a bit of a dude, or what?'

I had just begun to grapple with a reply to this weighty question when Chuck, his face puckered in concentration, chipped in with 'Hey, is that the guy they named Scott's hut after?'

'No,' I said, quickly grasping the opportunity to divert the conversation away from the dude issue. 'That was Mr Hut.'

It took us eight hours to get back, and then I had to put up my tent. It was snowing lightly, and I was too tired to dig out the igloo. I chose a place at the back of camp, facing the horizon. My metal tent pegs weren't deep enough, so I hijacked a bunch of bamboo flagpoles, and after the bottle-green and maroon tent was up I collapsed into a deep sleep.

When I woke up, a face was hovering a foot above mine.

'Hi Woo,' it growled. 'Didn't want to wake you.'

'This is a funny way to go about not waking me,' I said as the face drew closer.

They were using explosives to find out what the ground was like under 6,000 feet of ice. 'We're not particularly interested in ice,' someone commented breezily. Because of the inconvenient ice cover, most Antarctic geology can only be studied by remote-sensing methods like seismology. This involves setting off explosions, bouncing the soundwaves down through the ice to the earth's crust, and recording them on their way back up.

Before they could be detonated, the explosives had to be buried, and twelve itinerant drillers had been travelling around the ice sheet within a 200-mile radius of CWA boring a series of ninety-foot holes. They began each hole using a self-contained unit which heated water and sprinkled it on the ice like a shower head. This unit fulfilled a secondary function as a hot tub, and we got in four at a time, draping our clothes carefully over the pipes to prevent them from turning to deep-frozen sandpaper. This was a task requiring consummate skill. A square inch of fabric inadvertendy exposed to the air could have excruciating consequences.

Five members of the drill team were women, and in the hot tub one day I found myself next to Diane, a lead driller. She was tall and willowy with long hair the colour of cornflakes. I asked her how long she had been away.

'Thirty-five days,' she said. 'And my feet were never dry.'

'What did you do out there?' I asked. 'I mean, when you weren't drilling?'

'Well, just living took all our time. We worked twelve-hour shifts on the drill, and then we'd have to set up the cook tent and all that. We had to plan what we were going to eat carefully, as even if it was going to be a can of peaches it had to be hung up in the sleep tent overnight to thaw.'

'Was it your, er, ambition to do this kind of work?' I asked, struggling to grasp the concept that a woman could enjoy spending weeks in sub-zero conditions manipulating a drill for twelve hours a day.

'I do love it,' she said. 'I think this is the most magical place in the world. People say – "But all you can see is white!" That's true, but I could never, ever get bored on the drill when I can watch the dancing ice crystals, and the haloes twinkling round the sun. It's another world.'

The evening before they flew back to McMurdo, the drillers brought in ice from a deep core and hacked it up on the chopping board in the galley. It was over 300 years old, and packed with oxygen bubbles. It fizzed like Alka-seltzer in our drinks. Diane was baking cinnamon rolls. When she opened the oven door a rich, spicy aroma filled the Jamesway. It was like a souk.

Diane inhaled deeply. 'Heaven!' she said.

The next day I moved into the igloo. It was at the back of what they called Tent City, and it took me two hours to dig out the trench leading down to the entrance. Like all good igloos, the sleeping area was higher than the entrance, thereby creating a cold sink. Inside, there was a carpet of rubber mats, and a ledge ran all the way round about six inches off the floor. I spent a further two hours clearing away the pyramids of snow that had accumulated through the cracks. When my new home was ready, I spread out my sleep kit and sat on it. The bricks spiralled to a tapering cork, filtering a blue fluorescent light which threw everything inside into muted focus. I was filled with the same sense of peace that I get in church. Yes, that was it – it was as if I had entered a temple.

The previous inhabitant had suspended a string across the ceiling like a washing line, so after hanging up my goggles, glacier glasses, damp socks and thermometer, I fished out the beaten-up postcards that I always carry around. These could be conveniently propped on the ledge. The blue light falling on the 'Birth of Venus' highlighted her knee-length auburn hair with an emerald sheen, and the flying angels had never looked more at home. I felt that Botticelli would have approved.

In the mornings I sat underneath rows of cuphooks at one of the formica tables in the galley Jamesway, watching the beakers making sandwiches and filling waterbottles before setting out to explode their bombs. The cooks were the fixed point of camp. Bob and Mary were a great team. Every morning they dragged banana sledges over to what they called their shop, a storage chamber seventeen feet under the ice from which they winched up filmy cardboard boxes on a kind of Antarctic dumb waiter. Mary was relentlessly cheerful, and she loped rather than walked. Bob had an Assyrian beard, a penguin tattoo on his thigh and a reputation as the best cook on the ice. He was hyperenergetic, very popular, and seven seasons in Antarctica, including two winters, had left him with a healthy disrespect for beakerdom.

'What's going on out there?' someone asked one day after an explosion of historic volume.

'They're just trying to melt the West Antarctic ice sheet,' Bob said, scrubbing a frozen leg of lamb. He could seem abrasive, but really he was as soft as a marshmallow.

Seismic Man had spent so long in the field over the past six weeks that he said 'Over' as he reached the end of whatever he was saying. When he had to set off an explosion we rode far out from camp on the back of Trigger, his snowmobile. The ice was mottled and ridged like a relief map, and a hint of wind blew a fine layer of white powder over the surface. You could almost absorb the psychic energy out there.

'You know what?' I said to him one day as I unpacked orange sausages of nitroglycerine. 'People call this a sterile landscape, because nothing grows or lives. But I think it's *pulsating* with energy – as if it's about to explode, like one of these bombs.'

'Hell, yes,' he drawled. 'I've often felt as if it's alive out here. Hey, look at that,' he said, pointing to where the china-blue sky grew pale.

'It looks like a bunch of fuel drums,' I said.

'Ha!' he replied. 'It's the distorted image of camp, thrown up by refraction of the light. It's caused by temperature inversion in the atmosphere.'

Every few minutes a sharp tirade would issue forth alarmingly from somewhere within the folds of Seismic Man's parka. The beakers were forever gabbling to each other over the radio. They had developed their own language, and entire conversations took place between Lars and Seismic Man consisting of acronyms, nicknames and long-running, impenetrable jokes.

I had never met anyone who found life as effortless as Seismic Man. He approached everything with a positive attitude, and saw something to laugh about in every situation. As a result, everyone loved him. In addition, he was disarmingly perceptive. He seemed to have got me taped, anyway. He exemplified the easy-going languor I associate with Texas, without any of the cowboy-hat brashness.

'Can you tape the explosives into bundles of three?' he said, handing me a roll of tape. 'I have to set up the shotbox.'

The drillers had already made a hole, and after attaching the first two orange bundles to an electric line, we lowered them both into it. Then we tossed down the other 400 pounds of explosives. When the time came to initiate the detonator, I pressed the button on the shotbox and a black plume shot up like a geyser. A sound that could have come from Cape Canaveral followed in a second.

'Wow,' I said.

'That's it, Woo!' said Seismic Man throwing an empty tube of explosive into the air and heading it like a football.

'How are we measuring the soundwaves, then?' I asked. 'When they bounce back up from the earth's crust?'

'Well,' he said, packing up the shotbox, 'what we're trying to do here is image the geology under 6,000 feet of ice. Seismology is the tool we use, and it operates either by refraction or reflection, the difference between the two being largely a function of scale in that reflection facilitates the imaging of a smaller area in greater detail. With me so far?'

I nodded.

'What you've just been doing is refracting. The soundwaves we send down are refracted back to the surface from the earth's sediment and recorded by a line of Ref Teks, the soundwave equivalent of the tape recorder. The Ref Teks contain computers hooked up to geophones, and we have 90 Ref Teks 200 yards apart on a line right now, recording away. So all you and I have left to do is pack up!'

On the way back we stopped about ten miles from camp to eat our sandwiches (tinned ham and mustard). A narrow strip of incandescent purply blue light lay on the horizon between ice and sky, looking for all the world like the sea. It seemed to me that it would be almost impossible, in this landscape, not to reflect on forces beyond the human plane. Here, palpably, was something better than the realm of abandoned dreams and narrowing choices that loomed outside the rain-splattered windows of home.

'You're right,' said Seismic Man when I mentioned this. 'It's like plugging yourself in to the spiritual equivalent of the National Grid out here. Wasn't it Barry Lopez who wrote that Antarctica "reflects the mystery that we call God"?'

I called what I sensed there God too; but you could give it many names. It was more straightforward for me than it had been for some, as I brought faith with me. I can't say where the faith came from, because I don't know; it certainly wasn't from my upbringing, since neither of my parents have ever had it. I remember first being aware of it when I was about fourteen, the same time that a lot of other things were happening to me. At first, it embarrassed me, like a virulent pimple on the end of my nose. I have no problems of that kind with it now, though I have persistently abused the giver by following the siren voices of the opposition, also dwelling in the rocky terrain of my interior life and determined to fight to the death.

Despite a good deal of high-mindedness and a sprightly ongoing dialogue with God, in the day-to-day hustle I constantly failed to do what I knew to be the right thing. A sense of spirituality all too often stopped short of influencing action. I was a hopeless case. But I believed that what mattered to God was the direction I was facing, not how far away I was. Sin, it seemed to me, was the refusal to let God be God. I admit that it was a handy credo to espouse – but I did it from the heart. The inner journey, like my route on the ice, was not a linear one. It was an uncharted meandering descent through layers and layers of consciousness, and I was intermittently tossed backwards or sideways like a diver in a current.

On Friday 13 January a Hercules appeared in the sky. It was going to take the drill team and a few others back to McMurdo. When it landed, incoming mail was borne inside in a metal turquoise-and-red striped crate like a crown before a coronation. Everyone leapt up, plunging their arms into the crate and calling out names as packages were passed eagerly from hand to hand.

My own mail was supposed to be waiting back at base. It could have been worse: Shackleton and the crew of the *Endurance* missed their mail by two hours when the ship sailed out of South Georgia, and they got it eighteen months later. Then I heard my name being called. Someone in the post room must have known where I was and slung my bundle into the metal crate. It was like a minor Old Testament miracle. The bundle included eight Christmas cards, three of them featuring polar bears, two pairs of knickers from my friend Alison and a bill from the taxman, the bastard. I took the cards to the igloo later and put them up to block the cracks between the ice bricks, and blue light shone through the polar bears.

We went out to wave goodbye to the drillers. The plane attempted to take off four times. It was too light at the back, so the drillers, we heard over the radio, had to stand in the tail.

That night I found a hillock of snow on my sleeping bag and was obliged to reseal the igloo bricks from the outside. It was perishing cold in there all the time and getting to sleep was an unmeetable challenge. I tried to listen to my Walkman to take my mind off the pain but the earphones got twisted under my balaclava and the batteries died in minutes. All my clothes froze in the night. Besides the waterbottle, I was obliged to stow my VHF radio and various spare batteries in between the bag liner and the sleeping bag to prevent them from freezing.

'It's like sleeping in a cutlery drawer,' said Seismic Man, who had made valiant efforts to stay in the igloo. 'Why are you putting yourself through it, when there are warm Jamesways a few hundred yards away?'

It was the romance of it, if I was honest. I liked the idea of living in my own igloo, slightly apart from camp, on the West Antarctic ice sheet. Besides that, during the periods when I didn't have to devote every ounce of energy to maintaining my core temperature, I did love the blue haze very much. I had noticed that when the sun was in a certain position it was faintly tinted with a deep, translucent claret. The surface of the bricks gleamed like white silver all around me. When I crawled out in the mornings (this had to be accomplished backwards) and twisted round on my sunken front path, I looked up and blinked at a pair of pale sundogs glimmering on either side of the sun, joined by a circular rainbow.

Each night, however, produced a new torment. That evening my knees got wet (this was caused by a rogue patch of ice on the bag liner), so I moved the windpants doing service as a pillow down under them. This meant that the mummy-style hood of the bag flopped down over my head, raising the problem (they were queuing up for recognition now) of imminent suffocation. The digital display on my watch faded. Out of the corner of my eye I spied a fresh cone of snow on the floor near the entrance. Forced out of the bag to plug the hole with a sock, I brushed my head against the ceiling and precipitated a rush of ice crystals down the back of the neck. I began nurturing uncharitable thoughts about Eskimos.

The morning after the departure of the drillers I went straight to the galley to thaw out, noting that I had forgotten to stand the shovel upright with the result that it was now lost in accumulated snow. Camp had shrunk from forty-five to twenty-two overnight. Patsy Cline was blaring out of the speakers and Bob and Mary were playing frisbee with a piece of French toast.

In the end, the igloo defeated me. As I walked back to it the next night I eyed the drums nestling in cradles outside the Jamesways, pumping diesel into the Preways. Sneaking guiltily into one of the two berthing Jamesways, I lay on the floor behind a curtain. It was so easy.

※

Ice streams A, B, C, D and E were located on the West Antarctic ice sheet. There was also a little F, but no one ever talked about that. Hermann, the moon-faced *Road to Oxiana* scientist, was investigating Ice Stream B. He wanted me to go out there with him and his team – they were staying for a week – but I knew I wouldn't be able to get back easily, and I couldn't risk being stranded anywhere at that point in the season. I was sad.

'Just come for the put-in,' he said. I looked at him. It was an extraordinarily kind gesture: the put-in involved two Otter flights, and taking me along would seriously complicate logistics. 'You must see it,' he said. '*I must support you as a writer.*'

Hermann was buzzing around his pallets like a wasp as the Otter arrived. When we took off, I sat in the back of the hold with him. The Whitmore Mountains appeared in the distance. Hermann's eyes lit up.

'Look!' he said, pointing to a hollow above a deeply crevassed area. 'The beginning of Ice Stream B!' The ice there looked like a holey old sheet. Hermann pressed a hand-held Global Positioning System unit against the pebble window and said solemnly, 'We are entering the chromosome zone.' It sounded like the opening sequence of a science-fiction movie. 'The crevasses change direction as the glacier moves,' he said, 'and they turn into thousands of Y chromosomes.'

After that we entered the transition zone between the moving ice and the stable ice. It was called the Dragon, a highly deformed, heavily crevassed area streaked with slots. Hermann tapped his

propelling pencil against the thick glass of the porthole and held
forth. 'The ice streams are not well understood. The boreholes we
have drilled to the bottom of this stream reveal that the base of the
stream is at melting point. So they move' – tap, tap, tap – 'these
motions provide a process for rapid dispersal and disintegration of
this vast quantity of ice. I mean that most of the drainage of this
unstable western ice sheet occurs through the ice streams. The
mechanics' – tapping – 'of ice streaming play a role in the response
of the ice sheet to climactic change. In other words the ice streams
are telling us about the interactive role of the ice sheet in global
change.'

So it seemed that if the ice melted, resulting in the fabled Great
Flood of the popular press, water would pour out of the continent,
via the ice streams, on to the Siple Coast, virtually the only part of
Antarctica not bounded by mountains.

Hermann settled back in his seat. 'The aim of investigating ice-
stream dynamics,' he concluded, 'is to establish whether the ice
sheet is stable.'

'Geology,' Lars had told me, 'is an art as well as a science.'

Hermann stowed the pencil in his top pocket, my ears popped
and we landed at a few dozen ragged flags on a relatively stable
island in the middle of Ice Stream B. This island, shaped like a
teardrop, was called the Unicorn, and Hermann's eye glittered
like the mariner's at three or four flags flapping on bamboo poles
in the distance. 'The flags mark our boreholes,' he said, 'and we
have left equipment down in these holes, gathering data. Those
two boreholes' – he pointed to a pair of ragged red flags – 'are
called Lost Love and Mount Chaos.' It was like entering a private
kingdom. The Dragon, which resembled a slender windblown
channel of ice you could walk over in five minutes, was really a
two-mile-wide band of chaotic crevassing running for forty miles
down one side of the Unicorn. It was a dramatic landscape, its

appeal sharpened by the fact that fewer than twenty people had ever seen it.

Hermann's longstanding field assistant, who had travelled with us, was a gazelle-like woman called Keri. When the plane took off and the sound of the engines faded she began spooling out the antenna.

'You be my deputy field assistant,' Hermann said to me. We crunched off to a flag where he dug around until he found a plywood board encrusted with crystals. Fishing out a skein of wires from underneath it, and attaching them to a small measuring device, he began sucking up data. After a few minutes he beamed, an expression he retained until I left the camp, and possibly much longer. He started inscribing a neat column of figures in pencil in a yellow waterproof notebook.

'These bits of data,' he said, 'are all little clues to the big puzzle.'

Back at CWA they were detonating the last blasts of the season. Everyone went outside one morning to watch 750 pounds of explosives go up half a mile away. The blaster was close to the site. A black and grey mushroom cloud surged 500 feet into the air, followed, seconds later, by a prolonged muffled boom.

'One less for lunch, Bob,' said José.

I skied out to see the crater. It was forty-five feet in diameter with a conical mound in the middle, and a delicate film of black soot had settled over the ice. The blaster was admiring his work. 'My hundredth of the season,' he said proudly.

He was taciturn, as cold as the ice in which he buried his explosives, but once I showed an interest in his bombs his face mobilised and he began opening boxes to show me different kinds of powder and expounding on the apparently limitless virtues of nitroglycerine.

'Largest charge I've used this season,' he intoned with the treacly vowels of Mississippi, 'was 9,000 pounds,' and I tut-tutted admiringly as he ran his fingers through baby-pink balls of explosive which looked like candy and smelt of diesel.

As the days were slipping away from me, I decided I ought to catch a lift back to McMurdo in the Otter, rather than wait for a Herc which might not come. I whipped up a bread-and-butter pudding as a farewell gift. While they were eating it, Jen, a feisty individual working her second season as a field assistant, filled a tin bowl with hot water, rolled up her long-johns and perched on a chair in the galley shaving her legs.

'But who's gonna see those legs, Jen?' someone yelled. This was followed by a ripple of laughter.

'Get outta here,' she called. 'I wanna be a girlie for once.'

I went over to the igloo and lay down one last time, looking up at the spiral of bricks and the blue haze.

Everyone came over to the Otter to say goodbye. 'See you in Mactown,' said Seismic Man, squinting into the sunlight.

I watched them get smaller and smaller until they disappeared into the ice.

The pilot wanted to play cards with the air mechanic, so I moved into the cockpit. A stack of cassettes were jammed between the front seats – most of it was 1970s stuff I hadn't heard since school, and it was perfect cruising music. *Crime of the Century*, *The Best of the Eagles*, early Bowie, that Fleetwood Mac album we all had.

Looking down at the earth from 12,000 feet, I felt then that my life was in perfect perspective. It was a sense of oneness with the universe – I belonged to it, just like the crystals forming on the wing tip. At that moment I knew that all my anxieties and failures and pain were shadows on the wasteland.

CHAPTER 18

'BLUE COLLAR'

from *Big Dead Place* (2005)

Nicholas Johnson

Far beneath the scientists and the administrators, down at the bottom of the status pyramid, contemporary Antarctica also contains a little world of contract workers, for whom the continent can be less a wide-open wilderness than a screw-top jar full of managerial idiocies you just can't escape. Nicholas Johnson's scabrous memoir of working through the winter at McMurdo today is a kind of Dilbert *on ice.*

McMurdo lies in the shadow of Mount Erebus, a smoldering volcano encrusted with thick slabs of ice. To make room for McMurdo, a ripple of frozen hills on the edge of Ross Island have been hacked away to form an alcove sloped like the back of a shovel, and then affixed with green and brown cartridges with doors and windows. Silver fuel tanks sparkle on the hillside like giant watch batteries. As if unloosed from a specimen jar, a colony of machines scours the dirt roads among the simple buildings, digesting snow and cargo dumped by the wind and the planes, rattling like cracked armor and beeping loudly in reverse. In the distance, framed by ratty utility poles and twisted electrical lines, the gleaming mountains of the Royal Society Range spill glaciers that glow like molten gold onto the far rim of the frozen white sea. Near Castle Rock, skiing toward Mount Erebus, in the middle of nowhere, you can stop at the bright red emergency shelter that looks like a giant red larva and call your bank to dispute your credit card fees.

Most of the population work for NSF's prime support contractor, which employs everyone from dishwashers and mechanics, to hairdressers and explosives-handlers. While the National Science Foundation is known as a proud sponsor of public television programming, Raytheon is known for making the Exoatmospheric Kill Vehicle and other top-shelf weapons systems. In Antarctic parlance, all of the United States divides into 'Washington,' referring to NSF's sphere of influence, and 'Denver,' referring to a vague suburban belt of Sheratons and brewpubs on the outskirts of Denver, where the support contractor has long been headquartered. Toward Denver is the most immediate over-the-shoulder check for the Antarctic lackey. 'I'm going to have to "okay" that with Denver first,' they say, or 'I'm not the one who made the decision – if you have a problem with it, talk to Denver.' Denver is where most of the managers and full-time employees work, and where strategies for improving morale are formulated. Some of the clocks in McMurdo are set to Denver time.

One Saturday in mid-May we had an All-Hands Meeting, our first since the medevac plane had left in late April. We crowded into the Galley in our work clothes. The first speaker was the technician who maintains lab equipment. There was not a single scientist in McMurdo this winter, but if anyone could be labeled a 'researcher' to make it easy on the newspapers in the U.S., it would be he. He showed us some video footage of the volcanic activity in Mt. Erebus accompanied by the Pink Floyd song 'One of These Days (I'm Going to Cut You Into Little Pieces).' Afterwards he told us that the green laser in the Crary Lab had been fixed, and that if we wanted to see it we could call him and he would turn it on for us.

He reminded us not to climb on the roof to look at it from above, because it would permanently blind us.

In the winter the green laser shoots from the top of Crary into the sky while everyone goes about their business. To see this green laser while I hauled garbage was the central reason I had decided to winter. In a strange world hardened by routine, the rub between the fantastic and the mundane creates a spellbinding itch.

The next speaker was the winter Galley Manager, with whom I had worked my first year down here, when he was the baker. I would take breaks from washing pots to hear his stories about being a chef in the Playboy Mansion, where he spent much of the time making hot dogs and PBJs. Now he told us that his new oven had been stolen. Parts of it had been sent to him with ransom notes, threatening its destruction unless he sang 'I'm a Little Teapot' at the All-Hands Meeting. He sang one verse and sat down, but everyone cheered for more, so he did it again, and we cheered even louder.

Then the Operations Manager took the floor and reminded us to check the hours on our machines, and to remember to bring in our machines for PMs, or Preventive Maintenance. 'Also,' he said, 'if you have an accident, you need to report it.'

Then Franz, the new Station Manager, stood up to talk. He had replaced the previous station manager, who went out on the medevac flight. Before his new appointment he had been working as a supervisor in Materials. Though he was a fingee, Denver liked him for his management experience in a hotel in suburban Denver.

I had first met Franz in the summer, when he was Butch's roommate. One day after work Butch and I were hanging out in his room shooting the shit. When Franz came in from work, he busied himself on his side of the room for a while before saying to Butch:

'So, I'm going to take a shower now. I'll be five or ten minutes. Then the place is yours.'

Butch looked at him without understanding.

'I'll just be five or ten minutes,' Franz repeated, suggesting that we leave the room so he could take a shower, in the bathroom, behind a closed door that had a lock.

Franz read some statistics from a study he had scavenged on the Internet concerning the psychological effects of wintering in Antarctica. 'Many of you at this time of year will have sleeping problems,' he said, 'and may become depressed, irritable, or bored. Five percent of you,' he said, 'will suffer effects that will clinically categorize you as in need of psychological treatment.'

I was excited to see what personal dementias I would face, and realized that if my disrupted circadian rhythms or thyroid activity were to show any symptoms, since it was May now, they should be kicking in any day. I wondered if I would collect pictures of animals, or draw eyes on all my belongings, or come to despise asymmetrical shadows.

In the dark ages a withered priest might have warned us that the Devil was on the loose and that we had to purge ourselves of sin. Now we had scientific evidence to remind us, via a former hotel manager, that the individual's predetermined behavior and aberrations are the product of devilishly powerful external forces, such as the planet's tilt. There was little practical reason for any manager to warn us of winter psychological effects, since they are disregarded in daily affairs. You would still be written up for tardiness, regardless of 'sleeping problems.' A 'support program' for the 'depressed' would not be authorized until the end of winter. And 'irritability' would still be met with dorm room inspections in your absence. Whatever the initial intent of these academic psychological studies, their field application is as an orientation to employee culpability.

❃

After the meeting I stopped at the store to see if *Rosemary's Baby* was in the video collection and to buy some Skoal. The McMurdo store is miraculously well-stocked. Though someone is always likely to complain that this or that item has run out, the store has Pringles and Rolos and jars of hot salsa. There are a half dozen kinds of beer, most common types of liquor, and a considerable selection of red and white wine. (Every fourth bottle will be rancid by the end of the winter, because the wine is stored upright and the arid air will have ruined the corks.) There are hundreds of videos for free checkout just by giving the liquor clerk the last four digits of your Social Security number. There are windscreen facemasks for sale. There are aerial posters of Ross Island, a few kinds of soap and shampoo, nail clippers, and anti-fart medication. For years there have been hundreds of unsold postcards of a velvet Elvis painting that someone photographed at the Pole. When the Navy first opened the store, they stocked mosquito repellent that no one bought because there are no mosquitoes in Antarctica.

Much of the souvenir merchandise in the store is contracted for manufacture to a company in Denver. The souvenir t-shirt selection is large, but with two basic varieties. The first and most common variety centers around the penguin. These shirts may also include icicles or the sun, and their style staggers toward stark romance. They might say 'Wild Antarctica' or 'The Last Frontier' on them. The second variety may also include the penguin, but the styles imitate tired surf or snowboard designs. These designs include men in parkas with surfboards, or 'Antarctica' written in the style of the Ford logo. They refer to Antarctic 'powder' and say things like 'eternal sun' and 'chill out.'

Some of the goods at the store are depressing, like the bumper sticker that says, 'Antarctica: Been There, Done That,' and some are confusing, like a cap embroidered with a colorful bass biting a fishhook and the text 'Bite Me – Antarctica.'

At the counter I browsed the Antarctica pins that I never buy, and scrutinized one that depicted the Antarctic continent flanked by American flags. The clerk told me that last summer NSF, which usually has little to do with the running of the store, instructed her to remove the 'Made in Taiwan' sticker from the backs of the pins before displaying them.

The next day, in the middle of a Sunday afternoon, on a dark road coming down from T-site, Bighand flipped a truck. He came down too fast and went over the embankment by the Cosmic Ray Lab, launching the acetylene and oxygen tanks into the air from the back of the pickup. The truck rolled but landed on its wheels, and Bighand drove it back to town after gathering the pressurized canisters of volatile gases. He hid the truck behind one of the orange fish huts where scientists in summer stay warm while fishing for specimens (there are no Antarctic bass) through the sea ice. Then he found his boss at the bar and reported the incident.

The Heavy Shop assessed the truck's extensive damage. HR summoned Bighand for questions as to why the cab of the truck smelled like beer, and he said that the mechanics must have poured beer in the truck to frame him.

The grapevine lurched into action. At dinner the next day someone said, 'Shit, I didn't even hear about it until after lunch.' Bighand was in and out of the HR Office all day, and at break we speculated on the company's strategy. We determined that since Bighand was a foreman he wouldn't be fired straight away. He would stay on to work and would probably be sent out at Winfly in August. Had he been in some menial position, he might have been made an example of and put on minimum wage until he could be flown out, but since he was a foreman and necessary for construction of JSOC, he would be kept on until someone new could be brought in. HR would give him the impression that he had been forgiven, but he would be fired just before the first flight out.

The next few days were marked with investigations by HR and Safety. Both of those departments this winter totaled two people. They brought in everyone who was at T-site on Sunday and pumped them for information with which to convict Bighand.

T-site is the hub of all radio transmission in The Program. The road up to it is long and windy, with signs along the way warning of exposure to hazardous doses of radiation should you stray into the garden of transmitters. Because of the importance of uninterrupted communication around the continent, a couple of people, one of whom must always remain on-site, live at T-site in swank and roomy quarters. They have a pool table, a band room stocked with instruments, supplies for brewing beer, a well-stocked pantry and kitchen, and comfortable couches. Just off the ordinary living room lie corridors lined with banks of transmitter components: some of it state-of-the-art, some of it antiquated but reliable gear from the early Cold War era. One can get up from the couch in the warm and carpeted living room, pad in one's socks down the corridor full of vigilant technology sprouting bundles of wires and silently ricocheting voices or strands of data around the continent, and seat oneself on another couch by the pool table in the equally comfortable rec room. Looking out the window in the summer, one's view weaves through the dozen or so enormous spidery transmitters nearby for an otherwise clean view of the Transantarctics and of White Island and Black Island, where another transmission outpost stretches the range of communication from T-site. Going to visit the comm techs at T-site brings a change of scenery, where the relentless sound of loader back-up beepers in town is faint.

Bighand had been driving down from a band rehearsal held that afternoon in the T-site rec room. Franz, the new Station Manager, and the HR Guy called everyone who had been at T-site that day into the HR Office one by one to sign a 'warning' acknowledging that the signer had violated an NSF policy by using government vehicles to enter a restricted area; presumably this aimed to fill a hole somewhere in the documentation of T-site's restricted status. Franz told Nero that HR was 'just going to shred them up at Winfly anyway,' but Nero didn't see why he should sign a 'warning.' Many people did sign it, but many refused.

By the time he flipped the truck, Bighand was already notorious around town. His drink of choice was a tall glass of Jim Beam topped with Wild Turkey and a splash of Sprite. Then several more. When I wore a skua'd priest shirt to the bar one night, he got down on one knee before me with his eyes rolling back in his head and began babbling incoherently, so I blessed him and howled 'Demons be gone!' When he tried to leave, he walked into the door and almost fell over before going outside. I didn't think he would make it home, so I followed him outside, where he was just getting up from a fall on the ice, and walked him to his dorm. One time Bighand filled a truck with diesel instead of mogas. That's a pain in the ass for the Heavy Shop, who must then drain the lines. Now that he'd also flipped one of the new red trucks, he was a bona fide public buffoon. Trying to blame the Heavy Shop for the beer in the cab had also created enemies, as well as a potential rift between Ironworkers and Mechanics. Perhaps this was why someone crept into the JSOC job shack one night and took a shit in Bighand's hardhat, wiping their ass with a piece of the project's blueprint.

Aside from 'Been there, done that' and 'We need to touch base,' managers are particularly fond of the phrase 'It's a harsh continent,' which has two uses. The first meaning is that of the manager speaking of some hassle or burden on himself. In this case, the manager says, 'But hey, it's a harsh continent,' expressing a noble resignation. In the other case, the manager, awed by the big decisions coming down from someone more powerful than herself and fantasizing about making such decisions herself, says, 'Well, it's a harsh continent,' which translates as 'Tough shit for all of you.' Though these uses may seem opposed, they really express different shades of the same sentiment: submission is survival. To work hard and increase one's competence is nearly irrelevant. The most important things are to occasionally seek decisive assistance, to mimic the mannerisms of the immediate superior, and to occasionally let out a squeak or yelp of fear or pain.

Managers also like to joke about 'putting out fires.' Fire is the direst threat at an Antarctic station, where the dry air makes the buildings tinderboxes that can crumple minutes after the first flame. In manager parlance, though, 'fires' are problems of any kind, and the manager knows there is no end to the fires, so he usually follows the reference to extinguishing them with a fatigued sigh. Once a fire is put out, he moves onto the next fire. Each new flame is addressed as a unique problem, unrelated to anything that came before it. He rushes around the room extinguishing isolated flames, emphatically smothering anything in the vicinity of the smallest wisp of smoke, lest the snoozing overhead detector be aroused and its shrill scream betray his failure to control his sector.

By June our routine was hopelessly solid. Each of us in Waste could distinguish the sounds of different loaders even from afar. Every Saturday we checked the glass and aluminum bins at the bars to make sure they were empty. Every Monday we checked the same bins to see if they were full. The Galley pumped out a daily stream of Burnables and Cardboard and a medium stream of Plastic and Light Metal. FEMC produced a lot of Wood and Light Metal and Construction Debris. The Firehouse hardly put out anything at all, but when they did, they separated their trash poorly. The Heavy Shop made a lot of Construction Debris, and we had to make sure to pick up their Heavy Metal when it was only half-full; otherwise we might have trouble dumping it, because one of our loaders had some hydraulic problems at max capacity. The Carp Shop could fill a Wood dumpster in a day or two. The dorms were steady with Burnables and sporadic with everything else. The Coffeeshop Glass bin only filled with wine bottles, and we appreciated the bartenders' separating by glass color even though it wasn't their job. The power plant dumpsters had been requiring attention this winter, because the engineers were cleaning house, and they called us to pick up their cardboard frequently, but that's because they didn't break down their boxes. Crary Lab took forever to fill anything but Haz Waste or Plastic.

Passing conversation ever more often involved Christchurch, an Antarctican's Heaven, where the year's grinding work would be rewarded with sushi and botanical gardens, Thai food and titty bars. There would be rain on windows and the sound of wet tires on pavement. Fresh off the plane, we would seep into Christchurch like diesel into snow. We would be full of money. We would scatter about the hostels and hotels, then clump again into smaller groups at restaurants throughout the city. Ice people would be everywhere, stopping on the sidewalks to ask each other what they ate for lunch, because now lunch would not be the same for everyone. To avoid tables for ten with confusing bar tabs, one would avoid the Monkeybar Thai restaurant. Bailey's, a bar at the edge of Cathedral Square, draws so much business from the USAP that they have sent kegs of Guinness down to special parties on the ice. Bailey's would replace Southern Exposure, but without parkas by the door, and the work stories would be full of nostalgia instead of details. The talk would concern beautiful future beaches and bloodless Antarctica.

In Christchurch we look pale, weird, and menacing, but soft as adult-sized newborns. People who were attractive in thick brown

Carhartts and all manner of accessories to cover necks, faces, and hands appear in the Christchurch summer as a mass of elbows, kneecaps, and toes. People wear shorts and sandals, exposing pasty flesh and propensities for camping. We are no longer Carps or Fuelies or Plumbers. Our cold-weather clothes are taken away, our intertwining community vines pruned; we suddenly have separate destinations.

By June, work was sometimes a wearisome prospect. I was sleeping longer on weekends and tired on weekday mornings, even when I went to bed early. When I did laundry, the clean clothes got put away just in time to do laundry again. Shaving was a chore. My room was getting messier. My memory seemed weaker.

One day while I was welding a dumpster I had problems explaining something to Jane.

'In this case it'd be better to hold the steel plate than to . . .' I hawed. Jane waited patiently. I couldn't think of it. I pointed to the clamp lying on the floor. 'What's that called?' I asked her.

'Clamp,' she said.

'. . . than to clamp it,' I finished. Jane said that pretty soon we would be speaking in grunts, merely pointing at things to name them, and staring into space.

CHAPTER 19

'IN THE FOOTSTEPS OF AMUNDSEN, 2016'

from *Antarctica* (1997)

Kim Stanley Robinson

The best nature-writer in the US at the moment happens also to write science fiction: this is a strand from the novel he wrote after a polar sojourn courtesy of the National Science Foundation's Artists & Writers Program. A wilderness adventure in the near future is going wrong for a group of wealthy clients and their burned-out guide, just as the party reaches the top of the Axel Heiberg Glacier, but as it does so, it generates a kind of tough-minded Californian elegy for the Heroic Age, wise about the difference between then and now, and about the space we ought to allot in our lives for Antarctic beauty.

The others had all gone around the ice block to the higher belay and got off the rope, and Val and Jack had clipped their harnesses onto the belay rope and were just beginning to pull the sledge into line, when the ice block above them leaned over with a groan and fell. Val leapt into the crevasse to the left, her only escape from being crushed under falling ice. She hit the inner wall of the crevasse with her forearms up to protect her. The rope finally caught her fall and yanked up by her harness; then she was pulled down again hard as Jack was arrested by the same rope below her. For a second or two she was yanked all over the place, up and down like a puppet, slammed hard into the wall. The rope was stretching almost like a bungee cord, as designed – it was very necessary to decelerate with some give – but it was a violent ride, totally out of her control.

But the belay above held, and the belayers too. As soon as she stopped bouncing, however, she twisted and kicked into the ice wall with both front-point crampons, then grabbed her ice axe and smacked the ice above her with the sharp end to place another tool.

A moment's stillness. Nothing hurt too badly. She was well down in the crevasse, the blue wall right in front of her nose. Ice axe in to the second notch, but she wanted more. Below her Jack was hanging freely from the same rope she was, holding onto it above his head with one hand. No sign of the sledge.

Voices from above. 'We're okay!' she shouted up. 'Hold the belay! Don't move it!' Don't do a thing! she wanted to add.

'Jack!' she called down. 'Are you okay?'

'Mostly.'

'Can you swing into the wall and get your tools in?'

'Trying.'

He appeared to be below a slight overhang, and she above it. A very pure crevasse hang, in fact, with the rest of the group on the surface several metres above them, belaying them, hopefully listening to her shouts and tying off, rather than trying to haul them up by main strength; it couldn't be done, and might very well end in disaster. Val didn't even want to shout up to tell them to tie off: who knew what they would do? Not wanting to trust them, she took another ice-screw from her gear-rack, chipped out a hole in the wall in front of her, set the screw in it, then gave it little twists to screw it into the ice. Its ice coring shaved out of the aluminium cylinder. A long time passed while she did this, and it became obvious that they were underdressed for the situation; it was probably twenty below down here, and no sun or exertion now to warm them; and sweaty from adrenalin. They were chilling fast, and it added urgency to her operation. She had to perform a variation of the operation called Escaping the Situation – a standard crevasse technique, in fact, but one of those ingenious mountaineering manoeuvres that worked better in theory than in practice, and better in practice than in a true emergency.

The screw was in, and she clipped onto it with a carabiner and sling attached to her harness, then eased back down a bit. Now both she and Jack had the insurance belay of the screw.

From the surface came more shouts.

'We're okay!' she shouted up. 'Are the belay-screws holding well?'

Jim shouted down that they were. 'What should we do?'

'Just hold the belay!' she shouted up anxiously. 'Tie it off as tight as you can!' More times than she cared to remember she had found herself in the hole with the clients up top, and they had often proved more dangerous than the crevasse.

She tied another prussik loop to the belay rope, then reached up and put her right boot into it. Then she stood in that loop, jack-knifing to the side, and unclipped her harness from the ice screw, then straightened out slowly as she slid the prussik attached to her harness as high on the rope as it would go. When she was standing straight in the lower loop, she tightened the upper prussik, then hung by the waist from it, and reached down and pulled the lower one up the rope, keeping her boot in the loop all the while. There was the temptation to pull the lower loop almost all the way up to the higher one, but that resulted in a really awkward jack-knife, and made it hard to put weight on her foot so she could move the higher one up. So it was a little bit up on each loop, over and over; tedious hard work, but not so hard if you had had a lot of practice, as Val had, and didn't get greedy for height.

'Jack, can you prussik up?'

'Just waiting for you to get off-rope,' he said tightly.

'Go ahead and start!' she said sharply. 'A little flopping around isn't going to hurt me now.'

Soon enough she reached the edge of the crevasse, and the others on top helped haul her over the edge, where she was blinded by the harsh sunlight. She unclipped from the rope and went over to check the belay. It was holding as if nothing had ever even tugged on it. Bombproof indeed.

Then it was Jack's turn to huff and puff. Prussiking was both hard and meticulous, accomplished in awkward acrobatic positions while swinging in space all the while, unless you managed to balance against the ice wall of the crevasse. Jack appeared to be making the classic mistake of trying for too much height with each move of the loops, and he wasn't propping himself against the wall either. It took him a long, long time to get up the rope, and when he finally pulled up to the point where the others could haul him over, he was steaming and looked grim.

'Good,' she said when he was sitting safely on the ramp. 'Are you all right?'

'I will be when I catch my breath. I've cut my hand somehow.' He showed them the bloody back of his right glove, a shocking red. The blood was flowing pretty heavily.

'Shit,' she said, and hacked some firn off the ramp to give to him. 'Pack this onto it for a while until the bleeding slows.'

'A sledge runner caught me on its way down.'

'Wow. That was close!'

'Very close.'

'Where is the sledge?' Jorge said.

'Down there!' said Jack, pointing into the crevasse. 'But it got knocked in and past us, rather than crushed outright by the block. I gave it a last big tug when I jumped in.'

'Good work.' Val looked around. 'I'll go back down and have a look for it.'

'I'll come along,' said Jack, and Jim, and Jorge.

'You can all help, but I'll go down and check it out first.'

So she took from her gear-rack a metal descending device known as an Air Traffic Controller, and attached it to the rope, then to her harness using a big locking carabiner. She leaned back to take the slack out of the rope between her and the anchor, then started feeding rope through the Air Traffic Controller as she walked backward toward the crevasse, putting her weight hard on the rope. Getting over the edge was the tricky part; she had to lean back right at the edge and hop over it and get her crampon bottoms flat against the wall, legs straight out from it and body at a forty-five degree angle. But it was a move she had done many times before, and in the heat of the moment she did it almost without thinking. After that she paid the rope slowly up through the descender, one hand above it and one running the rope behind her back for some extra friction. Down down down in recliner position, past the ice-screw she had placed, down and down into the blue cold. She was keeping her focus on the immediate situation, of course, but her pulse was hammering harder than her exertion justified, and she found herself distracted by an inventory that part of her mind was taking of the emergency contents of everyone's clothing. This was no help at the moment, and as she got deeper in the crevasse she banished all distracting thoughts.

Just past the tilt in the crevasse that blocked the view from above, there was a kind of floor. Her rope was almost entirely paid out, and she had not tied a figure of eight stopper-knot in the end of the line, which was stupid, a sign that she wasn't thinking. But it got her down to a floor, and it was possible to walk on this floor, she saw, still going down fairly steeply; and as she saw no sight of the sledge, but a lot of chunks of the broken ice block leading still onward, she called up that she was going off-rope, then unclipped, and moved cautiously over the drifted snow and ice filling the intersection of the walls underfoot – a floor by no means flat, but rather a matter of Vs and Us and Ws, the tilts all partly covered by drift. There was also no assurance at all that it was not a false floor, a kind of snow-bridge in a narrow section, with more open crevasse below it; she would have stayed on-rope if there had been enough of it. As it was she crabbed along smack against the crevasse wall, hooking the pick of her axe into it as she went, testing each step as thoroughly as she could and hoping the bottom didn't drop out from under her.

She moved under the snowbridge she had noted from above, and the crevasse therefore became a tall blue tunnel. She moved farther down into it. Sometimes ice roofed the tunnel, at other times snow-bridges, their white undersides great cauliflowers of ice crystal, glowing with white light. The view from below made it clear why snowbridges over crevasses were such dangerous things, so tenu-ous were they and so fatally deep the pits below them. But that was why people roped up.

The tunnel turned at an angle, and then opened downward into a much larger chamber. Val kept going.

This new space within the ice was really big, and a much deeper blue than what she had come through so far, the Rayleigh scatter-ing of sunlight so far advanced that only the very bluest light made it down here, glowing from out of the ice in an intense creamy-translucent turquoise, or actually an unnamed blue unlike any other she had seen. The interior of the space was a magnificent shambles. Entire columns of pale-blue ice had peeled off the walls and fallen across the chamber intact, like broken pillars in a shattered temple. The walls were fractured in immense translucent planes, everything elongated and spacious – as if God had looked into Carlsbad Caverns and the other limestone caverns of the world and said *No no, too dark, too squat, too bulbous, I want something lighter in every way,* and so had tapped His fingernail against the great glacier and got these airy bubbles in the ice, which made limestone caves look oafish and troglodytic. Of course ice chambers like these were short-lived by comparison to regular caves, but this one appeared to have been here for a while, perhaps years, it was hard to tell. Certainly all the glassy, broken edges had long since sublimed away in the hyperarid air, so that the shatter was rounded and polished like blue driftglass, so polished that it gleamed as though melting, though it was far below freezing.

Val moved farther into the room, enchanted. A shattered cathedral, made of titanic columns of driftglass; a room of a thousand shapes; and all of it a blue that could not be described and could scarcely be apprehended, as it seemed to flood and then to over-flood the eye. Val stared at it, rapt, trying to take it all in, realizing that it was likely to be one of the loveliest sights she would ever see in her life – unearthly, surreal – her breath caught, her cheeks burned, her spine tingled, and all just from seeing such a sight.

But no sledge. And back at the entrance to the blue chamber, there was a narrow crack running the other way, not much wider than the sledge itself; and looking down it, into an ever darkening blue, Val saw a smear of pale snow and ice shards, and below that, what appeared to be the sledge, wedged between the ice walls a hundred feet or more below; it was hard to judge, because the crevasse continued far down into the midnight blue depths below. There was no way she could get down there and get back up again; and even if she could have, the sledge was corked, as they said. Stuck and irretrievable. In this case crushed between the walls, it looked like, and broken open so that its contents were spilled even farther down. A very thorough corking. No – the sledge was gone.

At first they walked over firn, which took their weight like a pavement. There were sastrugi of course, but they could easily step over them, and the different angles of hardpack that their boots landed on actually gave their feet and ankles and legs some variety in their work, so that no one set of muscles and ligaments got tired, as when pounding the pavement in cities or in the endless corridors of a museum. So in these sections it was good walking.

They spread out in little clumps: Jack and Jim up with Val, Jack going very strong, even pushing the pace a bit; Jorge and Elspeth behind them; Ta Shu back farther still, rubbernecking just as he had before their accident. Val set the pace and did not allow Jack to rush them. 'Save it,' she said to him once a little sharply, when she felt him right in her tracks. 'Pace yourself for the long haul.'

'I am.'

But he dropped back a little, and on they walked. They were doing fine. As she always did on long hikes, Val stopped the group to rest for about fifteen minutes after every ninety of walking, in a system somewhat similar to Shackleton's. In ninety minutes their arm-flasks had melted the snow and ice chips stuffed into them, and so everybody had two big cups of water to drink. They could also eat a few inches of their belts, as Elspeth put it; their suits' emergency food supplies were sewn into an inner pocket wrapped all the way around the waist. The food was something like a triathlete's power bar, flattened and stretched into something very like a wide belt, in fact. It was good food for their situation. At some stops they chewed ravenously; during others their appetites seemed to Val suppressed, by altitude or exertion no doubt. She made sure they didn't force it. In truth it was water that was crucial to this walk; they were breathing away gallons of it in the frigid, hyperarid air, and they were sweating off a little bit as well. Two flasks every ninety minutes was by no means enough, but it certainly staved off the worst of the dehydration effects, which could devastate a person faster even than the cold, and made one more susceptible to the cold as well.

So between the walks and the breaks they made steady progress.

But after several of these had passed, they came upon swales of softer snow, which had been pushed by the winds into sastrugi like cross-hatched dunefields. These snowdrifts were new, the result of unusually heavy snowfalls on the edges of the polar cap in recent years, generally assumed to be an effect of the global warming generally, and of the shorter sea ice season in particular. Climatologists were still arguing what caused all the different kinds of superstorms, aside from the overall increase in the atmosphere's thermal energy. In any case the snow was here, one more manifestation of the changes in weather.

Val stopped for a meeting. 'Follow me and step right in my footsteps, folks, and it will be a lot easier.'

'We should trade the lead, so everyone saves the same amount of energy,' Jack said.

'No no, I'll lead.'

'Come on. I know we've got a long walk, but there's no reason to get macho on us.'

Val looked at him for a while, counting on her ski-mask and shades to keep her expression hidden. When her teeth had unclenched she said, 'I've got the crevasse detector.'

'We could all carry that when it was our turn.'

'I want to be the one using it, thanks. I know all its little quirks. It wouldn't do to have any falls now.'

'You having the radar didn't keep it from happening last time.'

They stood there under the low, dark sky.

'Go second, and make her steps better for us,' Ta Shu suggested to Jack.

'We shouldn't have anyone lose more energy than anyone else.'

'I have more energy than anyone else to start with,' Val said. 'Everyone except maybe you, but you're hurt. You cut your hand. You hit the wall of the crevasse. Let's not waste any more energy arguing about it. It'll work out.'

It was very hard to be civil to him. She couldn't think of anything else to say, and so took off before she said something unpleasant.

He stayed right on her heels, like some kind of stalker. She could hear his breathing, and the dry squeak of his boots on the snow. Untrustworthy, disloyal, unhelpful, unfriendly, discourteous, unkind . . .

They followed her through the soft snow dunes in single file. She kept the pace easy, resisting the pressure from Jack. Never was the snow as soft as Rockies powder, of course, but it was extremely dry, and already had been tumbled by the winds until it was on its way to firn. It was more like loose sand than any snow back in the world, loose sand that gave underfoot, thus much more work than the firn. Then in the areas where it adhered, she had to pull her boots out of their holes after every step, and lift higher for the next one, which was also hard work. But she had put in her trail time – a lifetime's worth – and it would take many many hours of such walking to tire her. No, she would be fine; she could walk for ever. It was the clients she was worried about. She was responsible for them, and she had got them into trouble, as Jack had pointed out; but she couldn't carry them, they had to walk on their own. So it had to be made as easy for them as possible.

So she did what she could. But as they walked on, and hour after hour passed, under the sun that wheeled around them in a perpetual mid-afternoon slant, they began to lose speed and trail behind. Jack no longer trod in her bootprints the second she left them unoccupied, nor during the breaks did he again mention leading the way. In fact he spent the rest periods in silence now, a mute figure under his parka hood, behind his ski-mask and shades. He wasn't eating much of his belt, either. That worried Val, and she tried to inquire about it by asking the group generally how they were feeling, and getting a status report from everyone; Elspeth was developing blisters on her heels, she thought; Jorge's bad knee was tweaking; Jim and Ta Shu reported no problems in particular, but like everyone said they were tired, their quads in particular getting a little rubbery with all the loose, soft snow. Jack, however, only said, 'Doing fine. "Pacing myself for the long haul".'

So, okay. End of that break. On they walked.

Her GPS was still out of commission, but occasionally when she turned it on it flickered and gave a reading, then blinked out again. The last one that had come through indicated that they were averaging about three kilometres an hour, which was normal on the plateau; a bit slower in the soft snow no doubt, hopefully a bit faster on the hardpack.

Then they came to a patch of blue ice, and Val groaned to herself. They had to stop and put on crampons, then scritch cautiously across the ice, which here was pocked and dimpled by big, polished suncups. The nobbly surface gave their ankles a hard workout indeed, as their crampon points forced them to step flush on the terrain underfoot no matter its angle. It was best to step right on the cusps and ridges between the little hollows, crampons sticking into the slopes on both sides and keeping the foot level; but that took a lot of attention and precise footwork. So *scritch, scritch, scritch*, they stepped along, making perhaps two kilometres an hour at best. Val headed directly for the nearest stretch of snow in the distance, so that as soon as possible they reached the far side of the blue ice, groaning with relief, and could sit down and take the crampons back off, and drink what water had melted at the bottom of their flasks, then restuff the flasks with hacked chips of the blue ice, which would yield more water when melted than snow. Then they were up and off again, on what felt like land, after a precarious crossing over water.

Jorge and Elspeth were clearly tiring now, though they did not complain. Jim too was getting tired, and Jack stuck with him, arms crossed over his chest. Jack still wasn't eating very much compared to the others, but he still wasn't responding to her questions about it, either.

'Aren't you hungry?'

'I'm fine.'

'We're probably burning three or four hundred calories an hour doing this.'

'I'm fine. Don't bother me.'

So she shrugged and took off again. They were back on good firn again, and could make decent time with minimum effort. Just walking, a great relief after what had preceded it.

But now when she looked back, she saw that Jim and Jack were behind Ta Shu, bringing up the rear, and losing a couple of hundred yards per hour on all the rest of them. It didn't seem like much, but it added up. And it worried her. But there was nothing to do but carry on, and ratchet down the pace a bit so that no one pushed too hard, especially those bringing up the rear.

They had been hiking for ten hours when Val got another GPS fix. They had come some thirty kilometres, a good pace; but she had aimed them out to the south to avoid the crevasses at the top of the Hump Passage, at the head of the Liv Glacier. So they still had at least seventy kilometres to go, she reckoned, depending on how far south they would have to detour to get around the ice ridge extending southward from Last Cache Nunatak. Beyond that ice ridge lay the head of the Zaneveld Glacier, which was heavily crevassed;

they would have to stay south of that; and then on the far side of the Zaneveld was Roberts Massif. All those features lay below the horizon, of course; they could see only about ten kilometres in all directions, which meant that they could see nothing but the ice plain, except for occasional glimpses of the peaks of the Queen Maud Range, poking over the horizon to their right.

Into her rhythm, taking it slow. So far of all the clients Ta Shu seemed the least affected by their long march. He spent all his rest time contemplating the distant peaks of the Queen Maud Range. While walking he stumped along steadily, and at times caught up with her and walked by her side. 'We are doing well!'

'Yes.'

But this group had only one Ta Shu in it, and the rest were slowly losing steam. In fact Jack and Jim were falling behind faster than ever. Puzzled, Val stopped and watched them closely for a while. It was not Jim who was slowing them down: it looked as if Jack had hit the wall. 'Fuck,' she said. He had gone out too fast, perhaps, and burnt out. Or was feeling the loss of blood from the cut in his hand. Or both. Anyway he was slowing down markedly.

Val called an early break, and waited for the two men to catch up, cursing to herself. They joined the group twenty minutes after Jorge and Elspeth came in, and during that time the others had eaten and drunk their flasks and refilled them, and were beginning to freeze. This was a serious problem, and she couldn't help thinking that it was Jack's fault. So often it happened that men like him took off too fast, on an adrenalin rush, thinking their emergency energy would be inexhaustible, and then they were the first to hit the wall. Pacing took a lot of self-discipline. And big, muscular men were generally not so good in ultralong-distance events: they had too many muscles to feed, and when they ran out of the day's carbo-load, they had too little body fat to throw on the fire.

So when Jim and Jack clumped into the group, Val suggested that they have a bite of their belts to give themselves more energy. Jim nodded, and pulled out some of his belt and tore it off and stuffed it under his ski-mask into his mouth before it froze.

Jack just shook his head irritably. 'I'm just pacing myself,' he snapped. 'Like you said to do. Don't get neurotic about it, that's the last thing we need. Let people go what pace they want.'

'Sure, sure. Try eating some food, though. We need the group to stay more or less together, or the people in front will freeze waiting for the ones behind.'

'Don't wait then!'

She stared at him. 'You should eat,' she said finally. 'And drink your arm-flasks and refill them, for God's sake.'

And after a little while more she had taken off again, and was soon leading the way. No beeps, thank God; they were out on the big ice-cube itself now, a solid mass with very little cracking. Just a matter of walking. Pacing oneself, yes, and walking. Hour after hour. She shifted them to a ten-minute break every hour, which was exactly Shackleton's pattern. Frequently she glanced back over her shoulder, Jack was still falling behind, perhaps even more rapidly than before; and Jim was sticking with him.

At some time when she was not looking the sun was touched by a thin film of cloud, which had appeared out of nowhere. A white film, but heavily polarized by her sunglasses, so that it was banded prismatically.

As usual, it only took the slightest cloud cover for the day to go from blinding and hot to ominous and chill. Already they were pulling their ski-masks down over their faces, and zipping up their parkas; and as they did so the cloud thickened further, into a thin rippled patch thrown right over the sun, as if someone had tried to place it there. So often it happened that way; the cloud could have appeared anywhere in the sky, but ended up right between Val and the sun. It happened so frequently that she reckoned it must be some trick of perspective rather than a real phenomenon. In any case, there it was again.

Which was bad, bad news. The immediate effects were that their suits wouldn't be as warm, and worse, their arm-flasks would be much less efficient at melting snow and ice. It would take twice as long to melt snow now, maybe three times. So they were going to get thirsty.

The mental effect of the cloud was also bad. What had been a blazing plain was now shadowed and malign. Underfoot the beautifully elaborate crosshatching in the snow was revealed better than ever, a granulated fractal infinity of sharply cut micro-terracing. This complex world underfoot was as prismatic as any cloud whenever it flattened enough, and now when she looked in the direction of the sun Val saw diaphanous icebows, curving both in the cloud and across the snow itself. They walked forward into a geometry of rainbows. Val looked back at Ta Shu, and he raised a ski pole briefly, to let her know he had noticed the phenomena, and appreciated her thinking to bring it to his attention.

A beautiful sight; and yet still the world seemed dim and malignant. Clouds of any kind on the polar cap often presaged even worse weather, of course, which perhaps was part of the mood it cast. With luck her clients did not know that and so wouldn't be affected as much. They were still many hours' walk out from Roberts, and a lot could happen to Antarctic weather in that amount of time.

Nothing to do but forge on, of course, into a landscape turned alien; the awesome become awful, and all in the few minutes it had taken for a thin cloud to form. After which they were mere specks on a high plateau on Ice Planet, a place in which humans could not live except in spacesuits. And they could feel that palpably, in the penetrating cold.

At the next rest-stop they drank and ate in silence. There was no point, Val judged, in trying to cheer them on. She could have pointed out to them again that they were having an adventure at last, after trying so many times and paying so much money. But she doubted that would go over very well now. One of the distinguishing marks of a true adventure, she had found, is that they were often not fun at all while they were actually happening. And in one of their camp conversations Jim had quoted Amundsen to the effect that adventure was just bad planning. So that if she called it that, they might blame her for it. Jack was certainly ready to.

And she blamed herself. It had been a mistake to take the right-hand route, as it turned out. Although still – as she walked on thinking about it, trying to cheer herself up – it seemed that what had happened showed that Amundsen was wrong, and that adventures could also be a matter of bad luck as well as bad planning. You could plan everything adequately, and still get struck down by sheer bad luck. It happened all the time. Chance could strike you down; that was what made these kinds of activities dangerous. That was what made all life dangerous. You couldn't plan your way out of some things. You had to walk your way out, if you could.

In any case, while there was no obvious way to cheer them up during the rests, there was also no great need to urge or cajole them along. The situation was plain; they either walked on or died. The intense cold they were living in reminded them of that at every moment.

She tried her GPS and it gave her a reading, showing them on the 172nd longitude. About the halfway mark of their hike. Not bad at all, except that they were getting very tired. They had hiked around thirty miles, after all, and were beginning to run out of steam; she could see it in the way they moved. Jorge was limping slightly. Elspeth was letting her ski poles drag from time to time, no doubt to give her arms a rest. Jack was doing the same, and moving like a pall-bearer. Jim was trying to keep to his friend's slow pace, though often he pulled ahead and then stopped and waited, not a good technique. Only Ta Shu still had the contained efficiency of someone with some strength left in his legs, placing each step precisely into her bootprints, using his ski poles in easy short strokes. He looked as if he could stump along for a long time.

Val herself was feeling the work, but was well into her long-distance rhythm, a feeling of perpetual motion that was not exactly effortless but a kind of contained low-level effort, one that she could sustain for ever; or so it felt. Obviously there would come a time when that feeling would wear away. But she had seldom reached it, especially when guiding clients, and right now it was still a long way off.

Her endurance, however, was not the point. They could only go at the speed of the weakest members of the team, and there was nothing she could do for them. Well, she could give them her meltwater. And so at the next break she did that, giving one cup to Jack and another to Elspeth, over their objections. 'Drink it,' she ordered, her tone peremptory in a way she had not let it be until now. 'I'm not thirsty.'

The little cloud was thickening, a white blanket thrown right over the sun, holding its position with maddening fixity. You could laugh at the Victorians for talking about a battle with Nature, but when you saw a cloud hold its position like that, in the freshening wind now striking them, it was hard not to feel there was some malignant perversity at work there, a Puckish delight in tormenting humans.

It might be the pathetic fallacy, but when you were as thirsty as Val was it felt tragic.

❋

She slowed down to hike with each of the others in turn, inquiring after them. Except for Ta Shu, and perhaps Jim, they were hurting; nearly on their last legs, it appeared, with more than thirty kilometres to go. Well, she would shepherd them there. Bring them on home. Give them her water, give them her mental energy. There was something about taking care of clients in such a way that felt so good. Others before self. Being a shepherd, or a sheepdog. Husbanding them along.

❋

At the next stop, however, she tried again to give Jack her water, and suggested that he eat, and he refused the water and yanked the power bar out of his belt and tore off a piece savagely, muttering 'Lay off, for Christ's sake. We're doing the best we can!'

Jim and Elspeth and Jorge all nodded. 'This is hard for us,' Elspeth said to Val wearily.

'Of course,' Val said. 'I know. Hard for anyone. You're doing great. We're making a very long walk, in excellent time. No problem. Let's just keep taking it easy, we'll get there.'

And as soon as possible she had them moving again, despite Elspeth's suggestion that they take a longer break. That would only allow muscles to stiffen up; besides, the sheer impact of the cold made it impossible. They had to move to stay warm.

So she took off, trying to tread the fine line between going too fast and tiring them or going too slow and freezing them. She lost the glow she had felt during the previous march about the ethic of service and all that; in fact another part of her was taking over, and getting angry at these people for getting so tired so fast. Sure, she should have kept anything like this from happening. But they had no business coming down here to trek if they were not in shape. Even these so-called outdoorspeople were still very little more than brains in bottles – weekend warriors at best, exercising nothing but their fingertips in their work hours, the rest of their bodies turning as soft as sofa cushions. Watching computer screens, sitting in cars, watching TV, it was all the same thing – watching. Big-eyed brains in bottles. These clients of hers were actually among the fittest of the lot, they were the best the world had to offer! The best of the affluent Western world, anyway. And even they were falling apart after walking a mere seventy kilometres. And thinking they were doing something really hard.

But in their spacesuit gear the level of raw suffering was not that great, if they could just learn to thermostat properly. Indeed the whole idea of Antarctic travel as terrible suffering which required tremendous courage to attempt struck Val as bullshit, now more than ever. It was all wrapped up with this Footsteps phenomenon – people going out ill-prepared to repeat the earlier expeditions of people who had gone out ill-prepared, and thinking therefore that you were doing something difficult and courageous, when it was simply stupid, that was all. Dangerous, yes; courageous, no. Because there was no correlation between doing something dangerous and being courageous, just as there was no correlation between suffering and virtue. Of course if you went at it with Boy Scout equipment like Scott had, then you suffered. But that wasn't virtue, nor was it courage.

In fact, Val decided as she stamped along, most of the people who came to Antarctica to seek adventure and do something hard, came precisely because it was so much *easier* than staying at home and facing whatever they had to face there. Compared to life in the world it took no courage at all to walk across the polar cap; it was simple, it was safe, it was exhilarating. No, what took courage was staying at home and facing things, things like talking your grandma out of a tree, or reading the wanted ads when you know nothing is there, or running around the corner of the house when you hear the crash. Or waiting for test results to come back from the hospital. Or taking a dog to the vet to have it put down. Or taking a group of leukemia kids to a game. Or waiting to see if your partner will come home drunk that night or not. Or helping a fallen parent off the bathroom floor at four in the morning. Or telling a couple that their child has been killed. Or just sitting on the floor and playing a board game through the whole of a long afternoon. No, on the list could go, endlessly: the world was stuffed with things harder than walking in Antarctica. And compared to those kinds of things, walking for your life's sake across the polar ice cap was *nothing*. It was *fun*. It could kill you and it would *still be fun,* it would be a *fun death*. There were scores of ways to die that were immeasurably worse than getting killed by exposure to cold; in fact, freezing was one of the easiest ways to go. No, the whole game of adventure travel was essentially an escape from the hard things. Not necessarily bad because of that; a coping mechanism that Val herself had used heavily all her life; but not something that should ever be mistaken for being hard or heroic. It was daily life that was hard, and sticking it out that was heroic.

Val shuddered at this dark train of thought, stopped in her tracks. She looked back; she had been going too fast, and the people she was caring for had fallen far behind. 'Come on, goddamn it!' she said at them. 'You are so fucking slow. This is fun! This is your adventure! Are we having fun yet?' Almost shouting at them. But they were so far back there was no chance they would hear her.

APPENDIX

A BRIEF CHRONOLOGY OF ANTARCTIC EXPLORATION

1839–43	British naval expedition in HMS *Erebus* and HMS *Terror*, led by James Clark Ross, discovers the Antarctic mainland
1897–99	Adrien de Gerlache's *Belgica* expedition overwinters in the Antarctic pack ice
1898–1900	Australian/Norwegian/British *Southern Cross* expedition, led by Carsten Borchgrevink, spends first winter on the continent
1901–03	German expedition under Erich von Drygalski maps Kaiser Wilhelm II Land. First Antarctic balloon flight
1901–04	British *Discovery* expedition, led by Robert Falcon Scott and based on Ross Island. Southern journey reaches 82°17′S
1903–05, 1908–10	French expeditions led by Jean-Baptiste Charcot aboard the *Francais* and the *Pourquoi-Pas?* map the coast of the Antarctic Peninsula
1907–09	Ernest Shackleton's British *Nimrod* expedition at Cape Royds, Ross Island. Polar journey reaches 88°23′S
1910–12	Norwegian expedition led by Roald Amundsen reaches South Pole (90°S) on December 14th 1911
1912	Japanese expedition led by Nobu Shirase

1910–13	R. F. Scott's *Terra Nova* expedition at Cape Evans, Ross Island. Scott's party die on the return journey from the Pole, 1912
1911–12	German expedition in the Weddell Sea discovers the Filchner Ice Shelf
1911–14	Australian/New Zealand expedition, led by Douglas Mawson, in Adelie Land
1914–17	Shackleton's 'Imperial Transantarctic Expedition', failed attempt to cross the continent from Weddell Sea to Ross Sea
1922	Shackleton dies in South Georgia
1928–30	American expedition, led by Richard Byrd, establishes Little America base on Ross Ice Shelf. First overflight of South Pole, November 28th 1929
1933–35	Byrd's second expedition. Byrd overwinters solo
1935	Lincoln Ellsworth makes first air crossing of Antarctica
1938–39	German expedition to Queen Maud Land, renamed 'Neuschwabenland'
1943–45	British Navy's 'Operation Tabarin' establishes bases on the Antarctic Peninsula
1946–48	US Navy's 'Operation Highjump' and 'Operation Windmill'
1955–58	Commmonwealth Trans-Antarctic Expedition, led by Vivien Fuchs, makes first land crossing of the continent
1955	US Navy's 'Operation Deep Freeze' begins
1956	Construction of South Pole base (US) and McMurdo Station (US)
1957	Construction of Vostok Station (USSR)
1961	Antarctic Treaty enters into force
1966	First ascent of Vinson Massif (16,067 ft), Antarctica's tallest mountain

1966	Regular tourist cruises begin
1969–1970	First women included in the United States Antarctic Program
1983	Lowest temperature ever recorded on earth (-89.2°C) at Vostok
1985	Discovery of hole in ozone layer announced by British scientists at Halley and Rothera bases
1987	Signing of Montreal Protocol banning ozone-depleting chemicals. Patriot Hills runway first used for private flights
1995	Collapse of 2000 km^2 Larsen A Ice Shelf, Antarctic Peninsula
1996	Ice core completed at Vostok, showing 420,000 years of earth's atmospheric history. Discovery of 'Lake Vostok', fresh water lake as big as Lake Ontario, sealed for 25 million years beneath nearly 4km of ice
1997	Kyoto Protocol negotiated, aimed at reducing emission of greenhouse gases
1998	Antarctic Treaty's Protocol on Environmental Protection enters into force
2002	Collapse of 3250 km^2 Larsen B Ice Shelf, Antarctic Peninsula. Records over 50 years show a 2.5°C rise in the Peninsula's average temperature
2007–09	International Polar Year